queer Indian defence

by Jacob Aagaard

EVERYMAN CHESS

Everyman Publishers plc   www.everymanbooks.com

First published in 2002 by Everyman Publishers plc, formerly Cadogan Books plc, Gloucester Mansions, 140A Shaftesbury Avenue, London WC2H 8HD

Reprinted 2002

British Library Cataloguing-in-Publication Data
A catalogue record for this book is available from the British Library.

ISBN 1 85744 300 4

Distributed in North America by The Globe Pequot Press, P.O Box 480, 246 Goose Lane, Guilford, CT 06437-0480.

All other sales enquiries should be directed to Everyman Chess, Gloucester Mansions, 140A Shaftesbury Avenue, London WC2H 8HD
tel: 020 7539 7600 fax: 020 7379 4060
email: chess@everymanbooks.com
website: www.everymanbooks.com

EVERYMAN CHESS SERIES (formerly Cadogan Chess)
Chief advisor: Garry Kasparov
Commissioning editor: Byron Jacobs

Typeset and edited by First Rank Publishing, Brighton.
Production by Book Production Services.
Printed and bound in Great Britain by The Cromwell Press Ltd., Trowbridge, Wiltshire.

Everyman Chess

Popular opening books:

1 85744 218 0	Unusual QG Declined	Chris Ward
1 85744 253 9	Alekhine's Defence	Nigel Davies
1 85744 256 4	Queen's Gambit Declined	Matthew Sadler
1 85744 232 6	French Classical	Byron Jacobs
1 85744 281 4	Modern Defence	Speelman & McDonald
1 85744 292 X	Symmetrical English	David Cummings
1 85744 290 3	c3 Sicilian	Joe Gallagher
1 85744 242 3	Offbeat Spanish	Glenn Flear
1 85744 262 8	Classical Nimzo-Indian	Bogdan Lalic
1 85744 291 1	Sicilian Grand Prix Attack	James Plaskett
1 85744 252 0	Dutch Stonewall	Jacob Aagaard
1 85744 257 1	Sicilian Kalashnikov	Pinski & Aagaard
1 85744 276 8	French Winawer	Neil McDonald

Books for players serious about improving their game:

1 85744 226 1	Starting Out in Chess	Byron Jacobs
1 85744 231 8	Tips for Young Players	Matthew Sadler
1 85744 236 9	Improve Your Opening Play	Chris Ward
1 85744 241 5	Improve Your Middlegame Play	Andrew Kinsman
1 85744 246 6	Improve Your Endgame Play	Glenn Flear
1 85744 223 7	Mastering the Opening	Byron Jacobs
1 85744 228 8	Mastering the Middlegame	Angus Dunnington
1 85744 233 4	Mastering the Endgame	Glenn Flear
1 85744 238 5	Simple Chess	John Emms

Books for the more advanced player:

1 85744 233 4	Attacking with 1 e4	John Emms
1 85744 233 4	Attacking with 1 d4	Angus Dunnington
1 85744 219 9	Meeting 1 e4	Alexander Raetsky
1 85744 224 5	Meeting 1 d4	Aagaard and Lund
1 85744 273 3	Excelling at Chess	Jacob Aagaard

queen's Indian defence

by Jacob Aagaard

EVERYMAN CHESS

Everyman Publishers plc www.everymanbooks.com

CONTENTS

PREFACE

The Queen's Indian Defence (arising after 1 d4 ♘f6 2 c4 e6 3 ♘f3 b6) is one of the most popular openings at both club and international level. The reason for this is obvious – ever since its introduction at the beginning of the century, the Queen's Indian has proved to be the most dependable defence for Black against 1 d4, together with its companion, the Nimzo-Indian (3 ♘c3 ♗b4). Additionally, most players like to create some kind of imbalance and avoid structures of a symmetrical nature, such as those found in the Queen's Gambit Declined and the Slav, although these openings also have their followers.

When I was originally asked to write a book about the Queen's Indian I asked if I could write a two volume work in order to delve deep into the different positional aspects of the opening. My publisher judged that most people would be more interested in a single volume, standard work, which is what I have ultimately agreed to. In order to achieve this I had to make some decisions concerning the structure of the book because it was evident that certain things which, in an ideal world, merited space, would have to be omitted. First, it was impossible to provide a deep positional study in a naturally restricted book form, as I did with the Dutch Stonewall. In this case I counted 19 different pawn structures that would have to be discussed, and the only way this could be done would be via a multitude of arrows and short, abstract words – something other writers have done before, but for which I have found little use for myself and, consequently, believe is the same for others. Therefore, other than brief discussions about the isolated pawn structures, below, this book is more a traditional work on the Queen's Indian. Moreover, when it came to the lines to include I had to make numerous decisions, minimising the material as much as possible. In *ECO* there are about 120 pages devoted to the QID and the positions that can result via transpositions which, in a book like this, would be around 300 pages. Meanwhile, *ECO* includes only those games that were previously published in Informant, so they actually exclude quite a lot of important games! I decided to include games from the very highest level – more or less all the games in this book, as well as all the sidelines, originate from Grandmaster competition. But this only got me down to 20,000 games! Then I made the obvious decision: only critical lines should be represented. But merely eliminating mistake after a mistake was far from enough. I also had to decide that some moves were not critical in any way and that, therefore, they had no role in the book because nobody would try to memorise the continuation, while looking it up afterwards also appears to me to be rather indifferent. Finally, in 'normal' positions, those 'normal' moves that give Black several ways to equalise have been omitted.

The result is a traditional work of theory, aimed at the tournament player and thus designed for practical use. I feel that I have been good at finding the critical lines in modern play, and picking out the most important games. I hope you will find this a useful and enjoyable book.

Jacob Aagaard
Copenhagen
July 2002

INTRODUCTION

Theoretical Overview

Here, briefly, is a an overview of the status of the various lines found in the following chapters.

Chapter 1

4 ♗f4 is by no means an attempt to create an opening advantage. I have a feeling that the bishop is not very well placed in this variation as Black can still play ...d7-d6 in order to limit its scope. In fact Black can equalise in more than one way.

4 ♗g5 should normally lead to transpositions because the best move for White on the next move is 5 ♘c3. Ideas with 5 ♘bd2 appear to be nothing other than a means of avoiding opening theory and promise White nothing.

Chapter 2

4 a3 is, generally, an interesting system. As there is no line that guarantees an advantage against the Queen's Indian White should select his approach based on style and taste, although I do feel that 4 a3 is not the most annoying move order for Black. 4 ♘c3, with the idea of meeting 4...♗b7 with 5 a3!, appears to avoid some of Black's most popular, fashionable lines.

Anyway, after 4 a3 Black has the following possibilities.

4...d5!? leads to standard positions after 5 cxd5 exd5; these are normally very slightly better for White, but are ultimately a matter of taste. Such positions are discussed throughout the book and are examined in some detail in Chapter 1.

4...c6?! has been played only once at the top level and will rarely be repeated. White should secure a small plus in a symmetrical position, which is always unpleasant for the second player.

4...c5!? leads to a sort of Benoni set-up with the bishop on a6 after 5 d5 ♗a6 where, for the time being, theory promises Black a good game (yet nothing more). I have a feeling that White will eventually find a way to prove a small plus here, although this has yet to happen. This line has gained significantly in popularity thanks to Kasparov's convincing victory against Gelfand.

4...♗a6 is the most popular system these days, leading to a variety of different positions, both hedgehog and the more flexible systems with ...c5 and cxd4. This should lead to equality and pleasant play for Black if he is sufficiently prepared, but it is a system that is still open for improvements and new ideas.

4...♗b7 is the other main line (besides 4...♗a6), and a solid reply. White has tried a number of different ways to gain an advantage but it still seems that Kasparov's idea from the 80's with 5 ♘c3 d5 6 cxd5 exd5 7 ♕c2! is the only real chance of giving Black a headache. I believe that these positions are, perhaps, equal after correct play, but it should be borne in mind that this correct play could often prove difficult to produce.

Chapter 3

4 ♘c3 ♗b7 5 ♕c2 is harmless and Black equalises easily, but the chapter is also mainly about **5 ♗g5**. If Black has played 4...♗b7, then 5 a3! is the best way to fight for an advantage, and the move order I consider the most dangerous for Black (what White should play after 4...♗b4 is another question – see below). This particular move order gives Black the chance to equalise with 5...h6 6 ♗h4 ♗e7!, after which there are no problems for the second player.

4...♗b4 is a logical response, often played to avoid the 5 a3 transposition after 4...♗b7. These positions can arise after 1 d4 ♘f6 2 c4 e6 3 ♘c3 ♗b4 4 ♘f3, where both 4...c5 and 4...b6 are main lines, the latter obviously transposing to the QID.

5 ♗g5 and now Black has two ways to equalise. The first is 5...h6 6 ♗h4 ♗b7 7 e3 (the move that has been proven to give Black most problems, unlike7 ♕c2, for example, which does not impress) 7...♗xc3 8 bxc3 d6 when a Nimzo-Indian structure has emerged, with Black being quite comfortable. The other comes after 7...g5 8 ♗g3 ♘e4. Although this has been played many times and the 'opening' theory can continue to 30 moves or more, I still feel that there is room for improvement and that Black should not trust the verdict of equality completely. It should be noted that White must play 9 ♕c2 and that the gambit with 9 ♘d2 seems rather dubious.

Chapter 4

4 ♘c3 ♗b4 5 ♕b3! – I have given this

move an exclamation mark simply because it is the most unpleasant for Black to meet. This hitherto offbeat line became a main line with the match Timman-Seirawan, Hilversum 1990, where Seirawan employed it in all his White games with convincing results. Since then it has been played by some of the other world's elite, with varying degrees of success. Black has three main options.

5...a5 does equalise but the resulting positions seem to be a little passive for Black because he will often have to play on against the two bishops.

5...♕e7 is also sufficient for equality. However, one should always remember that if Black first has to fight to solve various problems before equalising, then this only means that both players have equal chances in the position itself, the assessment excluding other factors such as familiarity with the position, time used on the clock and playing strength. Consequently, in the reality of competition, it is not necessarily always 'happiness' when one equalises.

5...c5 is the main move and, it seems, also the best. After 6 a3 ♗a5 (the point) Black is allowed to keep the two bishops for the time being, and he will exchange only if doing so leads to a clear gain of some sort. Then comes 7 ♗g5 ♗b7!, as played several times in the match between Seirawan and Adams in Bermuda 1999. Black should be able to keep the game level, but this line is still in its early childhood, and new discoveries will most certainly emerge with time. It should be noted that this line is full of all kinds of tactical tricks and options, which is a major reason why I recommend it. Better preparation will pay off.

Chapter 5

4 e3. This chapter provides some easy to use ways for Black to equalise against this (from a theoretical point of view) harmless system. This might be a good place for a little warning: If you (as Black) do not know what you are doing against this system, you can quickly find yourself in terrible trouble. See, for example, Yusupov-Beliavsky (Game 33), where top players produce moves about which a deeper theoretical knowledge would have made them think twice.

Chapter 6

4 g3 sees the beginning of the great saga of White's most popular. I have always played 4 g3 when facing the QID, but I have never mistaken the great taste I had for the positions with an advantage, and neither, I am sure, have the majority of the players who employ the fianchetto. Black has a considerable variety of choices, but I would recommend playing something along the main lines with 4...♗a6 while, for White, I would seriously ask you to consider 4 ♘c3. Of course, perhaps you play these lines to avoid fun, just like I do on a bad day.

4...♗b4+: The lines with ...♗b4+ generally benefit from the inclusion of the preparatory 4...♗a6. The only exception is 4...♗b4+ 5 ♗d2 ♗xd2+ 6 ♕xd2 ♗a6!, which transposes to 4...♗a6 5 b3 ♗b4+ after 7 b3, which is the best move. Generally these lines seem to be me to be slightly worse for Black, but never anything less than that. They are not very exciting and the second player rarely has any reason to hope for a full point.

4...♗a6 is probably a better move than 4...♗b7, and certainly more modern. The reason why this appears to be so clever is that almost no matter which way White protects the c4-pawn, Black can always play 5...♗b7 and claim that the white pieces are no better placed than they were the previous move. The idea certainly appeals to many players. Black should equalise in all the main lines; perhaps there is a theoretical plus in the main line, but that is only something for players to worry about if they cannot draw drawn endgames... We will come to this but, first, let us look at White's options to be presented in this chapter.

5 ♕c2 is completely harmless. Black probably has several ways to equalise, but the simplest is 5...d5!, when there is no doubt about the evaluation of the position.

5 ♕b3 might look stupid and, after 5...♘c6! (best) Black is able to exploit the misplacement of the queen immediately to further his own development. However, White's move should not be mistaken for being bad since Black only equalises – nothing more.

5 ♘bd2 is my own choice, although it should not give Black any problems. Black has some different and interesting choices here. 5...♗b4!? is very interesting and leads to an unbalanced situation in which, while White might be slightly better, the stronger player will be in the driving seat. All the lines with a quick ...c7-c5 seem a bit dangerous to me, but (of course) I might be mistaken. It all comes down to an evaluation of Game 39 and the lines featured therein. Finally 5...d5 should equalise without too much effort, and that is the main reason why this is not a main line.

5 ♕a4 is popular but simply lacks punch. 5...c6 is rather dubious, but after 5...c5! Black has several ways to generate a good game. Actually I am normally pleased when I see this move from Black as I simply cannot see how White can play for a win in the resulting positions – there is no pressure.

Chapter 7

5 b3 is the main line. And actually the only argument I see for playing the sytem with 4 g3 is to prove that this move is an advantage for White rather than a weakening of the dark squares. Having investigated the relevant variations I must say that I still cannot see this as anything other than a weakness, and it is for this reason that I recommend that everyone dump 4...♗b7 and choose a line from below.

5...d5!? is not in itself poor but the idea is to answer 6 ♗g2 with 6...dxc4, which is unsound. 6...♗b4+ might still be theoretically okay, but I do not know many people who like to play such positions.

5...c5 also looks slightly fragile, although it might work as a surprise. But if you are looking for good positions, look elsewhere.

5...b5!? is Adorjan's move, about which a positional verdict is quite simple. If Black finds success in ...a5-a4xb3 he can look forward to a good position. But why should White allow this? Against a logical treatment Black should be suffering from his inferior pawn structure and be slightly worse. However, 5...b5 is not a poor move and it does offer Black chances to steer the game away from more theoretical lines.

5...♗b7 6 ♗g2 ♗b4+ is an interesting option which promises something close to equality after both **7 ♗d2 a5** (Adams' choice) and **7...c5** (Korchnoi's choice). The struggle often hinges on deep strategic understanding, and I would not recommend that you undertake the responsibilities of Black if this book is the only material you will look at. But if you work through the games and find them interesting, then I will certainly not discourage you from seeking further knowledge and subsequently including these lines in your repertoire. In fact most players with White are unaware of what is best after **5...♗b7** and can thus find themselves on unfamiliar territory when Black refrains from entering the long main lines.

The main lines after **1 d4 ♘f6 2 c4 e6 3 ♘f3 b6 4 g3 ♗a6 5 b3 ♗b4+ 6 ♗d2 ♗e7 7 ♗g2 c6** have been debated endlessly for the last decade, and the verdict is – not surprisingly – that it is very difficult for White to gain an advantage; and if he succeeds it is only of 'scientific' value – that is if Black is well prepared! I have looked at 8 0-0 d5 9 ♕c2, which is the new idea at the top level, but it seems to be harmless, and if anybody takes any risks in the games played, it has mainly been Black. 8 ♗c3 d5 9 ♘e5 is the main line and has been treated as something

which is highly respected yet no longer has any place among the living. The story of the main line is a funeral – I know that this is an easy thing to say for a believer, so let us keep it blurred for now, and see if the evaluation should ever change.

Chapter 8

4...♗b7 is still popular with some top grandmasters. Only the absolute elite such as Kramnik, Anand and Karpov stick to 4...♗a6, while Tiviakov, Timman and Korchnoi still have some affection for this old main move. Personally I have no doubt about the correctness of 4...♗b7, but I do feel that the play after 4...♗a6 is more flowing and should suit most players – at least those who I know – better. But there are some players with a very relaxed attitude to chess, and these do best with the calm and strategic 4...♗b7. Anyway, let us turn to the lines arising after **5 ♗g2**:

5...c5 is simply positionally suspect and Black has nothing to show for it but a very modest – and very temporary – initiative. Stay away from this move.

5...♗e7 is the main move (5...♗b4+ belongs to the comments given above for 4...♗b4+). Now White has two paths. First, after 6 0-0 0-0, there are some minor sidelines.

7 b3 is harmless. Actually, I play this occasionally in order to reach an equal endgame (you know – hot summer days when you would like to be at the beach...). Nonetheless, do take a quick look at the easiest equalising methods.

7 d5!? was once wildly popular. First Polugaevsky used it, then Kasparov. Now – it's a joke. Black has several ways to equalise and can probably also play for a win without any great risks – if he is well prepared.

7 ♖e1 was modern a few years ago. The problem seems to have been solved with 7...♘a6!, after which the new try is 8 a3. Come on guys! Call that an advantage?

7 ♘c3 raises numerous issues. First White has 6 ♘c3 with some different ideas, and this is the most popular line at the moment. In the event of 7 ♘c3 I would go for the highly exciting 7...♘a6!? – which is quite complicated – rather than the somewhat drawish 7...♘e4. Anyway, after 6 ♘c3 Black usually replies 6...♘e4. Then 7 ♕c2 is harmless. Instead after 7 ♗d2 it seems to me that only 7...♗f6! guarantees Black a good game. Of course this is tested again and again at the top level, but it seems to me that those lines that are given as leading to an advantage for White (8 ♕c2 ♘xd2 9 ♕xd2 is an example) are often the lines I would fear least, while those given as harmless might conceal a trick or two. There are some tricks involving delaying castling but after 7...♗f6 these do not pay off (as they do against all the other lines).

That's all folks. Enjoy your games, no matter what faith or choice or line you might take.

The isolated d5-pawn

The QID is characteristic for its many different lines and prototypical positions. It can be compared to the Sicilian, where the structures after the opening vary from, for example, the wildly different Sveshnikov, Dragon and Hedgehog variations. In the QID I have found 19 different prototypical variations which, of course, might themselves contain numerous variations. Only one pawn structure (along with its distinct variations) is transcendental universal and appears, in some form, in all lines. I am referring to a situation such as the following example:

Gelfand-Leko
Cannes 2002

1 d4 ♘f6 2 c4 e6 3 ♘f3 b6 4 g3 ♗a6 5 ♕a4 ♗b7 6 ♗g2 c5 7 dxc5 ♗xc5 8 0-0 ♗e7 9 ♘c3 0-0 10 ♗f4 ♘a6 11 ♖fd1 ♘c5 12 ♕c2 ♕c8 13 ♖d4 d5 14 cxd5 exd5 15 ♖dd1

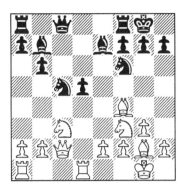

This is it! Black has accepted an isolated pawn on d5. As is usually the case this gives Black considerable free play for his pieces, but he will have to keep them active or use them appropriately before White's permanent advantage of a superior pawn structure begins to tell. Normally exchanges tend to favour White, as the removal of pieces serves to enhance the significance of the static aspects of a given position. This does not necessarily mean that endgames are bad for Black. Typically White might have weakened his queenside with b2-b3 at some point, when Black will be able to gain counterplay with a knight placed on e4, heading for c3. Gelfand-Karpov, Game 31 is an example of how activity can last long into the endgame.

In this game Black creates compensation for the isolated d-pawn by advancing his g-pawn, creating some potential threats on the light squares around White's king. Gelfand then decides to eliminate the g-pawn and, in return, takes a weak pawn on e3 (which is just as weak as d5).

15...♘ce4 16 ♖ac1 ♗c5 17 e3 ♘xc3 18 ♕xc3 ♘e4 19 ♕d3 ♕e6 20 ♗e5 ♖ac8 21 ♗d4 ♗e7 22 ♕f1 ♖xc1 23 ♖xc1 ♖c8 24 ♕d1 ♗d6 25 ♗f1 ♕f5 26 ♔g2 ♖xc1 27 ♕xc1 f6 28 ♗d3 ♔f7 29 ♕c2 g5 30 ♕e2 h5 31 ♘d2 g4 32 f3 gxf3+ 33 ♕xf3 ½-½

In the following game Black places all his

pieces in a more or less ideal way. I recommend you play through this game carefully and note how Black's pieces generate pressure.

Kramnik-Hübner
Yerevan 1996

1 ♘f3 ♘f6 2 c4 b6 3 g3 ♗b7 4 ♗g2 e6 5 0-0 ♗e7 6 ♘c3 0-0 7 ♖e1

This is Kramnik's way of playing the 7 ♖e1 variation. The threat of 8 e4 often makes Black respond with 7...d5, but 7...c5, along the lines of the hedgehog set-up, is a sensible move.

7...d5 8 cxd5 exd5 9 d4 ♘a6!

This is where the knight belongs. Black has no reason to fight for d4 in these positions because it is a fight he will only very rarely win. Rather he focuses on bringing the knight to an active post, the ideal spots being c5 and, primarily, e6.

10 ♗f4 c5 11 dxc5 ♘xc5 12 ♖c1 ♘fe4 13 ♘b5 ♘e6 14 ♗e5 ♕d7 15 ♘bd4 ♖ac8 16 ♖xc8 ♖xc8 17 ♗h3 ♗c5 18 a3 a5 19 e3 ♖e8 20 ♗g4

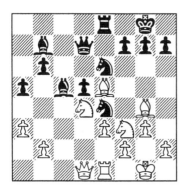

Here a draw was agreed.

If we look at the final position we see that all Black's pieces have a function. The knight on e6 monitors both d4 and f4 and can, potentially, jump to c5, from where an invasion might be possible. The knight on e4 keeps a good eye on f2 and also prevents White from putting his pieces completely at ease. The bishop on c5 exerts pressure on d4 and e3 and will, in the long run, prevent White from playing f2-f3, or at least serve to remind White that e3 would then become a weakness. The bishop on b7 looks bad but can often come into play with ...♗a6 or, perhaps, even the pawn sacrifice ...d5-d4 on some occasions. Only the heavy pieces are not easy to place. Usually the rooks should be at d8 and e8 if Black is playing for ...d5-d4, and at c8 and e8 if he (like here) has more or less ignored the fight for the d4-square.

White, on the other hand, tends to have problems in finding a good square for the dark-squared bishop. Principally it is best placed on b2, but that, of course, cannot happen without White weakening his queenside with b2-b3 at some point. As I mentioned above, this will give the knight, which is usually placed on e4, a future. Additionally, the bishop on g2 can often find that it is nicely placed, but with the knight on e4 it tends to be looking at a piece that cannot realistically be removed (the exchange would be far from ideal anyway) for fear of the resulting weaknesses on the light squares.

Let us take a look at another variation of the structures after ...d7-d5 and cxd5 exd5, where White is in no hurry to exchange on c5.

Karpov-Spassky
Riga 1975

1 d4 ♘f6 2 c4 e6 3 ♘f3 b6 4 g3 ♗b7 5 ♗g2 ♗e7 6 ♘c3 0-0 7 ♕c2 d5 8 cxd5 ♘xd5 9 0-0 ♘d7 10 ♘xd5 exd5 11 ♖d1 ♘f6

Where should White place his pieces here? I could use this as an exercise for my pupils because the answer is not so obvious if you are unfamiliar with the position. Well, the queen is fine (f5 or d2 look appropriate for later), the queen's rook goes to c1, the other rook is already perfectly placed, the queen's bishop has no obvious post and the other bishop is good. But what about White's knight? As Black will not fight for d4 the knight is not required on f3, but where would we prefer it to be? The correct answer is f4, from where it exerts considerable pressure on d5. The following manoeuvre is standard and will not have come as a surprise for Spassky.

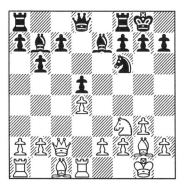

12 ♘e5 c5 13 dxc5 ♗xc5 14 ♘d3 ♗d6 15 ♗f4!

This bishop has no ideal square so seeking to remove it is quite logical.

15...♖e8 16 e3 ♘e4 17 ♗xd6 ♕xd6 18 ♘f4

White has an advantage. The d4-square is a good outpost for the heavy pieces and both the knight and the bishop are well placed. But most importantly – all the play will revolve around White's pressure on the d5-pawn, so Black will not be able to generate sufficient active play to compensate for the weakness.

18...♖ac8 19 ♕a4 ♕e7 20 ♕xa7 ♘xf2 21 ♘xd5 ♗xd5 22 ♕xe7 ♘xd1 23 ♖c1 ♖b8 24 ♕b4 ♗xg2 25 ♔xg2 ♘xe3+ 26 ♔g1 ♖e6 27 ♕f4 ♖d8 28 ♕d4 ♖de8 29 ♕d7 ♘g4 30 ♖c8 ♘f6 31 ♖xe8+ ♖xe8 32 ♕b7 ♖e6 33 ♕b8+ ♘e8 34 a4 g6 35 b4 ♔g7 36 ♕b7 h5 37 h3 ♔f6 38 ♔g2 ♖d6 39 a5 bxa5 40 bxa5 ♖e6 41 a6 ♘c7 42 a7 ♖e7 43 ♕c6+ ♔e5 44 ♔f3 1-0

The same manoeuvre is also possible even if the pair of knights has yet to be exchanged. The following example illustrates how White handles the possibility of ...c5xd4.

Beliavsky-Chuchelov
Ohrid 2001

1 d4 ♘f6 2 c4 e6 3 ♘f3 b6 4 g3 ♗a6 5 b3 d5 6 cxd5 exd5 7 ♗g2 ♗b4+ 8 ♗d2 ♗e7 9 0-0 0-0 10 ♘c3 ♗b7 11 ♖c1 ♘a6 12 ♗b2 ♖e8 13 ♖c1 ♗f8 14 ♘e5 c5 15 ♘d3 cxd4

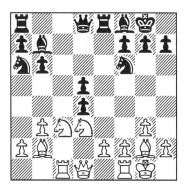

Black's trade in the centre is probably not the best. Clearly Black was familiar with the following manoeuvre, but it still seems to be a particularly unnecessary concession to give up the d4-square when having to face a well placed knight on f4.

16 ♘b5!

The main idea. In this position the knight transfer is rather straightforward, but some players have a tendency to forget about this if White has the option of recapturing on d4 with the queen. Now White has an edge.

16...♕d7 17 ♘xd4 ♘e4 18 ♘f4 ♖ed8 19 ♗h3 ♕e8 20 a3 ♘g5 21 ♗g2 ♘c5 22 b4 ♘a4 23 ♗a1 ♘e4 24 ♖c7 ♖ab8 25 ♘f5 d4 26 ♕c2 ♖bc8 27 ♘xd4 a5 28 b5 ♖xc7 29 ♕xc7 ♕d7 30 ♕c2 ♘ac5 31 ♘d3 ♖c8 32 ♘c6 ♘xd3 33 ♗xe4 ♘c5 34 ♗xh7+ ♔h8 35 ♗f5 ♘e6 36 ♖d1 ♕e8 37 ♕e4 1-0

CHAPTER ONE

Opting for Nothing:
4 ♗f4 and 4 ♗g5

1 d4 ♘f6 2 c4 e6 3 ♘f3 b6 4 ♗f4/4 ♗g5

There are some players, no matter what their rating, who always try to avoid main line theory. This can be for different reasons, of course – one is simply a surrender to the modern reality of the enormous amount of games in a standard database, while another is the need for an independent and original way of playing, based more on psychology than actual playing style.

Both 4 ♗g5 and 4 ♗f4 are ways to stay clear of all established theory in the Queen's Indian. Neither is dangerous for Black, but if you are content to get your pieces out and then play a game on practically alien soil, then 4 ♗f4 in particular makes good sense, as can be seen from Miles' and Bareev's relative success with this approach.

Game 1
Miles-Unzicker
Johannesburg 1979

---

1 c4 ♘f6 2 ♘f3 b6 3 d4 e6 4 ♗f4

This move is mainly played by those wanting to avoid the extensively explored waters of opening theory. It is neither good nor bad, just a plausible option. The thing to do when you are preparing an opening system like the QID is to acknowledge that these possibili-

ties exist, take a look at them once or twice and then let your understanding of the position be your guide. The three games I have presented here should more than cover what you need to know about the system.

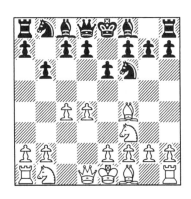

4...♗b7 5 e3 ♗b4+

This is an interesting choice. The simpler 5...♗e7 is presented in Game 3.

6 ♘fd2

The key reasoning behind this retreat is as follows:

1) The queen's knight belongs on c3 and not d2, and

2) White does not want doubled pawns.

There are two alternatives, each contradicting these points. Somewhat similar to the Nimzo-Indian and the lines in this book featuring 4 ♘f3 and 5 ♗g5 are the positions arising after 6 ♘c3 ♗xc3+ 7 bxc3 d6, when there are two set-ups for Black to choose between:

a) 8 ♗d3 ♘bd7 9 0-0 ♕e7 10 ♘d2 e5 11 ♗g3 0-0 12 ♖e1 c5 sees Black trying to dominate White's centre and bishops. In fact this seems to be rock solid, and Black had a good game in Ostenstad-Hjartarson, Gausdal 1985.

b) 8 h3 ♘bd7 9 ♗h2 ♕e7 10 ♖b1 0-0 11 ♗e2 ♘e4 12 ♖b3 f5 brings about another traditional set-up from the Nimzo-Indian. It is not clear that ♗h2 is, after all, such a great piece, but it is easy for Black to find good squares for his minor pieces, e.g. 13 0-0 e5!? (limiting the scope of White's bishop, although it was also possible to ignore it) 14 c5 ♗c6 and Black is fine, Agdestein-Yrjola, Gausdal 1985.

Meanwhile 6 ♘bd2 0-0 7 ♗d3 d5 8 0-0 ♘bd7 9 ♖c1 ♗d6 10 ♘e5 ♘e4 11 cxd5 exd5 12 ♘xd7 ♕xd7 gave Black full equality in Matera-Dzindzichashvili, New York 1980.

6...0-0 7 a3 ♗e7 8 ♘c3 d5

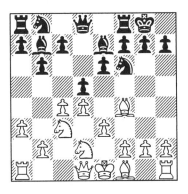

9 cxd5 ♘xd5!

This is the safe path to equality. Recapturing with the pawn would be ungrateful to the bishop on b7, although it has been tried. After 9...exd5 10 ♗d3 c5 11 0-0 ♘c6 12 ♘f3 White probably has a slight edge. In Meduna-Vilela, Leipzig 1980, play continued 12...a6 13 ♘e5 cxd4 14 ♘xc6 ♗xc6 15 exd4 ♖e8 16 ♖e1 ♗d6 17 ♕f3 with a slightly worse position for Black.

10 ♘xd5 ♗xd5 11 ♕c2

Here White has a serious alternative in 11 ♖c1. Then 11...♗d6!? 12 ♗xd6 cxd6 looks solid, while Miles-Hübner, England-West Germany 1979, continued 11...c5 12 dxc5 ♗xc5 13 ♗c4 ♗b7! 14 0-0 ♗d6 with approximate equality. Instead 13...♗xc4 14 ♘xc4 ♕xd1+ 15 ♔xd1 ♘d7 16 ♔e2 ♘f6 17 ♗d6 led to a lasting ending advantage for White in Miles-Ligterink, Amsterdam 1978, while 13...♘c6 14 b4 ♗e7 15 ♗b5! favours White as both ♗xc6 and e3-e4 are threatened..

11...c5

Equally good looks 11...♗d6 12 ♗xd6 cxd6 13 ♗d3 g6 14 0-0 ♘d7 15 ♖ac1 ♖c8 16 ♕a4 ♖c7 with equality in Meduna-Unzicker, Moscow 1982. Here 14 e4 ♗b7 15 0-0 ♘c6 16 ♘f3 ♕f6 also seems to fail to give Black problems in finding good squares for his pieces.

12 dxc5 ♗xc5 13 ♘e4

13 ♗d3 h6 14 0-0 ♘d7 15 ♖fd1 ♘f6 looked fine for Black in Meduna-Brynell, Leon 2001.

13...♘d7!

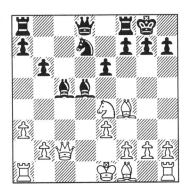

Black chooses to complete his development. This is more important than the two bishops. Now, thanks to the activity of the knight and the possibility of exchanging dark-squared bishops, Black can equalise.

**14 ℤd1 ♕c8 15 ♗d3 ♗xe4 16 ♗xe4 ♘f6
17 ♗d3**

The trick was, of course, 17 ♗xa8 ♗b4+!, and Black wins.

**17...♗e7 18 ♕e2 ♕c5 19 h3 ♘d5 20
♗g3 ℤad8 21 0-0 ♗d6 22 ℤc1 ♕a5 23
♗xd6 ℤxd6 24 ℤfd1 ℤfd8 25 ♗b5 ♘e7
26 ℤxd6 ℤxd6 27 ℤc3 ℤd5 28 a4 ♕b4
29 ℤc7 a5 30 g3 g6 31 ♔g2 ♕d6 32
ℤd7 ♕c5 33 ℤa7 ℤd8 34 ♕f3 ♘f5 35 e4
½-½**

After ...♘d6 Black has nothing to fear.

Game 2
Bareev-Karpov
Moscow (blitz) 1993

**1 d4 ♘f6 2 c4 e6 3 ♘f3 b6 4 ♗f4 ♗b7 5
e3 ♗e7**

This move is more natural than 5...♗b4+ and should lead to a good game without too much trouble.

6 ♘c3 ♘h5!

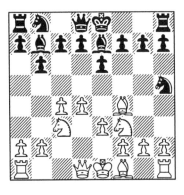

If White fails to address the well-being of the bishop then Black should, of course, attack it. Now White will anyway have to lose a tempo...

7 ♗g3 0-0

Karpov's strategy is logical and simple. The key idea is to develop, eliminating the bishop only when he is somehow forced to do so. Another possibility is to delay castling by exchanging the bishop immediately, e.g.

7...♘xg3!? 8 hxg3 ♗f6 9 ♕c2 g6 10 0-0-0 ♕e7 11 ♗d3 ♘c6 12 ♗e4 0-0-0, leading to an original position where both players had good chances in Rodriguez-Fedorowicz, New York 1987.

8 ♕c2

In this game Bareev elects, quite logically, to bury the bishop on b7 by advancing d4-d5. If he had not done so he might have played along the following lines: 8 ♗e2 g6! (a standard reaction; now the knight won't be hanging after surprises like ♘f3-e5) 9 0-0 d6 10 ℤc1 ♘d7 11 ♘d2 ♘xg3 12 hxg3 a6 13 ♗f3 c6 14 g4 ♕b8 15 a4 d5 16 cxd5 cxd5 17 ♗e2 ♕d6 with equality in Agdestein-Adorjan, Oslo 1984.

8...d6 9 d5

Essentially the same position as in the game, with the same players, arose after 9 ♗e2 g6 10 0-0-0 ♘d7 11 d5 e5 12 ♘d2 in Bareev-Karpov, Paris 1992. Now Black did not play the best move, 12...♘g7!, which he must have realised later (which brings us to the present game). Instead 12...♘df6 13 ♔b1 a6 14 f3 ♘xg3 15 hxg3 h5 16 e4 ♗c8 17 ♘f1 ℤe8 18 ♘e3 ♗f8 19 ♕d3 ♕e7 20 ℤh2 ♗d7 21 ℤdh1 ♗g7 22 ♘c2 ♘h6 23 ♘b4 ℤec8 24 ♘c6 ♕e8 25 g4 saw White being allowed to create a strong attack that was enough to win the game...

9...e5 10 ♗e2 g6 11 ♘d2

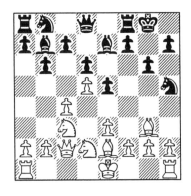

11...♘g7!

The correct decision. The g3-bishop is not

impressive and White would benefit tremendously from the opening of the h-file, as can be seen in the following game: 11...♘xg3?! 12 hxg3 ♘d7 13 0-0-0 ♔g7 14 g4 a6 15 g3 c6 16 ♗f3 ♖c8 17 dxc6 ♗xc6 18 ♗xc6 ♖xc6 19 ♕e4 with a clear advantage to White in Bareev-Karpov, Paris 1992. It should be noted that all these games were in 'active' chess of some form, and not played with the usual, longer time control.

12 e4 ♘d7 13 0-0

This looks very suspicious.

13...♗g5!

Compare the bishops on g5 and g3. Black has at least equalised.

14 b4 h5 15 h3 ♕f6 16 ♘f3 ♗f4!

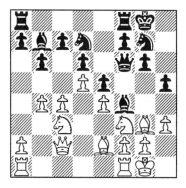

Exchanging the bishop to win the e5-square and making way for the g-pawn.

17 ♗xf4

17...g5, with an attack, was a serious threat.

17...exf4 18 ♕d2 g5 19 e5!?

White is worse and he knows it, so he decides to sacrifice a pawn in a bid to change the nature of the position and win some squares for his pieces.

19...♘xe5 20 ♘xe5 ♕xe5 21 ♖ae1 ♕f6 22 h4 gxh4 23 ♘e4 ♕f5 24 ♕d4 f6 25 ♘d2 h3!

Black uses his additional material to ruin White's king position. Black is winning.

26 gxh3 ♕xh3 27 ♕xf4 ♖ae8 28 ♕g3 ♕xg3+ 29 fxg3 ♖e5 30 ♘f3 ♖e3 31

♗d1 ♖fe8 32 ♔f2 ♖xe1 33 ♘xe1 b5

34 cxb5 ♗xd5 35 a4 ♖e4 36 ♗f3 ♖e5 37 ♘d3 ♖f5 38 ♘f4 ♗c4 39 ♖e1 ♔f7 0-1

Game 3
Nikolic-Lautier
Moscow (Fide knockout) 2001

---

1 d4 ♘f6 2 ♘f3 e6 3 c4 b6 4 ♗f4 ♗b7 5 e3 ♗e7 6 h3

Preserving the bishop, but this costs time, so Black decides to act at once in the centre.

6...c5!

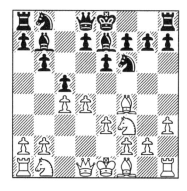

This is the easiest way to equalise. White's dark-squared bishop has left the queenside (g1-a7 and everything on the queenside as a result of e2-e3) so Black then operates on the dark squares there. This is perfectly logical.

The old way to play this was 6...0-0 7 ♘c3

d5 but this might result in a modest advantage for White in some cases. After 8 cxd5 ♘xd5 9 ♘xd5 ♕xd5 10 a3 c5 11 dxc5 ♕xc5 12 ♗e2 ♖d8 13 ♕b1 ♗a6 14 ♗xa6 ♕a5+ 15 ♔f1 ♕xa6+ 16 ♔g1 ♘d7 17 ♔h2, as in Meduna-Lerner, Lvov 1981, White's minor pieces are well placed, although Black should be okay. Perhaps if White plays something slower in the opening Black will have to face some problems.

7 d5?

This is completely suicidal. It is difficult to imagine a top GM playing something like this. There are two essentially different set-ups here.

a) 7 dxc5 bxc5 8 ♘c3 0-0 9 ♗e2 ♘c6 10 0-0 d6 11 ♕c2 ♕b6 is a universal approach for Black in the QID and almost always guarantees an equal position. Lputian-Mikhalchishin, Frunze 1979 continued 12 ♖ad1 ♖fd8 (12...♖ad8 13 ♖d2 h6 14 ♖fd1 ♖d7 15 ♘e1 ♖fd8 was equal in Langeweg-Timman, Leeuwarden 1980) 13 ♖d2 d5!? (an interesting decision, sharpening the position) 14 ♖fd1 ♘b4 15 ♕b1 dxc4 16 ♖xd8+ ♖xd8 17 ♘d2 (17 ♗xc4 ♗xf3 18 gxf3 ♘bd5) 17...♘bd5 18 ♘xc4 ♘xc3 19 bxc3 ♕xb1 20 ♖xb1 ♗e4 21 ♖b3 ♘d5 and here it is White who is fighting to keep the balance (which Lputian failed to do).

b) 7 ♘c3 cxd4 and now a possibility is 8 exd4, leading to a position similar to the Panov/Nimzo-Indian after 8...0-0 9 ♗d3 d5 10 0-0 dxc4 11 ♗xc4 ♘c6 12 ♖c1 ♖c8 13 ♗d3 ♘d5, Rivas Pastor-Hübner, Linares 1985. Here the moves h2-h3 and ♗f4 were clearly not very aggressive. Black has equalised. This leaves us with 8 ♘xd4 and a further branch:

b1) 8...a6 9 ♗e2 0-0 and now 10 ♗f3 is logical, dealing with Black's bishop, which has considerable influence on the centre. Gretarsson-Stefansson, Stockholm 1998 continued 10...♖a7 11 ♕a4 ♗xf3 12 ♘xf3 d6 13 0-0 ♕c8 14 ♖fd1 ♖d8 15 ♖d2 ♖c7 16 ♕d1 with an equal position, while Gretars-

son-Hansen, Gentofte 1999 went 10 0-0 d6 11 ♘b3 ♕c7 12 ♖e1 ♘bd7 with equality, although Black's game is probably the easier to conduct.

b2) 8...0-0!? is provocative but if White cannot exploit it then it is by far the most logical response. Miles-Kupreichik, Reykjavik 1980 continued 9 ♘db5 ♘e8 10 ♕d2?! (this move is obviously just losing time; better was 10 ♘d6 with an unclear position) 10...a6 11 ♘d6 ♘xd6 12 ♗xd6 ♗xd6 13 ♕xd6 b5! 14 a3 bxc4 15 ♖d1 ♘c6 16 ♗xc4 ♕g5 and Black has a useful lead in development.

7...exd5 8 ♘c3 dxc4!

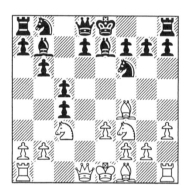

Black is testing the pawn sacrifice. Or he is just taking the pawn. You decide.

9 ♘b5

It is too late to play for compensation with 9 ♗xc4 because 9...d5 10 ♗b5+ ♗c6 gives White very little.

9...0-0!

Simple chess. White should not really take the exchange so Black simply makes the move from which he most benefits.

10 ♘c7?

The strategically decisive mistake. The only move here is 10 ♗c7! ♕c8 11 ♗d6, with ♗xc4 to come, trying for some kind of compensation.

10...d5 11 ♘xa8 ♗xa8

Black has two big central pawns and an enormous lead in development. The advantage is not in doubt.

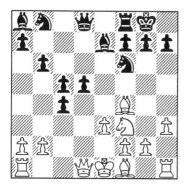

12 ♗e2 ♘c6 13 0-0 b5 14 a4 b4 15 ♕b1 ♘e4 16 ♖d1 ♘a5 17 ♘e5 ♘b3 18 ♗xc4

Who cares about pieces here? The pawns are doing the job!

18...♘ed2 19 ♕c2 dxc4 0-1

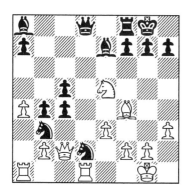

Game 4
Teske-Paehtz
East Germany 1988

(When one is confronted with a game such as this one always wonders whether the draw was pre-arranged, as well as the moves themselves – often this is the case, but you can never be really sure)

1 d4 ♘f6 2 c4 e6 3 ♘f3 b6 4 ♗g5

This move has less independent relevance than 4 ♗f4, as it often transposes to 4 ♘c3 ♗b7 5 ♗g5, which is treated in Chapter 3.

4...♗b4+

This is just as natural as 4...♗b7, although Black now loses the option of 5...♗e7 instead of ...♗b4. Of course if Black is not interested in 5...♗e7 the text is quite a funny move, threatening to engineer a win, as happens in this game.

4...♗b7 5 ♘bd2?! fails to impress. After 5...♗e7 6 e3 h6 7 ♗h4 0-0 8 ♗d3 c5 9 0-0 cxd4 10 exd4 d5!, as in Wuts-Matthias, Germany 1996, Black has at least equalised. The long-term potentials in the position are in Black's favour and the knight on d2 is not well placed in terms of the fight for the d5-square. Now Black will be able to take control over this quite easily and thus develop more freely than is usual in such positions.

5 ♘bd2

This move gives the line independent value, but it is not good. 5 ♘c3 ♗b7 leads us back to Chapter 3.

5...h6 6 ♗h4

6 a3!? is a possibility. If you are an occasional Bogo-Indian fan you can play 6...♗xd2+ 7 ♗xd2 ♗b7 with a good version!? Otherwise the simple 6...♗e7 should equalise directly.

6...g5 7 ♗g3 g4 8 ♘e5?

Losing. The only move is 8 a3!, with good prospects for Black after 8...♗e7 9 ♘e5 d6 10 ♕a4+ c6 11 ♘d3 ♕d7! followed by ...♗b7 and ...c6-c5.

8...♘e4 9 ♗f4 ♕f6 10 ♘d3 ♕xd4!

Capturing the pawn without releasing the pressure.

11 e3

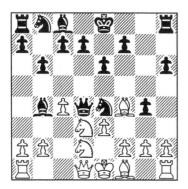

11...♘xd2??

What a blunder! After 11...♗xd2+! 12 ♕xd2 ♘xd2 13 exd4 ♘xf1 14 ♖xf1 ♗b7 Black is clearly better. White has some compensation on the dark squares but I, for one,

would take the risk!

12 exd4

Now we have a perpetual.

12...♘f3+ 13 ♔e2 ♘xd4+ 14 ♔e3 ♘f5+ 15 ♔e2

15 ♔e4 ♗b7+ 16 ♔e5 d6+ 17 ♔f6 ♘d7 mate(!) is a sour way to end your days.

15...♘d4+ 16 ♔e3 ♘f5+ 17 ♔e2 ♘d4+ ½-½

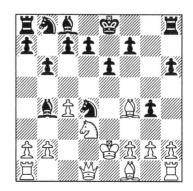

Summary

4 ♗f4 is a rather harmless move and after 4...♗b7 5 e3 both 5...♗b4+ and 5...♗e7 lead to safe equality. Still it is a good idea to check out the most important ideas here, or White might be able to pose Black some problems. 4 ♗g5 should not gain any independent significance, but simply transpose to Chapter 3. After 5 ♘bd2 Black is always going to be fine.

1 d4 ♘f6 2 c4 e6 3 ♘f3 b6 4 ♗f4 *(D)*

       4 ♗g5 *(D)* ♗b4+

            5 ♘c3 ♗b7 – Chapter 3

            5 ♘bd2 – *Game 4*

4...♗b7 5 e3 ♗e7 *(D)*

       5...♗b4+ 6 ♘fd2 – *Game 1*

6 ♘c3 – *Game 2*

       6 h3 – *Game 3*

    4 ♗f4   *4 ♗g5*   *5...♗e7*

CHAPTER TWO

The Petrosian System: 4 a3

1 d4 ♘f6 2 c4 e6 3 ♘f3 b6 4 a3

The Petrosian System had its heyday in modern times during the 1980's, when Kasparov – still a boy – blew away the world's strongest GMs. Today the variation does not enjoy the same status and is regarded as one of several options, not necessarily offering White an advantage, but leading to positions where many players feel comfortable. And, of course, new ideas are constantly produced.

In Game 5 we see what happens when Black pushes with ...d7-d5 and recaptures with the e-pawn. White might have a slightly more comfortable game but Black should do okay with decent play. Game 6 features an idea, 4...c6, tried once and not again (for good reasons), while Game 7 introduces a very interesting, dynamic system, namely 4...c5!?, a line that resembles the Benoni, which seems to be totally playable at the moment. In Game 8 we just glance at what happens if White is unambitious against 4...c5 –and not surprisingly, nothing happens. Game 9 includes the minor lines against 4...♗a6, which is one of Black's main replies, while we discuss the direct assault 5 ♕c2 ♗b7 (5...c5 leads to Game 7) 6 ♘c3 c5 7 d5?! in Game 10. Game 11 features one of the main lines, 7 e4 cxd4 8 ♘xd4 ♗c5, and Game 12 investigates 8...♘c6 9 ♘xc6 ♗xc6

10 ♗f4 ♘h5, which currently looks like the most promising system for Black in the 4...♗a6 line. In Game 13 it is time for 10...♗c5, which seems to give White an edge.

Game 5
Portisch-Nikolic
Ljubljana 1985

1 d4 ♘f6 2 c4 e6 3 ♘f3 b6 4 a3

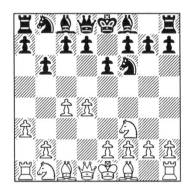

4...d5!?

This move is not the standard theoretical recommendation, but such great players as Petrosian, Larsen, Karpov and Bronstein, have given it a strong vote of confidence, simply by employing it against fellow players from the world's elite. Besides this, 4...♗b7 and 4...♗a6 are the standard moves. 4...c6 and 4...c5 are treated in the following games, while 4...♘e4 5 ♘fd2! d5 6 e3 ♗b7 7 cxd5! exd5 8 ♘xe4 dxe4 9 ♘c3 ♗d6 10 ♗b5+ ♔f8 (10...c6 11 ♗a4! and e4 is in trouble, unless Black accepts something along the lines of 11...f5 12 ♗b3!, and the king is caught in the middle) 11 ♕c2 ♕g5 12 g3 a6 13 ♗f1 f5 14 ♗g2 gave White the advantage in Glek-Rozentalis, Lvov 1985.

4...♗e7 5 ♘c3 0-0 is a strange and alternative way to play. After the logical 6 d5!? (taking control over the light squares in the centre, hoping to bury the bishop on c8) 6...♖e8! (directed against 7 e4) 7 g3 ♗a6 8 ♗g2! ♗xc4 (8...d6 9 dxe6 fxe6 10 ♘d4 seems risky) 9 ♘e5 ♗xd5 10 ♘xd5 exd5 11 ♗xd5 ♘xd5 12 ♕xd5 c6 13 ♕xf7+ ♔h8 14 ♕h5 ♕c8 15 ♗f4 d5 16 ♖c1 ♗f8 Black might have been okay in Gofshtein-Vitolinsh, Beltsy 1979, but the general impression of the game is that Black had to take risks without ever having a genuine opportunity to obtain more than an equal position..

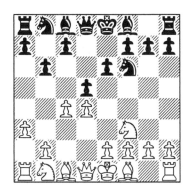

5 cxd5

White decides not to give his opponent the chance to return to the main lines with 5 ♘c3 ♗b7, although most players would probably stick with their choice and play 5...♗e7, with a transposition. However, after the usual 6 cxd5 Black can remain within the lines here with 6...exd5, but there are some things with ♕a4+. All these nuances are treated under 7 ♕a4+ in Game 15.

5...exd5

5...♘xd5 6 e4 is not relevant.

6 ♘c3 ♗e7 7 ♗f4

This is one of the two standard ways to place the pieces. 7 ♗g5 is also possible, of course, with a position from the Queen's Gambit Declined rather than the QID. The real alternative, and simply a matter of taste, is 7 g3 0-0 8 ♗g2 c5 9 0-0 ♗b7 10 ♗f4, but White cannot count on a significant advantage after 10...♘a6 11 ♘e5 (11 dxc5 bxc5 12 ♕b3 ♕b6 13 ♘d2 ♕xb3 14 ♘xb3 ♖ad8 15 ♘a5 ♗a8 was equal in Lputian-Nikolic, Sarajevo 1998, but 11 ♖c1! seems to be the most logical move) 11...♘c7. Note that here 11...♘e4? meets with 12 ♘xe4 dxe4 13 dxc5 ♘xc5 14 ♕c2 ♖c8 15 ♖fd1 ♕e8 16 ♗h3 ♘e6 17 ♕b3, which put Black under great pressure in Vaganian-Gulko, Lvov 1978. As we shall see it is a characteristic of these positions that ...♘e4 tends to be a clear positional error, and Black should be well aware of when it is playable and when it is not! Returning to 11...♘c7, with 12 dxc5 White chooses a forced continuation which ends with a completely level position, but ...cxd4 was a real threat now that the knight has control over b5. After 12...bxc5 13 ♘c4 ♖b8 14 ♗xc7 ♕xc7 15 ♘xd5 ♗xd5 16 ♗xd5 ♖fd8! (the most active, although 16...♖bd8 is also good enough) 17 e4 ♘xe4 we have the following:

a) 18 ♕h5?! g6 19 ♗xf7+ is given by Parma as leading to an advantage, but 19...♔g7 20 ♕e2 ♘d2! 21 ♖fe1 (21 ♘xd2?! ♖xb2 22 ♖ad1 ♔xf7 and here the bishop and the passed pawn must give Black a favourable position) 21...♗f6 22 ♗e6 ♘xc4 23 ♕xc4 ♖xb2 followed by ...♗d4 might even favour Black.

b) 18 ♕e2 ♖xd5 19 ♕xe4 ♕d7 20 ♖fe1 ♗f6 21 ♖ac1 h5 22 h4 ♗d4 23 ♖c2 a5 24 ♖ce2 ♖f5 with equality and a draw in Browne-Ljubojevic, Brasilia 1981.

7...0-0 8 e3

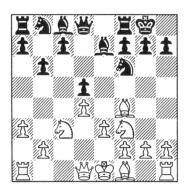

8...c5

The most active, but Black has more than one reasonable move here.

a) 8...♗f5 seems perfectly logical because the exchange has already been performed on d5 and, consequently, b7 is no longer a good square for the bishop. Still, the move does abandon the light squares on the queenside. Van der Sterren-Short, Baku 1983, continued 9 ♗e2 (9 ♗d3 also looks okay) 9...♘e4 10 ♕b3 c6 11 0-0 ♗d6 12 ♗xd6 ♕xd6 13 ♖ac1 ♘d7 with approximate equality.

b) 8...♗b7. This way of holding back the c-pawn makes sense. All the pieces can develop freely, so why not? Timman-Sunye Neto, Las Palmas 1982, went 9 ♗e2 (9 ♖c1!?, forcing Black to make a decision, is interesting) 9...♘bd7 10 ♘e5 (10 0-0 must be more testing) 10...♘e4 11 ♘xe4 dxe4 12 ♖c1 ♘xe5 13 ♗xe5 ♗d6 14 ♗xd6 cxd6 15 ♕a4 (this move does not impress; 15 0-0 must be better) 15...a6 16 0-0 ♗d5 17 ♖c3 b5 18 ♕c2 ♕b6 and Black looks more than fine. Bacrot-Röder, Spain 2001, saw positionally unsound play from Black: 9...a6 10 b4 ♗d6 11 ♗g3 ♕e7 12 ♕b3 ♘bd7 13 0-0 ♗xg3 14 hxg3 ♕d6 15 ♖fc1 ♖fe8 16 b5 c6 17 bxc6 ♗xc6 18 ♕b4 and Black had weaknesses in his pawn structure, while his bishop had no prospects.

c) 8...♗e6 seems illogical. The bishop is less well placed here than on f5 and b7. 9 h3 c5 10 ♗d3 ♘c6 11 0-0 a6 12 ♖c1 c4 13 ♗b1

b5 14 ♘e5 ♕b6 15 ♗g5 ♖fe8 16 f4 earned White an advantage in Wilder-Larsen, New York 1984.

d) 8...c6!? offers White some chances of a slight advantage if he plays 9 ♗d3. But after 9 ♘e5 ♗f5 10 g4!? ♗e6 11 ♗d3 ♘fd7 12 ♕c2, as in A.Petrosian-Short, Yerevan 1984, the situation is more difficult to evaluate, although White looks good here, too..

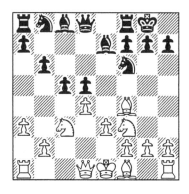

9 ♘e5

It may sound strange but this is the most flexible move available to White. Note that it is the only move that White is sure he will make, whereas the decision to put the bishop on e2 or d3, for example, can be made later. However, many games have been played using these moves directly:

a) 9 ♗e2 is the most serious alternative. After 9...♗b7 10 ♘e5 (10 0-0 ♘c6 or 10...♘a6, or 10...♘bd7 11 ♘e5 transposes) Black must make a choice – two options are interesting, the third less good.

a1) 10...♘a6!? is natural. It has not been properly tested in practice, only in this one game, Bacrot-Kurajica, Yerevan 1996, where White achieved nothing by playing 11 ♕a4 ♘c7 12 ♘c6 ♗xc6 13 ♕xc6 with the two bishops, being behind in development and already fielding threats – after 13...♘e6 14 ♗e5 cxd4 15 ♗xd4 (15 exd4!? is the testing move) 15...♖c8 16 ♕b5 ♘xd4 17 exd4 ♘e4 18 ♘xd5 ♗c5 19 dxc5 ♖xc5 20 ♕b4 ♕xd5 was equal. Instead 19 ♖d1! ♕xd5 20 dxc5

Wxc5 21 Wxc5 Xxc5 22 0-0 Xe8 23 Xfe1 gives White a tiny lead with bishop against knight in the endgame, although this will, in 99.9% of all cases, not influence the result.

a2) 10...♘bd7 seems to do less well with ...c7-c5 than the other knight moves. After 11 0-0 Xc8 12 dxc5 ♘xc5? (12...bxc5!? should keep the balance) 13 ♘b5! a6 14 ♘d4 White had the advantage in Ribli-Gligoric, Lucerne 1982. 11...♘xe5? is almost always bad when White's bishop is on e2: 12 dxe5 ♘e4 13 ♘xe4 dxe4 14 Wa4 a6 15 Xfd1 We8 16 Wb3 b5 17 e6 with advantage to White, Lputian-Zagrebelny, Lucerne 1993. The e4-square will always be weak in the endgame.

a3) 10...♘c6 11 0-0 cxd4 12 exd4 ♘e4 (as always with the bishop on e2 Black ends up in trouble after 12...♘xe5?! 13 dxe5 ♘e4 14 ♘xe4 dxe4 15 Wa4 a6 16 Xfd1 We8 17 Wb3, as in Timman-Larsen, Tilburg 1982) 13 ♘xc6 Xxc6 14 Xc1 Wd7 15 ♗a6 Xad8 16 Wd3 ♗d6 and now Farago-Matanovic, Vienna 1986 continued 17 ♘e2?! ♗xf4 18 ♘xf4 Wd6, when Black appeared to have survived the opening. With 17 ♘e2?! White completely lacked a plan; better was 17 ♗xd6 Wxd6 18 Xc2! to use the c-file in the near future!

b) 9 ♗d3 was played in Plaskett-Stefansson, Reykjavik 1992. There followed 9...♘c6 10 Xc1 (10 ♘e5 transposes to the main line) 10...♗b7 11 0-0 h6 12 ♘e5 ♘xe5 13 dxe5 (13 ♗xe5, with equality, is most likely superior) 13...♘e4 14 Wh5 We8!, preparing ...f7-f5 in the case of a sacrifice. After 15 ♘xe4 dxe4 16 ♗c4 b5 17 ♗a2 c4 Black was better.

c) 9 h3 ♘c6 10 ♗d3 should not be dangerous for Black, but after 10...cxd4 (a premature decision; 10...♗b7 offers good chances of equality) 11 exd4 ♗d6 12 ♗xd6 Wxd6 13 0-0 Xe8 14 ♗b5! ♗d7 15 ♗xc6 ♗xc6 16 ♘e5 White had an edge in Schandorff-Larsen, Denmark 1989.

d) Interesting is 9 Xc1 ♘c6 10 ♗e2 c4 (10...♗b7 is more natural). Now White can

choose a very interesting plan in 11 b4!?, with the idea that c3 will be a fine blockading square, and later e3-e4 will undermine Black's centre. Ostojic-Abramovic, Banja Vrucica 1991 was unclear after 11...a6 12 0-0 b5 13 ♘e5 ♗b7 14 ♗f3.

9...♗b7

Once the pawn has arrived on c5 this is the appropriate square for the bishop. After 9...♗e6 the c6-square is left weakened, something well illustrated in the following game: 10 ♗d3 Wc8 11 0-0 c4 12 ♗c2 ♘bd7 13 ♗a4 a6 14 ♘c6 Xe8 15 ♘xe7+ Xxe7 16 f3 b5 17 ♗c2 Wc6 18 Wd2 and the two bishops gave White good chances for an advantage in Bisguier-Villarroel, Caracas 1970.

10 ♗d3 ♘c6

10...♘bd7 is quite passive – as I mentioned earlier, ...c7-c5 and ...♘bd7 do not combine well. 11 Wf3 Xe8 12 0-0 a6 13 Wh3 created promising attacking chances for White in Tal-Bronstein, Tbilisi 1982.

11 0-0

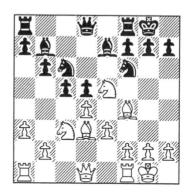

11...cxd4

This is the main line in *ECO* and other places, but I recommend 11...♘xe5! 12 dxe5 (12 ♗xe5, with equality, might be the best move) 12...♘e4!, the difference between this and other situations being that the bishop is now on d3. Browne-Frias, Santiago 1981 continued 13 Wc2 ♘xc3! 14 bxc3 (14 ♗xh7+ ♔h8 15 bxc3 g6 16 ♗xg6 fxg6 17 Wxg6 We8 and, as Black has control over all the light squares, there will be no attack, only three scattered pawns for the piece), and now not 14...g6? 15 ♗h6 ♖e8 16 ♗b5, when White was winning, but 14...h6, with an unclear position that Black should not fear. The alternative 12...♘e8?! was tried in Ligterink-Nikolic, Wijk aan Zee 1984, when 13 ♕g4 g6 14 ♖ad1 h5 15 ♕f3 ♘c7 16 ♗h6 was slightly better for White.

12 ♘xc6 ♗xc6 13 exd4 ♗d6?!

After this move Black will always face some problems. The exchange is illogical as it highlights the difference between the bishops on d3 and c6. An improvement is 13...♕d7! 14 ♕f3 ♖ae8! (the argument for using this rook lies in the following line: 14...♖fe8 15 ♖fe1 ♗d6 16 ♗g5! ♘e4 17 ♘xe4 dxe4 18 ♗xe4 ♖xe4? 19 ♖xe4 ♕b7 20 ♖ae1, where ...f7-f5 has no protection – with the rook on f8 this is not the case) 15 ♖fe1 ♗d6 16 ♗e5 (16 ♗g5? ♘e4! 17 ♘xe4? dxe4 18 ♗xe4 ♖xe4! 19 ♖xe4 ♕b7 and Black wins) 16...♗xe5 17 dxe5 d4 18 ♘e4 was Petursson-Larsen, Næstved 1988, and now Larsen writes that Black can keep the balance with 18...♘xe4 19 ♗xe4 ♗xe4 20 ♕xe4 ♖e6!, which looks correct as far as I can see. 21 ♖ad1 ♖d8 22 f4 d3 23 f5 ♖ee8! is an important line, when the e-pawn is getting as weak as the d-pawn, at least. Black should avoid 23...♖c6?? 24 e6 fxe6 25 fxe6 ♕e8 26 e7 ♖dc8 27 ♕xd3 and White wins.

14 ♗g5

14 ♕f3!? is also natural, preparing a future ♗e5!.

14...h6 15 ♗h4 ♖e8 16 ♗c2 ♗e7 17 ♖e1 ♘e4

This is the only move that, in the long run, frees Black from having to push with ...g7-g5.

18 ♗xe7 ♖xe7 19 ♕e2! ♖d7?!

Very passive. Now White gets time to strengthen his position without any worries. 19...♖e6 20 ♗xe4 dxe4 21 d5 ♗xd5 22 ♖ad1 ♖d6 23 ♕d2 ♕h4 24 ♘xd5 ♖ad8 25 g3 ♕g4 26 ♘e7+ ♔f8 27 ♕xd6 ♖xd6 28 ♖xd6 ♔xe7 29 ♖d3 might give White a small advantage

in the endgame, but only if he manages to penetrate to the 7th rank will he be able to win.

20 ♕d3 g6 21 ♗b3 ♔g7 22 ♖ac1 ♖c8 23 f3 ♘d6 24 ♕e3 ♘c4?!

Forcing this exchange only benefits White. After a more careful move Black should be only slightly worse.

25 ♗xc4 dxc4 26 ♖cd1 ♕g5!?

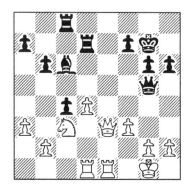

Introducing a tactical endgame in which Black is on the receiving end.

27 ♕xg5 hxg5 28 d5 ♗b7 29 ♖e5 ♖c5?

Here 29...♔f6 is the appropriate move, after which White maintains some pressure.

30 ♖xg5 f5 31 h4 ♔f6 32 d6 ♖e5 33 ♔f2 ♖e6 34 ♘e2 ♖dxd6 35 ♘f4 ♖xd1 36 ♖xg6+ ♔f7 37 ♖xe6 ♖d4

38 ♖h6 ♖xf4 39 ♔g3 ♖d4 40 ♖h7+ ♔g6 41 ♖xb7 ♖d2 42 ♖xa7 ♖xb2 43 ♖c7 b5 44 ♖c6+ ♔g7 45 ♖c5 ♔g6 46 ♖c6+

♞g7 47 ♜c5 ♞g6 48 h5+ ♘xh5 49 ♜xf5+ ♘g6 50 ♜c5 ♘f6 51 a4 bxa4 52 ♜xc4 a3 53 ♜a4 ♜a2 54 ♜a5 ♘g6 55 f4 ♘f6 56 ♜a6+ ♘e7 57 ♘f3 ♘f7 58 g4 ♘e7 59 g5 1-0

The lesson provided by this game, from a theoretical point of view, is that when White puts his bishop on d3 Black should consider ...♞xe5 followed by ...♞e4, but with the bishop on e2 Black will have to unravel more slowly, although he should be able to maintain the balance.

Game 6
Dreev-Seirawan
Wijk aan Zee 1995

---

1 d4 ♞f6 2 ♞f3 e6 3 c4 b6 4 a3 c6?!

One of those ideas that is tried once for the sake of originality, and never tried again for the sake of results...

5 ♞c3 d5

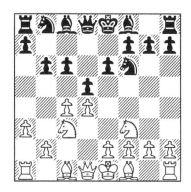

6 cxd5!

Letting Black choose at once.

6...cxd5

This was the reasoning behind 4...c6, of course. Otherwise the move would have contributed nothing to Black's cause. 6...exd5 meets with 7 ♗g5, when White has the freedom to play as he likes in the centre.

7 ♗f4!

The bishop takes up residence on what is now the most dangerous diagonal for Black.

7...a6 8 ♜c1! ♗b7

8...♗e7? is very bad in view of 9 ♞a4!!, when Black is forced into 9...♗d7 10 ♗c7 ♗xa4 11 ♕xa4+ ♕d7 12 ♕b3 b5 13 ♞e5 with a significant advantage to White. After e2-e3 comes a3-a4.

9 e3 ♞c6?!

Failing to appreciate the immediate danger on the c-file. With this in mind 9...♞bd7 followed by ...♜c8 is absolutely necessary. Now White springs a wonderful combination.

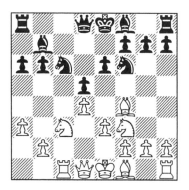

10 ♞b5! ♜c8

10...axb5 11 ♗xb5 ♜c8 12 ♞e5 sees White win the piece back with interest.

11 ♕a4 ♞d7

11...♞h5 12 ♞c7+! ♜xc7 13 ♗xc7 ♕xc7 14 ♗xa6 ♗xa6 15 ♜xc6! and White wins.

12 ♞c7+ ♜xc7 13 ♗xa6!

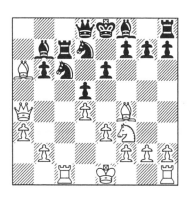

Precisely played. After 13 ♗xc7? ♕xc7 14

♗xa6 ♘db8 15 ♗xb7 ♕xb7 Black is ready with ...b6-b5, breaking the pin. And after 16 ♕b5 ♗d6! Black prevents ♘e5.

13...♗xa6

There is no alternative. 13...♘db8 14 ♗xb7 ♖xb7 15 ♗xb8 b5 16 ♕a6 and White regains his piece, or 13...e5 14 ♗xb7 ♖xb7 15 ♕xc6 and White wins.

14 ♗xc7 ♕xc7 15 ♖xc6 ♕b7 16 ♘e5 ♗e7 17 b4! f6

17...♗c4 would lead to serious trouble after 18 ♖xb6!, but not 18 ♘xc4 dxc4 19 b5 as indicated by Dreev. Then 19...♘b8! 20 ♖xc4 ♕xg2! by no means looks bad for Black!

18 b5?

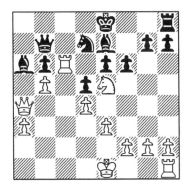

This is simply a mistake. After 18 ♖xb6! ♕xb6 19 ♕xd7+ ♔f8 20 ♘c6 ♕b7 21 ♕xe6 ♕c7 22 ♔d2! ♕d6 23 ♕xe7+ ♕xe7 24 ♘xe7 ♔xe7 25 a4 White has very good chances in the endgame.

18...♗xb5 19 ♕xb5 fxe5 20 0-0

20 ♖xe6 exd4 21 0-0 ♔f7 22 ♖c6 ♘f6 is okay for Black.

20...exd4?

The decisive mistake. Dreev must have not seen that Black is absolutely fine after 20...0-0 21 ♖fc1! ♗d8 22 ♖xe6 e4, instead giving 21 ♖xe6 as a simple explanation, but after 21...♗xa3 22 ♖a1 ♖c8! all Black's pieces are playing.

21 ♖fc1! ♔d8?!

Another grave error. After 21...♗d8 22 ♖xe6+ ♔f7 23 ♖cc6 ♘f6 24 e4!? ♕d7 25

exd5 ♗e7 Black is starting to unravel.

22 exd4 ♖f8 23 a4!

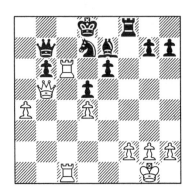

Now Black can do nothing to stop the a-pawn.

23...♗g5 24 ♖1c2 ♖f4 25 a5 ♖xd4 26 g3 ♖d1+ 27 ♔g2 ♖a1 28 axb6 ♘b8

28...♕a6 29 ♕xa6 ♖xa6 30 b7 ♖xc6 31 ♖xc6 ♗f6 32 ♖d6 and White wins.

29 ♖d6+ 1-0

Game 7
Gelfand-Kasparov
Novgorod 1997

1 d4 ♘f6 2 c4 e6 3 ♘f3 b6 4 a3 c5!?

The alternative continuation 4...♗a6 5 ♕c2 c5 6 d5 is seen just as often.

5 d5

5 e3 is considered in Game 8.

5...♗a6 6 ♕c2

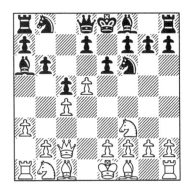

6 b3 has been played a few times but the pawn structure is not really suited for a bishop on b2 as d6 is the weak spot in Black's camp.

6...exd5

Black can try to prevent e3-e4 with 6...♕e7?! but experience shows that this move, which hinders development, is rather risky if White reacts with determination. Miles-Kudrin, London 1982, went 7 ♗g5 exd5 8 ♘c3! ♗xc4 (8...♗b7 9 cxd5 h6 10 ♗xf6 ♕xf6 11 e4 was a shade better for White in Vyzmanavin-Rozentalis, Lvov 1987) 9 e4! (Kasparov's contribution) 9...h6 10 ♗xf6 ♕xf6 11 exd5 ♗xf1 12 ♔xf1 d6 13 ♖e1+ ♗e7 14 ♕a4+ ♔f8 15 ♕g4 and Black was under a lot of pressure. Returning to the position after 9 e4!, Black has a couple of alternatives to 9...h6. 9...♕e6 10 ♗xc4 dxc4 11 0-0-0 ♘c6 12 e5 ♘h5 13 ♘d5 ♖c8 14 ♕xc4 ♗e7 15 g4 was terrible for Black in Hernandez-Ortega, Cuba 1982, but 9...dxe4! 10 0-0-0 ♗e6 11 ♘xe4 ♕d8 12 ♗c4 ♗e7 13 ♗xf6 ♗xf6 14 ♘d6+ ♔f8 15 ♗d5 ♗xd5 16 ♖xd5 gives White compensation for the material rather than an enormous advantage.

7 cxd5 g6

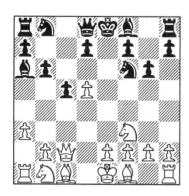

This only serious move. The bishop never belongs on e7 in a Benoni set-up and winning a pawn with 7...♗b7?! 8 e4 ♕e7 9 ♗d3 ♘xd5 looks unhealthy. After 10 0-0 ♘c7 11 ♗g5! f6 12 ♗f4 d6 13 ♘c3 ♘d7 14 b4! Black was under pressure in Sakaev-Ruban,

Elista 1995. And 7...♘xd5 8 ♕e4+ ♘e7 9 ♕xa8 ♘ec6 10 ♘e5 ♕c7 11 ♗f4 ♘xe5 12 ♕e4 simply wins for White, as in Einarsson-Thorhallsson, Reykjavik 1996.

8 ♘c3

There is an alternative set-up both here and on the following move, designed to take immediate advantage of the weaknesses of the d6-square and the a4-e8 diagonal. Luckily for Black, he also has his resources. 8 ♗f4!? d6 9 ♘c3 ♗g7 10 ♕a4+ ♕d7! 11 ♗xd6 ♕xa4 12 ♘xa4 ♘xd5 13 0-0-0 ♘e7! is very important, for if the knight goes to f6 it blocks the bishop and does not possess any mobility. About 6-7 serious games have been played with 11 ♗xd6, and in all of them where the knight went to f6 (mainly after 13 e4) Black did badly, while in the rest, where the knight went to e7, Black equalised. Browne-Timman, Las Palmas 1982 continued 14 e4 ♗xf1 15 ♖hxf1 ♘bc6 16 ♘c3 ♗xc3! 17 bxc3 ♖d8 18 ♗c7 ♖d7 19 ♗f4 f6 with an equal ending which Black went on to win. Less ambitious is 11 ♕xd7+ ♔xd7, when Black should be doing fine. In Garcia Trobat-Rodriguez, Malaga 1991 White even got into trouble after 12 g3 ♔e7 13 ♗g2 ♘bd7 14 0-0 ♖he8 15 h3 ♘h5 16 ♗e3 ♔f8! etc. Finding a good move for White here is by no means easy.

8...♗g7 9 g3

White can also give up the right to castle in order to gain immediate control over the centre with 9 e4 ♗xf1 10 ♔xf1, but this neglects the fact that in Benoni positions Black is normally thrilled to exchange the light-squared bishop for any piece. Consequently, without any weak light squares, this makes little sense from a positional point of view. Of course this is my way of thinking. A number of the world's top players think differently, and the variation has been tried by better players than I. Arencibia-Almasi, Elista 1998, for example, continued 10...d6 11 ♗f4 0-0 12 h3 ♖e8 13 g4 b5! 14 ♘xb5 ♘xe4 15 ♖e1 a6 16 ♘c3 ♘xc3 17 ♖xe8+ ♕xe8 18 bxc3 ♘d7 19 ♔g2 (White should avoid 19 ♗xd6 c4 20 ♗g3 ♘f6 21 d6 ♘e4, where the importance of the inactive rook is all too evident) 19...c4 20 ♖e1 ♕d8 21 ♗xd6 ♘f6 22 ♗e5 ♕xd5 23 ♕d2 ♕xd2 ½-½. Cebalo-Tukmakov, Pula 1994 saw Black enjoy a pleasant position after 14 ♔g2 ♕b6, with all his pieces being able to find good squares. Who knows – Black might even be a little bit better here.

9...0-0 10 ♗g2

The automatic square for the bishop, and also the best. However GM Neverov has experimented with 10 ♗h3 b5!, but now Black does not rush with ...d7-d6 as there is no pressure on the g2-a8 diagonal. Play might continue 11 0-0 ♖e8 (Also good looks 11...b4 12 axb4 cxb4 13 ♘d1 ♘xd5 14 ♗g5 ♕c7 15 ♕d2 ♗b7 16 ♖c1 ♕a5 17 ♘e3 ♘xe3 18 ♗xe3 ♗xf3 19 exf3 ♘c6 with a very complex position, which ended with a draw in Neverov-Onischuk, Donetsk 1998) 12 b4!? (the e2-pawn needs protection, and ruling out ...b5-b4 safeguards the d5-pawn) 12...d6 13 ♗f4 ♘h5 14 ♗g5 ♕c7 15 bxc5 ♕xc5 16 ♖fc1 ♗c8 17 ♗g2 and now instead of 17...♘a6, as in Neverov-Nisipeanu, Koszalin 1998, 17...♗b7!? looks best, with at least equality for Black.

10...d6

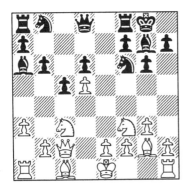

11 0-0

An understandable mistake would be 11 a4?. The problem here compared to normal Benoni set-ups is that Black has not yet played ...a7-a6 or ...♘d7. Now the knight comes to b4 in a second, and White experiences problems with the a6-f1 diagonal (d3) and the d5-pawn. 11...♗b7! 12 ♘d2 ♘a6 13 0-0 ♘b4 14 ♕b3 ♕e7 15 ♖d1 ♗a6 gave Black a clear advantage in Marjanovic-Timman, Bled 1979.

11...♖e8

This is the exact developing move. It is a question of timing and the deeper details in the position. After both possible knight moves Black comes under pressure. 11...♘bd7?! 12 ♕a4! ♗b7 (12...♕c8?! 13 ♗h3! and Black is under irritating pressure, with ♗f4! coming soon) 13 ♕h4! and Black has some problems, as has been demonstrated in many games, one such being Grooten-Riemersma, Holland 1993. 13...♘xd5? loses at once to 14 ♘xd5 ♗xd5 15 ♘g5!, for example.

Nor does 11...♘g4?! 12 ♖e1 improve Black's situation because after the natural 12...♘d7?? White might consider 13 ♕a4, when Black resigned in Korotylev-Kiselev, Moscow 1996. Sometimes it is nice to see 2545 players blunder like we might do in 1-minute games on the Internet Chess Club! It makes me feel that the game is still alive for humanity...

12 ♖e1

Clearly the most natural move, and by far the most popular. Others:

a) 12 ♗f4 ♘h5 13 ♗g5 ♕c8 14 ♖fe1 ♘d7 15 g4?! ♘hf6 16 ♗f4 (16 h3 h5! is also bad for White) 16...♘xg4 17 ♘e4 ♖xe4! 18 ♕xe4 ♗xb2 and Black was better in Zhu Chen-Ehlvest, Beijing 1998. Look at the prospects for the queenside pawns!

b) 12 b4!? was original and not unsuccessful in the following game but, as we shall see, Black had some promising improvements: 12...♘bd7 (12...♘xd5 13 ♗g5!, or 12...♘e4 13 ♘xe4 ♗xa1 14 ♗g5 f6 15 ♖xa1 fxg5 16 ♘fxg5, followed by ♘e6 or ♕c3, with good compensation) 13 ♗b2 ♗c4 14 ♖fd1 cxb4

(14...b5!?) 15 axb4 ♖c8 (15...a5, gaining c5 for the knight) 16 ♕d2? (16 e4 ♘xe4 17 ♘xe4 ♗xb2 18 ♘xd6 with a mess) 16...♗xe2? (16...♘xd5! wins a pawn!) 17 ♘xe2 ♘e4 18 ♕d3 ♗xb2 19 ♖xa7 and the position was rather unclear in Krasenkow-Emms, Hastings 1990.

c) 12 ♖b1 ♘bd7 13 ♖e1 b5 14 b4 ♖c8 15 ♕d3 ♘g4 16 ♘e4 ♕e7 saw White already experiencing problems in Zhu Chen-Alterman, Beijing 1997.

12...♘bd7

This is the standard move. There are some transpositions with 12...b5, but they are not so relevant. Yet one idea does look interesting: 12...h6!?, playing against the c1-bishop. 13 e4 ♗b7 14 ♗f4 ♘h5 15 ♗e3 ♘a6 16 ♖ad1 ♕d7 led to an interesting position in Touzane-Bauer, France 1996. However, I have a feeling the bishop's value on b7 has declined here.

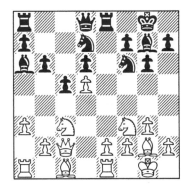

13 h3!

By far the most logical option. White wants to play e2-e4 without allowing ...♘g4-e5-d3. Others:

a) 13 ♗f4 ♕e7, and now:

a1) 14 e4 ♘g4! 15 ♗g5 f6 16 ♗f4 ♘ge5 17 ♘xe5 ♘xe5 18 ♖ad1 ♕d7 and Black has the better prospects, Kramnik-Timman, Linares 1993. White's pieces are nicely placed, but they are not really doing anything.

a2) 14 ♕a4 ♗b7 15 ♘b5 ♘xd5 16 ♗xd6 (16 ♘xd6 ♗xb2 17 ♘xb7 ♗xa1 18 ♖xa1

♘c3 looked better for Black in Riazantsev-Mitenkov, Moscow 1998) 16...♕f6 17 ♖ad1 ♗c6 and White's pieces are all tangled up, Szymczak-Panczyk, Poland 1982.

a3) 14 ♖ad1 ♘e4! 15 ♕a4 (15 ♘xe4 ♕xe4 16 ♕d2 ♕e7 with equality) 15...♗xc3! 16 bxc3 ♗b7 17 ♖d3 f5 and Black is by no means worse, Jusupov-Timman, Tilburg 1986.

b) 13 e4 ♘g4 14 ♗g5 ♕c7 15 ♗f4 ♘de5 16 ♖ad1 b5 gave Black excellent prospects in Popov-Kastanieda, St. Petersburg 1998.

c) 13 ♕a4?! ♗b7 14 ♕h4 does not work now as the rook is no longer on f8! After 14...♘xd5! 15 ♘xd5 ♗xd5 16 ♘g5 ♗xg2 17 ♕xh7+ ♔f8 18 ♔xg2 ♘f6 19 ♕h4 d5 Black has the advantage (...d5-d4 and ...♕d5 are coming, with total domination).

13...b5

Clearly the best move. After 13...♘e5?! 14 ♘xe5 ♖xe5 15 e4 ♖e8 16 ♗e3 ♘d7 17 f4 Black's forces had problems finding squares in Yusupov-Timman, Tilburg 1986.

14 e4

This was supposed to be the move for White until the present game was played. Now nobody really knows. Just as frequently played has been 14 ♗f4, but Black should be fine if he continues 14...♕b6 15 e4 ♖ac8 16 ♗e3 ♗b7!?, remembering to push with ...a7-a5 and then ...♗a6 in order to fight for control of the c4-square. Yevseev-Ionov, St. Petersburg 2000, went 17 ♘d2 a6 18 a4 b4 19 ♘c4 (19 a5 ♕c7 20 ♘cb1 c4 and Black is okay) 19...♕c7 20 ♘b1 a5! 21 ♘bd2 ♗a6 22 ♗f4 ♗f8 23 ♖ad1 ♘h5 with a sound position for Black. In Moreno-Emms, Mondariz 2000, 16...♕b7 17 ♗f1 ♘b8! also proved to be fine, e.g. 18 ♗f4?! b4 19 ♘d1 b3 20 ♕b1 ♗xf1 21 ♔xf1 ♕a6+ 22 ♔g2 ♘bd7 23 ♘c3 c4 and Black was better.

14...♕c8!!

I have used this position as an exercise in my positional training program on the Internet. The key idea is that the bishop should be supported so that Black can play ...b5-b4 as soon as possible. Kasparov's move is the only one that does this. The automatic 14...♖c8 15 ♗e3 ♕c7 (15...b4 16 axb4 cxb4 17 ♖xa6 bxc3 18 ♘d4! followed by ♘c6 has long been known to give White a good position) 16 ♗f1 ♕b7 17 ♗f4 gave White a good position in Van Wely-Kamsky, Amsterdam Donner 1996. 14...♕b6 15 ♗e3! also slows down the ...b5-b4 idea.

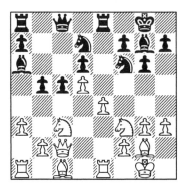

15 ♗f4

The aggressive approach, but after this it is White who must try to keep the balance. However, other games suggest that Black is absolutely fine. 15 ♗f1!? b4 16 ♘b5 ♗xb5!? 17 ♗xb5 ♖b8 18 ♗c6 b3 19 ♕d3 ♘e5 20 ♘xe5 ♖xe5 21 ♔g2 ♖e7 led to an interesting position (which Black went on to win) in Markos-Nisipeanu, Cappelle la Grande. The question is what is the most important here – the bishop on c6 or the weaknesses of the b2-pawn? The debate is most likely not over. 15 ♗d2? b4 16 ♘d1 b3 17 ♕b1 c4 was plainly good for Black in Tunik-Ionov, St. Petersburg 2001.

15...b4 16 ♘a4

16 ♘d1 b3 17 ♕b1 ♕c7 18 ♘c3 ♖ab8 did not look impressive in Zhu Chen-Zatonskih, Istanbul 2000.

16...b3!

This is the idea – now White loses control over e4.

17 ♕xb3

I am one of those people who does not

need to see variations to see that 17 ♕b1? is bad. Just look at the white pieces!

17...♘xe4 18 ♕c2

18 ♘c3? ♖b8 19 ♕c2 ♖xb2! pockets a pawn for Black.

18...♘df6

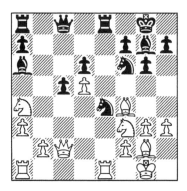

Here White needs to do something to challenge the power of the e4-knight. The way he does it is terrible, as it serves only to weaken his king.

19 g4?!

19 ♘g5! was the only move.

19...♕d7 20 g5?!

Still 20 ♘g5!? is necessary.

20...♘h5 21 ♗h2

21 ♖xe4 ♖xe4 22 ♕xe4 ♖e8 23 ♘xc5 ♖xe4 24 ♘xd7 ♖xf4!? leads to a very clear advantage for Black. White's pieces could hardly be worse.

21...f5!

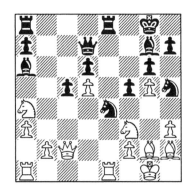

With complete domination.

22 ♘c3 ♖ab8 23 ♖ab1 ♗xc3!

Securing the difference between Black's majestic knight and the bishop on h2.

24 bxc3 ♖xb1 25 ♖xb1 ♗c4 26 ♘d2 ♘xd2 27 ♕xd2 f4! 28 ♖e1 ♖e5!? 29 ♖e4? ♖xe4 30 ♗xe4 ♕xh3 31 ♗g2 ♕g4 32 ♕e1 ♘g7! 33 f3 ♕xg5 34 ♕b1 ♘f5 35 ♕b8+ ♔g7 36 ♕xa7+ ♔h6 37 ♕f7 ♗f1! 38 ♔xf1 ♘e3+ 39 ♔e1 ♕h4+! 40 ♔e2 ♕xh2 41 ♔d3 ♘f5 0-1

Game 8
Silman-Gheorghiu
Palo Alto 1981

---

1 d4 ♘f6 2 c4 e6 3 ♘f3 b6 4 a3 c5 5 e3

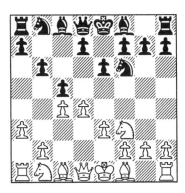

This move is less ambitious than 5 d5, and Black has no problems equalizing.

5...♗b7

5...g6!? 6 ♘c3 ♗g7 7 ♗e2 0-0 8 0-0 ♗b7 9 b4 (9 d5?! exd5 10 cxd5 ♖e8 gives Black a good version of the Benoni – where does White's queen's bishop belong and how is the other bishop contributing?) 9...cxd4 10 ♘xd4 (10 exd4!? d5 11 c5 bxc5 12 bxc5 ♘e4 should not certainly not be worse for Black) 10...♘c6 11 ♘xc6 ♗xc6 12 ♗b2 d5 13 ♕b3 (13 cxd5 ♘xd5 with at least equality, Browne-Timman, London 1980) 13...dxc4 14 ♗xc4 ♕e7 15 ♖ad1 ♖fd8 with an equal position (but also somewhat boring, with chances only for a draw) in Panno-Andersson, Bue-

nos Aires 1980.

6 ♘c3 cxd4 7 exd4 d5 8 cxd5

There has been an attempt to finish Black off immediately by weakening his light squares with 8 ♗g5 ♗e7 9 ♗xf6!? ♗xf6 10 cxd5 ♗xd5 11 ♘xd5 ♕xd5 12 ♕a4+ ♔e7 13 ♖c1, but time has shown that this is not possible. Christiansen-Gurevich, Parsippany 1996 went 13...♖d8 14 ♗d3?! a6! 15 0-0 ♖a7 16 ♖fe1 ♗xd4! 17 ♗xh7 ♕b5 18 ♕xb5 axb5 19 ♘xd4 ♖xd4, when Black was better placed for the endgame, while 14 ♗e2 a6 15 ♖c7+ ♖d7 16 ♖c8 ♖d8 17 ♖xd8 ♔xd8 18 0-0 ♘c6 results in equality according to Gurevich.

8...♘xd5

This is clearly the most flexible move, and as White has no way of troubling Black straight away there is no need to resort to 8...exd5?! 9 ♗b5+ ♘bd7 10 ♘e5 ♗e7 11 ♘c6 ♗xc6 12 ♗xc6, when White stood better in the game Eingorn-Lauber, Bad Wörishofen 1997.

9 ♗b5+ ♗c6 10 ♗d3 ♘d7!

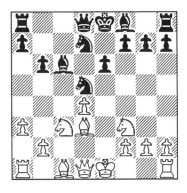

The bishop appears to be exposed on c6 but White has no way to exploit it, so Black maintains the balance.

11 0-0 ♗e7 12 ♗d2?!

This clearly shows that White lacks sufficient understanding of the positions arising with the isolated pawn. 12 ♕e2 is an improvement.

12...0-0 13 ♖c1 ♘xc3 14 ♖xc3 ♗b7 15

♗f4 ♘f6 16 ♗e5 ♖c8 17 ♖xc8 ♕xc8 18 ♕b1 g6 19 ♕c1

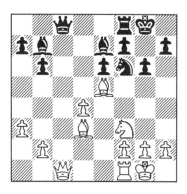

This looks just like a bad endgame, and guess what it is...?

19...♕xc1 20 ♖xc1 ♘d5 21 ♗e4 f6 22 ♗g3 ♖c8 23 ♖xc8+ ♗xc8 24 ♗b8 a6 25 ♗xd5 exd5 26 ♗c7 b5 27 b4 ♗f5

Here the bishop is better than the knight. Black has good practical chances, although White might have been able to hold it with best play.

28 ♘e1 ♔f7 29 ♔f1 h5 30 ♔e2 ♔e6 31 ♗f4 g5 32 ♗c1 ♗d6 33 h3 g4 34 h4 g3 35 f3 ♗b1 36 ♘d3 ♔f5 37 ♘c5 ♗a2 38 ♘xa6 ♗c4+ 39 ♔e1 ♗f4 40 ♗xf4 ♔xf4 41 ♘c5 ♔e3 42 a4 bxa4 43 ♘xa4 ♔xd4 44 ♘c5 ♔c3 0-1

Game 9
Barlov-Sakaev
Budva 1996

---

1 d4 ♘f6 2 c4 e6 3 ♘f3 b6 4 a3 ♗a6

The ...♗a6 system has gained much popularity over the last decade and is now the primary system for Black among top players. I think this has less to do with the actual worth of the move (both 4...♗b7 and 4...♗a6 probably lead to equal play) and more to do with the double-edged positions that we find in the critical lines. There are simply more chances to outplay your opponents in this variation.

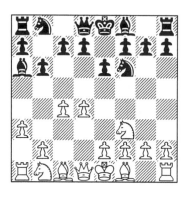

5 ♕b3

The queen is quite obviously less well placed here than on c2. Other moves have also been tried.

a) 5 e3 is really harmless, and often transposes to the 4 e3 line after 5...d5, where White has the extra move a2-a3, which hardly does him any good (Black can also play 5...c5 6 ♘c3 ♗e7 7 ♗e2 cxd4 8 ♘xd4 ♗b7 9 ♗f3 ♘c6 with total equality, as in Hort-Ljubojevic, OHRA 1988). And now:

a1) 6 b3 ♗e7 7 ♗d3 0-0 8 0-0 c5 9 ♗b2 dxc4 10 bxc4 ♘c6 11 ♘e5 ♘a5 12 ♘d2 ♖c8 13 ♖c1 ♘d7 and White's queenside weaknesses began to tell in Smolej-Siegel, Germany 1985.

a2) 6 ♘c3 ♗e7 7 ♘e5 (7 ♕a4+ c6 8 cxd5 ♗xf1 9 ♔xf1 exd5, Flesh-Romanishin, Lvov 1981, is simply better for Black – look at White's bishop) 7...0-0 8 ♗e2 c6 9 0-0 ♘fd7! and Black has solved all his opening problems, Browne-Benjamin, USA 1984.

a3) 6 ♘bd2 is the only move for people who want to play. Kholmov-Naumkin, Voskresensk 1990 went 6...♗d6 7 b3 0-0 8 ♗d3 ♗b7 9 ♕c2 ♘bd7 10 ♗b2 c5 11 0-0 ♖c8 12 ♖fe1 b5 13 dxc5 ♗xc5 14 ♕b1 with a draw, although I must say that as Black I would have considered playing on here.

b) After 5 ♘bd2 Black plays 5...♗b7! as the new arrival on d2 is poorly placed. Rohde-Miles, USA 1989 continued 6 ♕c2 d5 7 cxd5 exd5 8 g3 ♗d6! (controlling e5 and better than the old 8...♗e7) 9 ♗g2 ♘bd7 10 0-0 0-0 11 ♘h4!? ♖e8 12 ♘c4?! (not good; 12 ♘df3 gives both players chances) 12...♗f8 13 ♗f4? ♘e4! and Black was much better due to the threat of ...g7-g5.

5...g6! 6 ♘c3 ♗g7 7 e4 0-0 8 ♗e2 c5 9 d5 d6

9...exd5 would be too soon. After 10 exd5 ♖e8 11 ♕c2 White might be better as the bishop is misplaced on a6.

10 0-0 ♘bd7

Black is just developing and, as White has no active plans, the position is equal. Now White goes over the edge in an attempt to do something.

11 dxe6?! fxe6 12 e5 dxe5 13 ♘g5 ♕e7 14 ♗f3 e4!

Black will not allow White to occupy e4 with a knight without first opening up for his bishop on the long diagonal.

15 ♘cxe4?

This seems to be bad, but 15 ♘gxe4 ♘xe4 16 ♗xe4 ♘e5 17 ♘b5 ♖ad8 would also benefit Black.

15...♘e5 16 ♘xf6+ ♗xf6 17 ♗xa8 ♗xc4 18 ♕g3 ♗xf1 19 ♗e4 ♗d3!

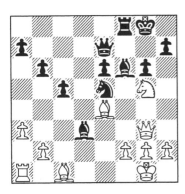

A very important simplification. Now White's hopes of an attack against the weakened king disappear together with the minor pieces.

20 ♗xd3 ♘xd3 21 ♕xd3

The last finesse is that 21 ♘xh7 ♕xh7! 22 ♕xd3 ♖d8! 23 ♕e2 ♕h5 gives White a terri-

ble problem on the first rank and on b2.

21...♗xg5 22 ♗xg5 ♕xg5 23 ♖d1 ♕e5

Black has a pawn and very good winning chances, which proved enough...

24 b3 ♔g7 25 a4 ♕f4 26 ♕d7+ ♖f7 27 ♕d2 ♕f6 28 h3 e5 29 ♖e1 ♕f4 30 ♕e2 e4 31 ♕b2+ ♔h6 32 ♕c2 ♖e7 33 ♕c4 ♕e5 34 ♕g8 ♕f5 35 ♕d8 ♕f7 36 ♕d2+ ♔g7 37 ♕e3 ♕d5 38 ♕g3 ♕d4 39 ♕h4 ♖e5 40 ♕g3 ♖f5 41 ♕h4 ♖e5 42 ♕g3 a6 43 ♔h2 ♖e7 44 ♕h4 ♕e5+ 45 ♔g1 b5 46 axb5 axb5 47 ♕g4 c4 48 bxc4 bxc4 49 ♕e2 c3 50 ♕c2 ♖d7 51 ♖xe4 ♖d1+

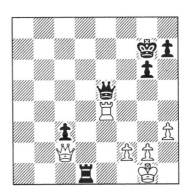

52 ♕xd1 ♕xe4 53 ♕d7+ ♔h6 54 ♕c8 c2 55 ♕f8+ ♔g5 56 h4+ ♔h5 57 ♕c5+ ♔xh4 58 ♔h2 g5 0-1

Game 10
Dzhandzhava-Chernin
Lvov, 1987

---

1 d4 ♘f6 2 c4 e6 3 ♘f3 b6 4 a3 ♗a6 5 ♕c2 ♗b7 6 ♘c3 c5 7 d5?

This should not be considered as a serious alternative to 7 e4, and nor should 7 dxc5 bxc5, e.g. 8 ♗f4 ♘h5 9 ♗g5 ♗e7 10 ♗xe7 ♕xe7 11 e3 0-0 12 ♗e2 ♘f6 13 0-0 d6 14 ♖fd1 ♖d8 15 ♖d2 ♘bd7 16 ♖ad1 and White realised that he had no advantage at all in Gavrikov-Yemelin, Tallinn 2000. Another game went 8 ♗g5 ♗e7 9 e3 d6 10 ♖d1 0-0 11 ♗e2 ♘bd7 12 0-0 ♕b6 13 ♖d2 ♖ad8 14

罩fd1 罩fe8 15 h3 公f8! with the idea of
...公g6 and ...h7-h6, winning the two bishops.
After 16 奧f4 公g6 17 奧h2 罩d7 18 豐b1
罩ed8 Black was no worse in Portisch-
Timman, Reykjavik 1988.

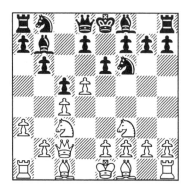

7...exd5 8 cxd5 公xd5 9 奧g5

9 豐e4+ 豐e7 10 豐xd5 is a silly blitz line.
Black just takes the money and runs.

9...奧e7 10 公b5 0-0 11 公d6

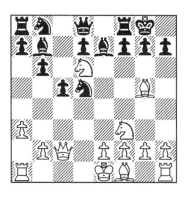

11...公e3!!

This was a serious new move at the time.
Now Black takes over the initiative.

12 fxe3

Practically forced as 12 豐d3 奧xf3 13
奧xe3 奧g4 14 豐e4 奧xd6 15 豐xa8 豐f6
looks extremely dangerous for White.

12...奧xf3 13 exf3

13 奧xe7 豐xe7 14 公f5 豐e4 and Black
wins.

13...奧xg5 14 奧c4

White must get going. The alternatives are
hopeless. After 14 f4 奧e7! 15 公f5 g6 there is
no compensation for the sacrificed material,
while 14 豐e4 豐e7! 15 豐xa8 豐xe3+ 16 奧e2
公c6 17 豐b7 豐d2+ 18 含f1 豐xd6 19 罩d1
公d4 is very close to winning for Black. The
domination of the dark squares and the misplacement of White's king will decide the
game.

14...公c6?!

Here Black could have buried 7 d5 once
and for all by simply playing 14...豐e7!, e.g. 15
豐e4 豐xd6 16 豐xa8 公c6 17 豐b7 奧xe3, or
15 公f5 豐e5 16 e4 g6, when Black has a
pawn plus an overwhelming positional advantage.

15 f4?

Here White could have fought back a little
bit with 15 h4! 奧xe3! 16 公xf7 罩xf7 17
奧xf7+ 含h8 18 奧d5, and Black has no clear
way to conduct the attack, although he has
good chances. Now the struggle is effectively
over...

15...奧xf4! 16 公xf7

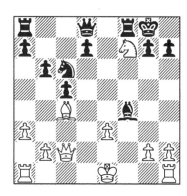

16 exf4 豐e7+ 17 公e4 公d4 18 豐d3 罩ae8
19 奧d5 豐h4+ 20 含f1 (20 g3 豐h5 21 奧b7
d5) 20...豐xf4+ 21 含g1 豐f5 22 奧b7 d5 23
公f2 豐e5 24 g3 c4 25 豐d1 f5 and the attack
wins by itself.

16...豐h4+ 17 g3

No alternatives: 17 含e2 豐h5+ 18 g4 (18
含e1 d5!) 18...豐xg4+ 19 含d2 奧xe3+! 20
含xe3 豐d4+ 21 含e2 罩ae8+ 22 含f1 d5 and

17 ♔d1 ♗xe3! 18 ♘h6+ ♔h8 19 ♘f7+ ♖xf7 20 ♗xf7 ♘d4 21 ♕d3 ♕g4+ 22 ♔e1 ♕xg2 both win for Black.

17...♗xg3+ 18 ♔d2

Black would also win after 18 ♔e2 ♕h5+ 19 ♔d2 ♗f2! (funnily enough Chernin makes the mistake of mentioning 19...d5 as winning, but 20 hxg3! is worth a try!!) 20 ♖af1 ♗xe3+! 21 ♔xe3 d5 and Black wins in the attack.

18...♗f2 19 ♔d1

19 ♕d3 ♖xf7 20 ♗xf7+ ♔xf7 21 ♕xd7+ ♘e7 22 ♖af1 ♖f8 and Black wins.

19...d5 0-1

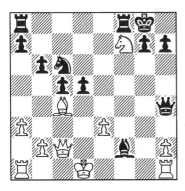

Game 11
Bacrot-Adams
Cannes (rapid) 2001

---

1 d4 ♘f6 2 c4 e6 3 ♘f3 b6 4 a3 ♗a6 5 ♕c2 ♗b7 6 ♘c3 c5 7 e4 cxd4 8 ♘xd4

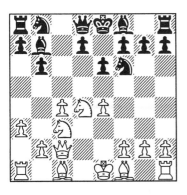

8...♗c5!?

Here the main line is 8...♘c6, but the text move and 8...d6!? have gained in popularity. After 9 ♗e2 ♗e7 White has played:

a) 10 ♗e3 a6 11 g4?! has been tried occasionally but it seems to be too dangerous for White in view of the weakening of his queenside with a2-a3. Dreev-Lerner, Vienna 1996 continued 11...♘fd7 12 0-0-0 ♘c6 13 ♘xc6 ♗xc6 14 f4 ♕b8 15 g5 0-0 16 h4 b5 17 h5 b4 18 axb4 ♕xb4 19 g6 ♗f6 20 gxf7+ (20 gxh7+ ♔h8 21 ♗d4 ♗xd4 22 ♖xd4 ♘c5 would also give Black a serious attack) 20...♖xf7 21 ♗d3 ♗xc3 22 ♕xc3 (22 bxc3 ♕a3+ 23 ♔d2 ♗a4 24 ♕c1 ♕a2+ 25 ♗c2 ♘c5 and Black is better) 22...♕xc3+ 23 bxc3 ♘c5 24 ♗xc5 dxc5 and Black was much better and went on to win.

b) 10 0-0 0-0 11 ♗e3 a6 12 ♖fd1 ♕c7 13 ♖ac1 ♘bd7 14 f3 ♖fc8! 15 ♗f1 ♕d8 16 ♕f2 ♖ab8 17 ♔h1 ♗a8 18 ♕g3 ♖c7 19 b4 ♕e8! with equality in Ljubojevic-Piket, Monaco. In these hedgehog positions a2-a3 tends to have pros and cons. It provides White with the opportunity to advance with a3-a4-a5 later to generate an attack against a6, but it also weakens the defence of a2-c4, and any pawns that might be placed on that diagonal.

9 ♘b3 ♘c6 10 ♗g5

This game illustrates quite clearly that this line is okay for Black. Here are the alternatives:

a) 10 ♗d3 0-0 11 0-0 h6!? 12 ♘xc5 bxc5 13 ♗e3 d6 14 f3! ♖b8 15 ♖fd1 ♕e7 16 ♗f1 ♖fd8 17 ♖ab1! with a very small advantage to White in Sakaev-Milos, Sao Paulo 1991. In Lputian-Adams, Wijk aan Zee 2000, 11 ♗f4 e5 12 ♗g5 h6 13 ♗h4 ♗e7 14 0-0 ♘h5 15 ♗xe7 ♕xe7 16 ♖ad1 ♘f4 17 ♘d5 ♕g5 18 ♘xf4 exf4 left Black slightly better.

b) 10 ♘xc5 bxc5 11 ♗d3 d6 12 0-0 0-0 13 h3 e5 14 ♕d1 h6 15 ♖b1 a5 16 f4 exf4 17 ♗xf4 ♘e5 and Black seems to be fine, Khalifman-Salov, Amsterdam 1995.

c) 10 ♗f4! is the real test of 8...♗c5, when wild and gruesome is 10...0-0 11 ♘xc5 bxc5

12 ♗d6 ♘d4 13 ♕d3 e5 14 ♗xc5! (the exchange does not appear to be so interesting when all the remaining pieces are good for Black) 14...♖e8 15 ♗xd4 exd4 16 ♕xd4 ♘xe4 17 0-0-0 and White had the advantage in Piket-Salov, Wijk aan Zee 1997. In Kramnik-Psakhis, Debrecen 1992, 10...♗e7 11 ♗e2 d6 12 ♖d1 ♕b8 was too slow, and White had 13 c5 e5 14 cxd6 exf4 15 dxe7 ♘xe7 16 ♗b5+ ♔f8 17 0-0 with a small advantage. This leaves 10...e5 11 ♗g5 h6 12 ♗h4, and now Black has the following options at his disposal.

c1) 12...0-0 13 f3 ♗e7 14 ♗f2 with advantage to White according to Dautov. And trust me, he is right, although Black should hurry with 14...a5!, with the idea of ...a5-a4 and ...♘d4 and, perhaps, ...d7-d5 to use his lead in development to blow the centre apart. 13 ♘xc5?! bxc5 14 ♗d3 ♘d4 15 ♕d1 a5 16 0-0 g5 17 ♗g3 d6 18 ♖e1 ♗c6 was better for Black in Christiansen-Seirawan, USA 1984.

c2) 12...♗e7 13 0-0-0!? 0-0 14 f3 was better for White in Notkin-Kiselev, Cappelle la Grande.

c3) 12...d6 13 0-0-0 a6 (13...0-0 14 f3 a5 15 ♕d3! gave White a serious advantage in Akopian-Salov, Wijk aan Zee 1993) 14 f3 ♖c8 15 ♔b1 ♘a5, Gruenenwald-Bischoff, Bundesliga 1988, and here White should have played 16 ♘xc5! bxc5 17 ♘d5 with an advantage.

10...♘d4!

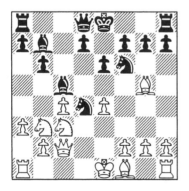

11 ♘xd4 ♗xd4 12 ♘b5

This is the test, but as we shall see it seems to be in Black's favour. 12 ♗d3 ♕b8 and the control over the dark squares guarantees Black equality.

12...♗c5!

12...♗e5 13 f4, with unclear play, was the main line before this game. But the bishop is better placed on c5.

13 e5 h6! 14 exf6

Also fine for Black is 14 ♗e3 a6! 15 exf6 axb5 16 fxg7 ♖g8, e.g. 17 ♕h7 ♔e7 18 ♕xh6 ♗xe3 19 ♕xe3 bxc4 and Black appears to be better as g2 is weak. 17 ♗xc5 bxc5 18 ♕h7 ♔e7 19 ♕xh6 ♕a5+ looks good for Black. White is severely behind in development and the potential pressure against g2 is strong.

14...hxg5 15 fxg7 ♖g8 16 ♕h7 ♔e7 17 b4 a6 18 bxc5 axb5 19 ♕h6 f6

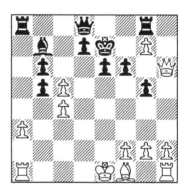

White has attacked with his lone queen and now his king is stuck in the centre. Black now wins almost by force from here.

20 ♗d3 ♗xg2 21 ♖g1 ♕c7! 22 cxb5

22 ♖xg2 ♕e5+ is easy.

22...♕xc5 23 ♕h7 ♗f3 24 ♖b1 ♖xa3 0-1

> *Game 12*
> **Bareev-Eingorn**
> *Kiev 1986*

1 d4 ♘f6 2 c4 e6 3 ♘f3 b6 4 a3 ♗a6 5 ♕c2 ♗b7 6 ♘c3 c5 7 e4 cxd4 8 ♘xd4

♘c6 9 ♘xc6

In practice this is the only move played by the top players; there are no serious alternatives. After 9 ♗e3 ♘g4! Black gains the two bishops without any concessions.

9...♗xc6

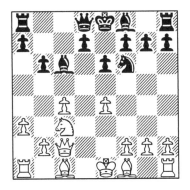

10 ♗f4

This is the main move, but not the only serious one.

a) 10 ♗e2 does nothing about the important dark squares. In fact White should now be careful if he is to maintain the balance:

a1) After 10...♕b8 we have 11 0-0?! ♗c5! 12 ♔h1 (12 b4 ♗d4 13 ♗b2 h5 and the attack continues) 12...h5 13 ♕d3 ♘g4, when Black was already much better in Fedorowicz-Miles, USA 1989, while 11 ♗e3 was equal in Christiansen-Miles, Linares 1985.

a2) 10...♗c5! looks best. Then 11 0-0?! is too dangerous. Now Black attacks on the dark squares (but what should White do?): 11...♕c7 12 ♔h1 h5! 13 f3 h4 14 b4 ♗d4 15 ♗d2 ♘h5! with a decisive attack in prospect, Farago-Grooten, Sas van Gent 1988.

b) 10 ♗d3 ♕b8 11 ♕e2! (no castling here!) 11...♗d6 12 ♗d2 0-0 13 h3 ♗f4 14 ♗xf4 ♕xf4 15 0-0 d6, as in Sakaev-Poluljahov, Vrnjacka Banja 1996, should be equal.

c) 10 ♗g5!? might give White something. It all comes down what happens after 10...♕b8. While 11 g3?! is not very good, the

refutation is not 11...♘xe4?!, as played in Lputian-Psakhis, Sochi 1987, but 11...♗e7! 12 ♗g2 ♘xe4!! 13 ♗xe7 ♘xc3 14 ♗xc6 ♕e5+ 15 ♔f1 dxc6 16 ♖e1 ♕d4 17 ♗h4 h6!! 18 g4 (18 ♕xc3 ♕xc3 19 bxc3 g5 20 ♖e4 ♖d8! and Black will have a better endgame) 18...♕xg4 19 ♗g3 ♕xc4+ 20 ♔g1 ♖d8 21 ♕xc3 ♕xc3 22 bxc3 ♖d3 23 ♖e3 ♖xe3 24 fxe3 ♔e7, and the three pawns look stronger than the bishop. Instead 11 ♗d3 ♗e7 12 ♕e2 h6 13 ♗d2, Klimov-Yemelin, St. Petersburg 2000, looks like a tiny edge for White.

10...♘h5

Whether this is the best move or not is very difficult to tell. The alternative, 10...♗c5, is treated in Game 13.

11 ♗e3

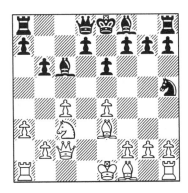

11 ♗d2 ♕b8 12 g3 f5 13 ♗d3 ♗d6 14 0-0-0 f4 gave Black good control over the dark squares in Polugaevsky-Arnason, Reykjavik 1987. Super-GM Curt Hansen evaluates the position as unclear, but I feel that Black should not fear such unclear situations.

11...♗c5?!

This is not the appropriate strategy. Karpov developed the correct approach over a few tries in the early 1990's. The first was 11...♗d6??, which ended quickly with 12 ♕d1!, when Black resigned in Christiansen-Karpov, Wijk aan Zee 1993. But the second attempt, 11...♕b8!, is here to stay. The strategy involves a fight for f4 with ...f7-f5 and

...♗f8-d6 coming. Black should equalise:

a) 12 g3 f5! 13 0-0-0 (13 ♖g1!? fxe4 14 ♘xe4 ♗xe4 15 ♕xe4 ♘f6 16 ♕f3 ♗c5 17 ♗f4 e5 18 ♗g5 0-0 with equality in San Segundo-Langeweg, Zaragoza 1995) 13...♘f6 14 ♗d3 ♕b7 15 f3 (15 ♘d5 fxe4 16 ♗xe4 exd5 17 cxd5 ♘xd5 does not work) 15...fxe4 16 ♘xe4 ♘xe4 17 ♗xe4! (17 fxe4?! hinders the bishop on d3; after 17...♗d6 Black was better in Lutz-Karpov, Dortmund 1993) 17...♗xe4 18 fxe4 ♗e7 19 ♖hf1 0-0-0 with an unclear game according to Karpov.

b) 12 ♖d1 validates 12...♗c5! 13 ♗xc5 bxc5 14 ♘b5 ♕e5 15 ♘d6+ ♔e7, when White has the most problems with his king. Bykhovsky-Soffer, Tel Aviv 1994 went 16 g3 ♖ab8 17 ♖d2 g5 18 ♗g2 f5 19 0-0 f4, with preference for Black.

c) 12 0-0-0 with a further branch:

c1) 12...♗c5 13 ♗xc5 bxc5 14 g3 0-0 15 f4 d6 16 ♗g2 ♘f6 17 ♖d3 ♖c8 18 ♖hd1 ♘e8 19 g4!, Gurevich-Korchnoi, Biel 1993, with aggressive ideas, as g4-g5 and ♖h3 look very good for White.

c2) 12...♗d6 13 g3 ♗e5 (13...f5 14 ♗e2 ♘f6 15 exf5! ♗xh1 16 ♖xh1 ♕b7 17 ♖d1 ♗e7 18 g4 0-0 19 g5 ♘e8 20 ♗d3 illustrates how the light squares can suddenly become so important; White is clearly better) 14 ♗d3 ♕b7 (14...♘f6 15 f4! ♗xc3 16 ♕xc3 ♕b7 [or 16...♗xe4 17 ♗xe4 ♘xe4 18 ♕xg7 with a clear advantage, and the same goes for 16...0-0 17 ♗d4!] 17 ♖he1 and White looks much better) 15 ♖he1 ♘f6 and now, instead of 16 f4, as in Kramnik-Lutz, Dortmund 1993, White could have claimed a large advantage with 16 ♗f4! d6 (16...♗xf4+ 17 gxf4 d6 18 e5 dxe5 19 fxe5 ♘d7 20 ♘e4 and Black is in deep trouble) 17 ♗xe5 dxe5 18 ♗f1 0-0 19 f3 ♖fd8 20 ♕f2. This structure is simply very bad for Black. Once all the heavy pieces are traded off the endgame will give White a strong passed pawn on the queenside and, potentially, pressure against the e5-pawn, or e6 if the first is protected with ...f7-f6.

c3) 12...♘f6! is probably the only good move here. Then 13 f4 ♘g4! does not work, so Arencibia-Bischoff, Havana 1998 continued 13 ♗e2 ♗d6 14 g3 ♗e5 15 ♖he1 0-0 16 f3 a6 17 ♔b1 ♖c8 18 ♗d4 ♗xd4 19 ♖xd4 d5 with equality.

12 ♗xc5 bxc5 13 g3 0-0

13...f5 14 0-0-0 f4 worked out well after 15 g4?! in Dreev-Supatashvili, Moscow 2001, but White could have used his lead in development more aggressively with 15 ♗e2! ♕g5 (15...♘f6? 16 gxf4 ♕c7 17 e5! ♗xh1 18 ♖xh1 followed by ♘e4-d6 and White is practically winning) 16 h4 ♕e5 17 g4 ♘f6 18 g5 ♘xe4 19 ♗h5+ g6 20 ♖he1 gxh5 21 ♘xe4 ♗xe4 22 ♖xe4 ♕f5 23 ♕c3, with an initiative and the safer king position.

14 ♗d3 ♘f6 15 0-0-0 d6 16 f4 ♖b8 17 ♖hg1 e5 18 g4

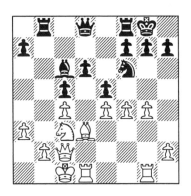

Here White's attack seems to be the most promising, as none of Black's minor pieces seems able to help on the kingside.

18...♘d7 19 f5 ♕a5 20 ♗e2 ♖b7 21 ♖xd6 ♖fb8 22 ♖gd1 ♖xb2 23 ♕xb2 ♖xb2 24 ♔xb2 ♕c7 25 g5 ♔f8 26 f6 gxf6 27 gxf6 ♔e8 28 ♔a2 a6 29 ♗h5 ♕b7 30 ♘d5 1-0

Game 13
Lautier-Timman
Amsterdam 1996

1 d4 ♘f6 2 ♘f3 e6 3 c4 b6 4 a3 ♗a6 5

♕c2 ♗b7 **6** ♘c3 c5 **7** e4 cxd4 **8** ♘xd4 ♘c6 **9** ♘xc6 ♗xc6 **10** ♗f4 ♗c5 **11** ♗e2

The best move. White does not want to allow 11 0-0-0 ♘h5!, when he has no advantage after 12 ♗d6 ♗xd6 13 ♖xd6 0-0 14 g3 f5 15 ♗g2 (15 f4?! fxe4 16 ♘xe4 ♗xe4 17 ♕xe4 ♖c8 is even more dangerous for White) 15...f4 16 ♖hd1 ♕g5 17 ♕d2 ♕e5, as in Greenfeld-Kindermann, Pardubice 1994.

11...0-0 12 0-0-0

This is by far the most promising continuation. After 12 ♖d1 a5 Black appears to be doing all right. Play might develop as follows: 13 ♗g5!? (13 ♗g3!? ♕e7!? 14 e5 ♘e8 15 ♘e4 f5 16 exf6 ♘xf6 17 ♗d3 ♗xe4 18 ♗xe4 ♘xe4 19 ♕xe4 and Black cannot be that much worse, if at all, Gurevich-Chuchelov, Germany 1995) 13...h6 14 ♗h4 e5? (Black is okay after 14...♕c7 15 ♗xf6 gxf6 16 ♖d3 ♔h7) 15 0-0 ♕e7 16 ♔h1 g5 17 ♗g3 ♖ab8 18 ♗f3 ♗d4 19 ♘e2 ♗c5 20 ♘c3 ♗d4 21 ♖fe1 g4 and now instead of 22 ♗e2?, as in Dreev-Adams, London (rapid) 1995, White could have won with 22 ♘d5!! ♗xd5 23 exd5 ♕c5 (23...gxf3 24 ♖xd4 and Black is on the wrong side of a strong attack) 24 ♕f5 gxf3 25 ♕xf6 fxg2+ 26 ♔xg2 ♕xc4 27 ♖xd4 ♕xd4 28 ♗xe5 ♕g4+ 29 ♔h1 ♔h7 30 ♖g1 etc. (Vaisser).

12 e5 meets with 12...♘h5! 13 ♗xh5 ♕h4 14 ♗xf7+ ♖xf7 15 ♗g3 ♕xc4, while in the vent of 12 0-0 Black has 12...♗d4!? with the wild idea of 13 ♗d6 ♗xc3 14 ♗xf8 ♘xe4 15

♗b4 ♗e5 16 ♗f3 f5, with strong compensation. For more cautious players I recommend 13...♖e8! 14 e5 (14 ♗d3 e5 looks even better for Black) 14...♗xc3 15 ♕xc3 ♘e4 with equality.

12...♘e8

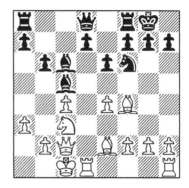

Also possible are one decent alternative and two mistakes:

a) 12...♖c8 13 ♔b1 a5 (13...♘e8 14 ♗g3!? f6 15 b4 ♗e7 16 ♗g4! ♘c7 17 b5 ♗a8 18 ♕d3 ♗xa3 19 ♕xd7 ♕xd7 20 ♖xd7 ♖f7 21 ♖hd1 with a clear advantage for White) 14 ♗g3 ♘e8 15 ♖he1 ♕e7 16 ♗d3 f6 17 f4 ♔h8 18 ♗f2 should supposedly give White a small advantage, as in Greenfeld-Yu, Beijing 1996, but it does not appear to be that clear, does it?

b) 12...e5? 13 ♗xe5 ♘g4 14 ♗xg4 ♕g5+ 15 ♔b1 ♕xg4 16 ♘d5 ♗xd5 17 cxd5 ♖ac8 18 f3 ♕g6 19 ♗c3 left White with an extra pawn in Krasenkov-Hellsten, Malmö 1995.

c) 12...♗xf2?! 13 ♗d6 ♖e8 14 e5 ♗xg2 15 ♖hg1 ♗xg1 16 ♖xg1 ♗b7 17 ♕d3 ♖c8 18 ♕g3 g6 19 ♕f4, with a very dangerous position for Black (Piket).

13 ♗g3

This appears to be the strongest. The alternative 13 ♔b1!? is probably not best met with 13...f6 14 ♗g3 e5 15 f4 ♗d4 16 ♘b5! ♗xb5 17 cxb5 ♖c8 18 ♕a4 ♘c7 19 ♖c1, with an advantage to White in Greenfeld-Tunk, Beersheva 1996. Instead Black has 13...e5 14 ♗xe5 ♗xf2 15 ♗d3 f6!? 16 ♗f4

♗d4 17 ♖hf1 with close to equality, or even 13...♗xf2! 14 ♗d3 ♗c5 15 e5 f5 and the pawn sacrifice gives White compensation, but not too much.

13...e5

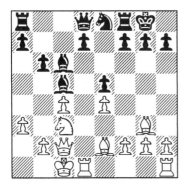

Here you can also take the direct route to the insane asylum with 13...f5!? 14 exf5 exf5 15 f3 ♕g5+ 16 ♔b1 f4 17 ♗d3 fxg3 18 ♗xh7+ ♔f7 19 f4 ♕f6 20 hxg3 ♘d6 21 g4 ♔e7, and who can tell what the hell is going on here without scanning all the other games in the database and spending two weeks with this position?! Piket-Timman, The Hague 1995 ended in a draw.

14 ♔b1

14 ♗xe5 ♕g5+ 15 f4 ♗e3+ 16 ♔b1 ♗xf4 17 ♗d4 ♗e5!? with equality according to Tiviakov.

14...♗d4 15 ♘b5 ♗xb5 16 cxb5 ♕e7

Here I prefer 16...♖c8 17 ♕a4, when Black has a couple of options. 17...♘f6 18 ♗h4 h6 (18...d5 19 f4 ♖c5 was played in Watson-Browne, USA 1996, and now White could probably have gained an advantage by bringing his last piece into play with 20 ♖hf1!) 19 f4 g5 was Van Wely-Adams, Wijk aan Zee 1998, and now White would have the advantage after 20 ♗g3! ♘xe4 (20...gxf4 21 ♗xf4 ♘xe4 22 ♗xe5 ♗xe5 23 ♕xe4 appears even more dangerous) 21 fxe5 ♘xg3 22 hxg3 ♗xe5 23 ♖xh6. Alternatively 17...♕e7 18 ♖c1 ♘d6 19 ♗d3 h5 20 h4 led to equality in Van Wely-Timman, Breda

1998.

17 ♖xd4!? exd4 18 ♖d1 d5!?

Black is trying to complicate the position. 18...♕c5 19 b4 ♕xc2+ 20 ♔xc2 ♖c8+ 21 ♔b2 ♘f6 22 ♖xd4 ♖fe8 23 ♗d3 gives White a small advantage in the endgame due to the two bishops.

19 exd5 ♘d6

19...♘f6 20 d6 ♕d7 21 ♖xd4 is just very good for White.

20 ♗d3! h6?

A grave error. After 20...♖fc8! 21 ♕e2 (21 ♕a4 ♖c5!) 21...♕xe2 22 ♗xe2 the chances are even (Lautier).

21 ♕a4 ♕f6?!

Black continues to hesitate about seizing the open file, and soon it is too late. After 21...♖ac8 22 ♕xd4 ♖fe8 23 ♕f4 ♖ed8 24 h4 ♖c5 25 a4 White is slightly better.

22 ♖c1! ♘f5?

Still not doing too well.

23 ♗c7! ♘h4? 24 f4! ♘xg2 25 ♗e5 ♕h4

25...♕d8 26 ♕xd4 f6 27 ♕e4 wins for White immediately.

26 ♕xd4 ♘e1

26...f6 27 ♕e4 fxe5 28 ♕h7+ ♔f7 29 ♖c7+ ♔e8 30 ♕g6+ and White mates.

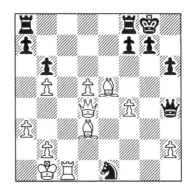

27 ♕g1!

27 ♗xg7?! meets with 27...♘f3!, when matters are less clear.

27...f6 28 ♕xe1?!

Here Lautier later felt his queen was better placed and that 28 ♖xe1 fxe5 29 fxe5 would have won easier as both the pawns march forward and the idea of ♖e1-e2 followed by ♕g1-g6-h7 seems to have deadly powers.

28...♕xe1 29 ♖xe1 fxe5 30 fxe5 ♔f7 31 h4! g5

31...♖ad8 32 d6 ♔e6 33 ♗c4+ ♔d7 34 e6+ ♔xd6 35 e7 and White wins.

32 hxg5 hxg5 33 ♗f5 ♖ad8

33...♔g7 34 ♗d7! followed by the e-pawn's march forward wins for White.

34 d6 ♔g7 35 ♗g4 ♖h8

35...♖f4 36 e6! ♖xg4 37 e7 and wins.

36 ♔c2 ♖h4 37 ♖e4 ♖xg4

37...♔f8 38 ♔c3 ♖h2 39 b3 ♔e8 40 a4 and the king marches to the centre to assist the pawns forward.

38 ♖xg4 ♔f7 39 ♖xg5 ♔e6 40 ♔d3 ♖h8 41 ♔e3 ♖h1 42 ♖g8 1-0

Game 14
Gershon-Anastasian
Saint Vincent 2000

---

1 d4 ♘f6 2 c4 e6 3 ♘f3 b6 4 a3 ♗b7 5 ♘c3

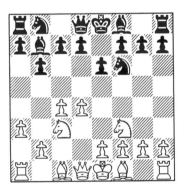

5...g6

This is the most serious alternative to 5...d5, although Black hardly ever equalises. The other option worth mentioning is 5...♘e4!?, a variation I have tried without any pleasure. Black has no real chance to fight for equality. A good, solid way for White to gain an advantage is 6 ♘xe4 ♗xe4 7 e3 ♗e7 8

♗d3, e.g. 8...d5!? (8...♗xd3 9 ♕xd3 d6 10 b4 c6 11 0-0 0-0 12 e4 ♘d7 13 ♗f4 gave White a safe plus in Browne-Trois, Buenos Aires 1979) 9 ♗xe4 dxe4 10 ♘d2 f5 11 f3 ♗d6!? (11...c5?! 12 fxe4 cxd4 13 ♕a4+! ♔f7 14 ♘f3 favours White, as does 11...e5 12 fxe4 exd4 13 exf5 0-0 14 e4) 12 ♕a4+ c6?! (12...♘d7! 13 fxe4 ♕h4+ 14 ♔d1 ♕g4+ 15 ♔c2 ♕xg2 16 ♖f1 also gives White a grip on the light squares, but still it was a fighting chance – now White is just much better) 13 0-0 ♕h4 14 f4 0-0 15 c5! bxc5 (15...♗c7 16 cxb6 ♗xb6 17 ♘c4 is also clearly better for White) 16 ♘c4 ♕e7 (16...♗e7 17 dxc5 ♘d7 18 b4 and Black has no compensation for his structural weaknesses) 17 dxc5 ♗xc5 18 b4 ♗d6 19 ♗b2 with a clear advantage for White in Kramnik-Vaganian, Horgen 1995.

6 ♕c2 ♗xf3

This is the only move that makes sense. After 6...♗g7?! 7 e4 The bishop is not very good on b7. 7...d5 (7...0-0 8 ♗g5!? h6 9 ♗e3 d6 10 h3 ♘bd7 11 ♗e2 was very good for White in Dreev-Sorokin, St.Petersburg 1993) 8 cxd5 exd5 9 e5 ♘e4 10 ♗d3 f5 (White also had a solid advantage after 10...♘xc3 11 bxc3 0-0 12 0-0 c5 13 ♗g5 ♕c8 14 ♕d2 ♗a6 15 ♗xa6 ♘xa6 16 a4 ♖e8 17 ♗h6 in Farago-Podlesnik, Bled 1996) 11 exf6 ♘xf6 12 ♕e2+ ♕e7 13 ♕xe7+ ♔xe7 14 0-0 ♖e8 15 ♗f4 ♔d8 16 ♘b5 and Black is in trouble, Christiansen-Schroll, Vienna 1991.

7 exf3

Also good is 7 gxf3 ♘c6 8 ♕d1!? ♗g7 9 ♗g5 0-0 10 f4 d5 11 cxd5 exd5 12 ♗g2 ♘e7 13 b4, when White had the advantage in Garcia Ilundain-Epishin, Manresa 1995. Romero Holmes writes that White is better in view of the superior bishop and the weakness of c6.

7...♗g7

This move has to be played, so just get it out. After 7...♘c6 8 ♗e3 ♗g7 9 0-0-0 ♘e7 (9...0-0 10 d5 ♘a5 11 h4 a6 12 g4 was good for White in Dreev-Korchnoi, Yalta 1995) 10 g4 d5 11 h4 h6 White had the upper hand in

Slobodjan-Speelman, Lippstadt 2000.

8 ♗e3

This is the most normal move. The alternatives just seem to be too premature. 8 g4 0-0 9 ♗e3 d5 10 g5 ♘e8 11 cxd5 exd5 12 f4 ♘c6 13 ♘e2 ♘e7 14 ♘g3 c5 15 dxc5 d4 gave Black good counterplay in Kozul-Romanishin, Yerevan 1996, while 8 d5 0-0 9 ♗e2 exd5 10 cxd5 c6 11 dxc6 ♘xc6 12 ♕a4 a6 13 0-0 b5 14 ♕h4 ♘h5 15 ♗g5 ♗f6 was certainly not worse for Black in Lalic-Romanishin, Germany 1996.

8...0-0 9 h4

Here it is actually most natural to castle first. In the following game Black chooses a good set-up compared to the main game: 9 0-0-0 d5 10 g4 dxc4 11 ♗xc4 c6 12 h4 ♘d5 13 ♘e4 ♘d7 14 h5 ♕c7 15 hxg6 hxg6 16 ♗xd5 exd5 17 ♘c3 ♕d6 with a good game for Black, Huzman-Van der Wiel, Pula 1997. 10 cxd5 ♘xd5 11 ♘xd5 ♕xd5 12 ♗c4 ♕d6 13 d5 e5 would be the critical position. I prefer White due to the control over the light squares.

9...♘c6

Here Black has 9...d5!? 10 cxd5 ♘xd5 11 ♘xd5 ♕xd5 12 ♗c4 ♕d6, with a slight edge for White.

10 0-0-0 d5

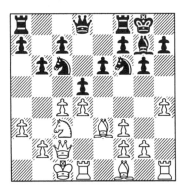

11 cxd5! exd5

11...♘xd5 12 ♘xd5 ♕xd5 13 ♗c4 ♕d6 14 d5 and now the knight is misplaced on c6.

12 g4 ♘a5 13 h5 ♖e8

Black is trying to defend. Active counterplay with 13...c5 14 hxg6 hxg6 15 dxc5 ♖c8 invites 16 g5, undermining the defence of the centre.

14 hxg6 hxg6

14...fxg6 15 g5 ♘h5 16 f4 and White has the advantage due to the weak light squares in the centre.

15 ♗d3

15 ♗e2!? makes more sense in some ways because it monitors the h5-square. But from d3 the bishop might be sacrificed on g6 later!

15...c6

Before he can think of any counterplay Black has to protect the d5-pawn

16 ♖h3!

16 ♗h6? ♗xh6+ 17 ♖xh6 ♘xg4! gives Black some interesting opportunities. For this there is no reason.

16...♘c4 17 ♗g5 ♕d6

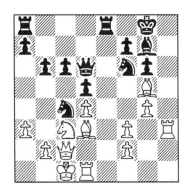

18 ♗xg6!?

This sacrifice does present Black with more problems than most players can solve at the board. But it does seem that as White does not have anything directly winning that it is not the objectively best continuation. 18 ♖dh1 ♘d7 19 ♘e2 followed by ♘f4 is also very dangerous for Black.

18...fxg6 19 ♕xg6 ♔f8

Better is 19...♘d7! 20 ♕h7+ ♔f7 21 ♖h6 ♖e6 22 ♕f5+ ♘f6 23 ♕g6+ ♔f8 24 ♖dh1 ♖ae6 25 ♖h8+ ♘g8 26 ♕f5+ ♖f6 27 ♗xf6 ♕xf6 28 ♖8h5, when White has some advantage.

20 ℤdh1 ℤe6

20...♘g8 21 ♕f5+ ♘f6 22 ♗h6 ℤe7 23 g5 and Black is just dead lost. 20...♕e6 seems to lose quite quickly to pressure on the 6th rank with 21 ℤh6! etc.

21 ♗xf6 ♕f4+

21...ℤxf6 22 ℤh8+ ♗xh8 23 ℤxh8+ ♔e7 24 ♕g7+ ℤf7 25 ♕g5+ ♕f6 26 ♕xf6+ ℤxf6 27 ℤxa8 ℤxf3 28 ℤxa7+ ♔e6 and Black has some good chances of a defence, although White has an obvious material advantage.

22 ♔b1 ℤxf6

22...♕xf6 –see the note to 21st move.

23 ℤh8+ ♗xh8 24 ℤxh8+ ♔e7 25 ♕h7+! ℤf7 26 ♕h4+ ♔d6?

26...♕f6! –see note to move 21.

27 ℤxa8 ♕d2 28 ♕d8+

Here moves were made in order to win time, as the game was being played with time increments.

28...♔e6 29 ♕e8+ ♔f6 30 ♕h8+ ♔e6 31 ℤe8+ ♔d7 32 ℤd8+ ♔e6 33 ♕e8+ ♔f6 34 ♕h8+ ♔e7 35 ℤe8+?

Still not finding the right path. Luckily the win did not go away.

35...♔d7 36 ℤd8+ ♔e6 37 ♕e8+ ♔f6 38 ♘e4+!

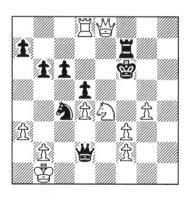

Addressing the ♘c4 problem and therefore winning the game.

38...dxe4 39 ♕xc6+ ♔g7 40 ♕xc4 exf3 41 ♕c8 ♕xf2 42 ℤg8+ ♔h7 43 ℤh8+ ♔g7 44 ♕g8+ ♔f6 45 ℤh6+ 1-0

With a mating attack. Black resigned.

Game 15
Neverov-Stefanova
Reykjavik 2002

---

1 c4 e6 2 d4 ♘f6 3 ♘f3 b6 4 a3 ♗b7 5 ♘c3 d5

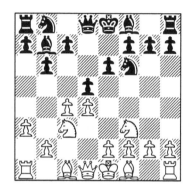

This is, of course, the main move here. Now White has a variety of choices, which will be discussed in the following seven games. The first of them is the popular...

6 ♗g5

...which should give White an advantage.

6...♗e7

6...dxc4!? also appears to be fully playable. After 7 e4 ♗e7 8 ♗xf6 ♗xf6 9 e5 ♗e7 10 ♗xc4 0-0 11 0-0 c5 12 d5 exd5 13 ♗xd5 ♗xd5 14 ♘xd5 ♘a6 15 ♕b3 ♘c7 16 ℤfd1 ♘xd5 17 ℤxd5 ♕c8 18 ℤad1 ♕e6, as in Van Wely-Korchnoi, Wijk aan Zee 1997, Black cannot be much worse, although White still dictates events.

7 ♕a4+!?

This was the major line in the 1990's. The key idea is that after 7... c6 8 cxd5 exd5 9 g3 0-0 10 ♗g2 White has gained a slightly improved version of the 4...d5 line. Here White has had many successes in practical play, but experience has shown that Black completely equalises after...

7...♕d7! 8 ♕c2

This is what Gelfand invented when Black

found sufficient defences after 8 ♕xd7+ ♘bxd7 9 ♘b5 ♗d8! (the most logical, and also the height of fashion), e.g. 10 cxd5 (10 ♗f4? dxc4 11 ♘xc7+ ♗xc7 12 ♗xc7 0-0 13 ♖c1 ♖fc8 14 ♗f4 b5 and Black is better. The control over the centre and the queenside majority is far more important than the dark squares, Van Wely-Gelfand, Monaco 2001) 10...♘xd5 11 e4 ♘5f6 12 ♖c1 with a draw agreed in Dreev-Anand, Moscow Knockout 2001. Then 12...0-0?! 13 ♘xc7 ♖c8 14 ♘b5 ♖xc1+ 15 ♗xc1 leads to the win of a pawn for White, but Bacrot-Gelfand, Leon 2001 continued 12...♗xe4! 13 ♘xc7+ ♗xc7 14 ♖xc7 ♘d5 15 ♖c1 h6 16 ♗d2 ♗xf3 17 gxf3 ♔e7, and the question here is whether White's two bishops can compensate for the poor pawn structure. Perhaps the answer is yes, but Black appears to have full control as c7 is his for keeps, meaning White cannot threaten him.

8...dxc4

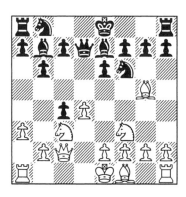

9 e4?!

This is an opening experiment we will not see Gelfand try again. White permanently sacrifices the c4-pawn and hopes to generate an initiative in the centre. I feel that it is doubtful whether he can prove any substantial compensation for the pawn. But the main line here has, by now, been more or less established as equalising for Black. After 9 e3 Black needs to go for the pawn, as 9...0-0?! 10 ♗xc4 c5 11 dxc5 was somewhat better for

White in Gelfand-Karpov, Dortmund 1997, when Black was still far from finishing his development. Here 11 0-0-0?! meets with 11...cxd4 12 ♖xd4 ♕c8 13 ♖h4 h6 etc. Instead 9...♗xf3! 10 gxf3 b5 is best, when 11 ♗xf6 ♗xf6 leaves White to make a choice. 12 ♕e4 0-0! 13 ♕xa8 ♘c6 14 ♕xf8+ (14 ♕b7 ♖b8 15 ♕a6 ♖b6 and the queen does not escape) 14...♔xf8 15 ♘xb5 ♕d5 sees Black win the f3-pawn, with dangerous threats on the dark squares.

This leaves 12 a4 c6 13 axb5 cxb5 14 ♕e4 0-0 15 f4! (White is playing for structure; after 15 ♖a5 b4 16 ♘a4 ♗d8! 17 ♘c5 ♕d5 18 ♖a4 ♘c6 19 ♗g2 ♗b6 20 f4 ♖fd8 Black is ideally placed according to Gelfand), and now time has validated 15...♖c8! (15...♘c6, as in Gelfand-Lautier, Biel 1997, has also been played). Now White has more than one possibility:

a) 16 ♕xa8 ♘c6 17 ♕xc8+ ♕xc8 18 ♗g2 a6 19 0-0 g6 and the primary factor in the position is Black's future on the queenside.

b) 16 ♗g2 ♘c6 17 0-0 (17 ♘xb5? ♘b4 18 ♕b7 ♕d8 and White is not well coordinated, nor fully developed) 17...♖ab8 18 ♗h3 shows that White can earn no advantage from 16 ♗g2. Bacrot-Gershon, Bermuda 1999 continued 18...b4 19 ♘a4 ♖d8 20 ♘c5 ♕d5 21 ♗g2 ♘xd4 22 exd4 ♗xd4 23 ♘a4 ½-½.

c) 16 ♗h3!? attacks on the light squares, where White is better. All other moves are harmless. Piket-Khalifman, Wijk aan Zee 2002, went 16...♘c6 17 ♘xb5 ♖ab8 18 ♘c3 ♖xb2 19 0-0 ♖b3 with a very promising position for Black, but best seems 19...♘xd4! with the idea of 20 exd4 ♕xd4 21 ♕xd4 ♗xd4 22 ♖ac1? (otherwise three pawns and the better structure should be important, too) 22...♖b3 and Black wins. 17 d5 ♘d8 18 0-0 is a suggestion – without an evaluation – of Gelfand. Black should be fine if he chooses to play 18...b4 19 ♘a4 exd5 20 ♗xd7 dxe4 21 ♗xc8 ♖xc8, when the passed pawns are of paramount importance, and White is struggling for survival.

9...b5 10 ♖d1 a6 11 ♗e2 h6 12 ♗h4 ♕d8 13 0-0 0-0 14 ♘e5

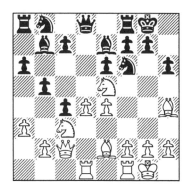

14...c5?

Here Black loses the chance to gain a clear opening advantage. After 14...♘c6! White has no better move than the exchange of knights, as d4 is hanging. After the trade Black needs slightly less space in which to manoeuvre, and the pawn grows in stature.

15 d5! exd5 16 exd5 ♘fd7?!

16...♘xd5!? 17 ♗g3 ♘xc3 18 ♖xd8 ♘xe2+ 19 ♕xe2 ♗xd8 with a situation that is very difficult to assess. Black is, in theory, better placed, with the large majority on the queenside, but there will be considerable problems completing development.

17 ♗xe7 ♕xe7 18 ♘g4

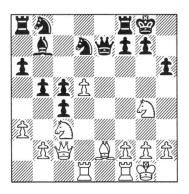

Here White finally has a very interesting position. For the pawn he has a strong passed pawn on d5, while Black's development difficulties remain.

18...f5 19 ♘e3 f4 20 ♘f5 ♕g5 21 ♘d6 ♘e5 22 f3 ♖a7 23 a4 ♕d8 24 ♘ce4 ♕b6 25 g3 ♘ed7 26 ♔h1 ♘f6 27 gxf4 ♘bd7 28 ♘f5 ♘xd5?!

28...♘h5 looks better, with a complex struggle ahead. Now White slowly takes over.

29 ♖xd5 ♗xd5 30 ♘e7+ ♔h8 31 ♘xd5 ♕e6 32 ♖d1 ♖f5 33 ♘dc3 b4 34 ♖d6 ♕f7 35 ♘d5 c3 36 ♗c4 ♕h5 37 ♔g2 ♖f8 38 bxc3 ♘e5 39 ♕e2 ♘xc4 40 ♕xc4 bxc3 41 ♕xc3 ♖b7 42 ♘g3 ♕h4 43 ♖e6 ♖d7 44 ♕e5 ♕d8 45 ♖xh6+

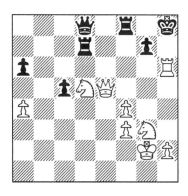

45...♔g8 46 ♕e6+ ♖ff7 47 ♖h5 ♖d6 48 ♕h3 ♖h6 49 ♖xh6 gxh6 50 ♕e6 ♕f8 51 f5 c4 52 f6 ♔h7 53 ♕e4+ ♔h8 54 ♕xc4 ♕b8 55 ♕e4 a5 56 ♕g6 ♖b7 57 ♘e7 ♖b2+ 58 ♔h3 ♕f8 59 ♘gf5 1-0

Game 16
Piket-Anand
Monte *Carlo (blindfold) 1997*

1 d4 ♘f6 2 c4 e6 3 ♘f3 b6 4 ♘c3 ♗b7 5 a3 d5 6 ♕c2!?

This move has been known ever since 1950, but it was only when Gelfand used it against Karpov in 1992 that it became fashionable. As with the 6 ♗g5 line its span in the great circulation of modern theory was short, as Black quickly found the right way to respond. In this game we shall see two such examples.

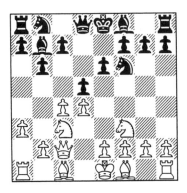

6...dxc4

This is the current trend, but I prefer 6...c5, although it is a matter of taste. However, not good for Black is 6...♘bd7?! 7 cxd5 ♘xd5 8 ♘xd5. Then 8...exd5 9 ♗g5 gives White a small edge, but 8...♗xd5? 9 e4 ♗b7 10 ♗b5! c6 (otherwise ♗c6 with a great advantage) 11 ♗xc6 ♖c8 12 d5 ♕c7 is a different story. Now instead of 13 ♘d4? as in Gelfand-Karpov, Moscow 1992, White should play 13 ♗e3! ♗xc6 14 ♖c1 exd5 (14...♘b8 15 dxc6! ♘xc6 16 0-0 e5 17 b4 and Black is still struggling to complete his development) 15 exd5 ♘b8 16 dxc6! ♕xc6 17 ♕d1 ♕e6 18 ♕a4+! with a lasting initiative.

Returning to 6...c5!, this is the tactician's preference. After 7 cxd5 cxd4 8 ♕a4+ ♘bd7 White has three logical options (of different value):

a) 9 ♕xd4?! ♗c5 10 ♕a4 exd5! 11 ♗g5 0-0 12 e3 ♗e7! and White needs to develop quickly, but chose not to in Gofshtein-Alterman, Israel 1997.

b) 9 dxe6 dxc3 10 exd7+ ♕xd7 11 ♕xd7+ ♘xd7 12 bxc3 ♗e7 13 ♗e3! ♖c8 14 ♗d4 0-0 15 e3 ♘c5 16 ♘d2 (16 ♗e2? ♘b3 17 ♖b1 [17 ♖a2? ♗d5 and Black is getting some action] 17...♘xd4 18 cxd4 ♗xa3 and Black is better due to the pawns and bishops) 16...♘a4! 17 c4 ♗c5 with good compensation for the pawn, Lputian-Dautov, Budapest 1996.

c) 9 ♘xd4 has become the critical move, although Black has nothing to fear after 9...♘xd5 10 ♘xd5 ♗xd5 11 e4 ♗b7, e.g. 12 ♗e3 a6 13 f3 b5 14 ♕d1 ♗e7 15 ♗e2 0-0 16 0-0 ♖c8 17 ♕e1 ♗g5 18 ♗f2 ♘e5 19 ♖d1 ♕e7 and Black had equalised so effortlessly that he became too ambitious in Dreev-Karpov, Cap d'Agde 2000. Cramling-Xu Jun, Yerevan 1996 went 12 ♗a6 ♗xa6 13 ♕xa6 ♗c5 14 ♗e3 0-0 15 0-0 ♘f6 16 ♖ad1 ♕c8! with equality.

6...♗e7 is dealt with in the next game.

7 e4 c5 8 d5

8 dxc5 seems to be rather harmless. After 8...♗xc5 9 ♗xc4 ♘bd7 10 0-0 ♕c7 11 ♗d3 a6 12 ♗g5 ♘e5! Black already has a pleasant position. In fact in Sokolov-Polugaevsky, Holland 1994 the sequence 13 ♘xe5 ♕xe5 14 ♗h4 ♘h5! 15 ♕a4+! ♔f8 16 ♕d7 g5! gave him a great position.

8...exd5 9 exd5 a6!

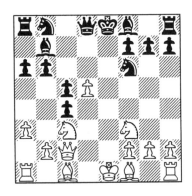

This is the way they are doing it these days. After the passive 9...♗d6 10 ♗g5 0-0 11 0-0-0 ♘bd7 12 ♗xc4 ♕b8 13 ♔b1 a6 14 ♘e4 ♘xe4 15 ♕xe4 ♖e8 16 ♕g4 ♘f8 17 ♗d3 ♗c8 18 ♕h5 ♕c7 19 ♖c1 White had a little pressure in Lautier-Karpov, Monte Carlo 1996.

10 ♗g5!?

The beginning of a wild stream of complications that ends with an equal position.

10 ♗xc4 b5 11 ♗a2 ♗d6 12 ♗g5 0-0 13 0-0 ♘bd7 14 ♖ad1 ♕c7 15 ♗b1 ♖fe8 and

Black was in no way worse in Avrukh-Anand, Haifa 2000. Instead 11...♗e7? is poor since the bishop belongs in front of the d-pawn. Sakaev-Veingold, Moscow 1994 went 12 0-0 0-0 13 ♗g5 ♘bd7 14 ♖ad1 ♕b6 15 ♘h4 with an advantage to White in view of 15...g6? 16 ♘xg6 hxg6 17 d6 ♗xd6 18 ♕xg6+, when White wins.

10...b5 11 0-0-0 ♗d6 12 ♘e4 ♗e7 13 ♗xc4?!

This attack seems incorrect. 13 ♗xf6 ♗xf6 14 ♘xc5 0-0 (14...♗c8 15 ♕e4+! with an attack) 15 ♘xb7 ♕c7 16 g4!? was a try for an advantage.

13...bxc4 14 ♖he1 0-0 15 d6 ♗xe4 16 ♖xe4 ♗xd6 17 ♘e5 ♘bd7?!

17...c3! would have disturbed White considerably. Now we are heading for a draw.

18 ♖xd6 ♘xe4

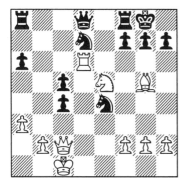

19 ♗xd8 ♘xd6 20 ♘xd7 ♖fxd8 21 ♘b6 ♖ab8 22 ♘xc4 ♘xc4 ½-½

Game 17
Cramling-Almasi
Horgen 1995

1 d4 ♘f6 2 c4 e6 3 ♘f3 b6 4 a3 ♗b7 5 ♘c3 d5 6 ♕c2

Another way to lead to the positions in the game (in fact the most common) is the following: 6 cxd5 ♘xd5 7 ♗d2 (7 ♕c2 ♗e7 8 ♗d2 has been seen, but the most popular replies to 7 ♕c2 are 7...c5 and 7...♘xc3,

while White often prefers 8 e4, transposing to 7...♘xc3) 7...♘d7 8 ♕c2. Now 8...c5 seems safe enough, albeit a little boring. Akopian-Gurevich, Haifa 1995 continued 9 e4 ♘xc3 10 ♗xc3 cxd4 11 ♘xd4 a6 12 g3 ♕c7 13 ♗g2 ♗e7!? 14 0-0 0-0 15 ♖ac1 ♖ac8 16 ♕e2 ♖fd8! (the x-ray finds no practical use, so Black ignores it) 17 ♘b3 ♘e5 18 ♗b4 ♕d7 19 ♗xe7 ♕xe7 with equality. Instead 8...♗e7 9 e4 ♘xc3 10 ♗xc3 0-0 would be a very natural transposition to our main game, which seems more interesting and equally sound.

6...♗e7 7 cxd5 ♘xd5

7...exd5 leads to positions similar to the 4...d5 lines. There is no need for exact theoretical knowledge there.

8 ♗d2 0-0 9 e4 ♘xc3 10 ♗xc3 ♘d7 11 0-0-0

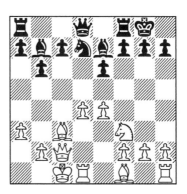

11...c6!

11...♕c8 12 h4 ♖d8 13 ♖h3 h6!? 14 d5 15 ♘g5! (threatening e4-e5) 15...hxg5 16 hxg5 ♘g4 (16...♘e8?! 17 f4 gives White a very strong attack as the black pieces are not playing) 17 f4 ♗c5! 18 ♗xg7!? ♔xg7 19 ♕c3+ and White had a very interesting attack in Akopian-Granda Zuniga, Groningen 1993. Best for Black here is 19...♔f8! 20 ♖h7 ♗e7, bringing the king to safety, when 21 ♗e2 exd5 22 f5 is messy indeed.

12 h4 b5 13 ♔b1

More direct is 13 ♖h3!? a5 14 d5 cxd5 15 ♗xb5, as in Kamsky-Anand, Sanghi Nagar

1994. Black defended well by taking the central squares with 15...♘f6 16 ♘g5 ♕b6 17 exd5 ♖ac8! 18 ♗d7 ♗xd5! 19 ♗xc8 ♖xc8 20 ♖xd5 (the bishop seems to be stronger than the rook, so this exchange is quite natural) 20...exd5 21 ♕f5 ♕a6, and now instead of the adventurous 22 ♔d2?! White should have settled for the repetition after 22 ♔b1 ♕f1+ 23 ♔a2 ♕c4+.

13...a5 14 ♗e1?

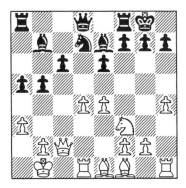

This move hurts my eyes. I cannot see how the bishop will ever be a useful piece on e1.

Better, in my opinion, is 14 ♗d2 b4 15 a4 c5 16 d5?! (this pawn sac seems wrong; 16 ♗g5! is obviously superior, getting all the pieces into action) 16...exd5 17 exd5 ♗xd5 18 ♘g5 ♘f6, Mikhalchishin-Petrosian, Lvov 1994, when Black has the initiative and a pawn and, therefore, the better prospects (his pieces are only temporarily awkwardly placed in the centre).

14 d5 cxd5 15 ♘g5 (15 ♗xb5 ♖c8 16 exd5 ♗xd5 17 ♗d3 ♕b6! looks good for Black) 15...dxe4 16 ♗xb5 ♗d5 17 ♘xe4 ♕c7 was good enough for Black in Tregubov-Akesson, Cap d'Agde 1994, although White has quite a bit of compensation for the pawn.

14...b4 15 a4 ♖c8 16 ♘g5 c5 17 d5 ♗xg5!

17...e5? fails to 18 ♘e6! fxe6 19 dxe6, when White is better.

18 hxg5

No improvement is 18 dxe6 fxe6 19 ♗b5 (19 hxg5 ♕e7 and Black's position is comfortably superior, with, among others, ...♘b6 and ...c5-c4 coming) 19...♗c6! 20 ♗xc6 ♖xc6 21 hxg5 ♕e7 and White is very weak on the highly important light squares.

18...exd5 19 exd5 g6 20 ♗b5

20 ♕b3 ♕xg5 21 ♕h3 ♘f6 and Black is close to winning. 20 f4 is met by 20...♘b6.

20...♘b6

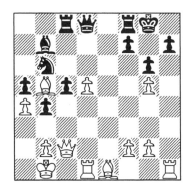

Black is clearly better according to Almasi.

21 d6 c4?

21...♗xg2! 22 ♖h2 ♗f3 and White is finished.

22 f3! c3! 23 b3

Forced. 23 d7 b3! wins on the spot for Black.

23...♘d5 24 ♗f2!

More tricks: 24 d7 ♘e3! and Black wins.

24...♕xg5 25 d7 ♖b8 26 ♗h4?

Here White had the chance to gain good counterplay with 26 ♗d4! ♘e3 27 ♗xe3 ♕xe3 28 ♖he1 ♕g5 29 ♖e8, although Black's chances are preferable after 29...♖d8 etc.

26...♕f4 27 ♖de1?

White is on the way, not to sacrifice an exchange, but to win a piece. The only problem is that a bishop on d5 together with the strong c3-pawn combine to provide Black with decisive compensation. 27 ♗f2 was better according to Almasi.

27...♘e3 28 ♖xe3 ♕xe3 29 ♖e1 ♕b6 30

♖e8?! ♗d5! 31 ♔a2 ♖bxe8 32 dxe8♕ ♖xe8 33 ♗xe8 ♕d4!

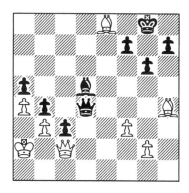

White has a piece but, as promised, Black is very close to winning.

34 ♗g3 ♕d2 35 ♔b1 ♕e3! 36 ♗b5 ♗xb3! 37 ♕xb3 ♕g1+ 38 ♔a2 ♕xg2+ 39 ♔a1 ♕xg3 40 ♕d1 ♕f2 41 ♗e2 b3! 42 ♕xb3 ♕xe2 43 ♕xc3 ♕d1+ 44 ♔b2 ♕d8 0-1

White has had enough.

Game 18
Timman-Polgar
Bali 2000

---

1 ♘f3 ♘f6 2 c4 b6 3 d4 e6 4 a3 ♗b7 5 ♘c3 d5 6 cxd5 ♘xd5 7 ♕c2!

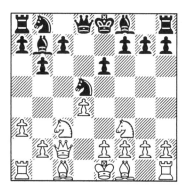

This is the most popular move in this position with GMs today, and for good reason. As we shall see Black has no clear-cut path to

development and, in fact, this is the main reason why I cannot fully recommend the system with 4...♗b7 followed by 6...♘xd5. I just do not feel comfortable about the resulting positions.

7...♘xc3

7...c5 is dealt with in the following game.

8 bxc3

This has become the only serious move. In the late 1980's 8 ♕xc3!? was also played quite a lot, but several methods to equalise were quickly found. The simplest is 8...♘d7 9 ♗g5 (9 ♗f4 ♗d6 is no problem at all for Black) 9...♗e7 10 ♗xe7 ♔xe7! (the king is not exposed, so this yields no problems) 11 e3 ♖c8 12 ♗e2 c5 13 dxc5? (this starts a kamikaze journey for the queen which leads only to problems; 13 0-0 is better) 13...♖xc5! 14 ♕xg7 ♖g8 15 ♕xh7 ♖xg2 (the white king is more awkward in the centre as Black is well developed) 16 ♕h4+ ♘f6 17 ♖d1 ♕c7 18 ♘d4 a5! and Black is clearly better according to Petursson. Portisch-Karpov, Biel 1996 saw White blunder with 19 ♘b5?? (19 h3!?) 19...♖xb5! 20 ♗xb5 ♖g4 0-1.

8...♗e7 9 e4 0-0 10 ♗d3 c5 11 0-0

Here there is a very interesting alternative. Of course this can also be played at move 13, but it is for some reason seen more often here – namely 11 ♗b2!, when Piket-Rau, Rotterdam 1988 continued 11...♕c8 12 ♕e2 ♗a6 13 0-0 ♗xd3 14 ♕xd3 ♕a6 (14...cxd4 15 cxd4 ♕a6 16 ♕e3 ♘d7 17 d5 gives White the initiative, while 14...♘c6? 15 d5 ♘a5 16 c4 is overwhelmingly better for White) 15 c4! cxd4 16 ♘xd4 ♕b7 (16...♖c8?! 17 ♘b5 ♘c6 18 ♕g3 e5 19 f4! was very promising for White in Piket-Polugaevsky, Aruba 1994) 17 ♕g3 (17 ♘b5!? also looks good) 17...♗f6 18 e5 ♗e7 19 ♖ad1 ♖d8 20 ♘b5 ♖xd1 21 ♖xd1 ♘a6 with an unclear game. I think that this is more unclear for White than for Black, if you get my drift. White has some strong plans involving the advance of the h-pawn. Note that 15 c4! is far stronger than 15 ♕e3 ♘d7 16 ♖ad1 ♖ac8 17 ♖d2 b5, where the bishop is poor on b2. Black has at least equalised, and won quite soon in Flear-Hjartarson, Szirak 1987. Nor does 15 ♕xa6 ♘xa6 16 ♘e5 ♖fc8 17 ♖fd1 cxd4 18 cxd4 ♖c2 present Black with anything but prospects, as in Malaniuk-Ehlvest, USSR 1987.

11...♕c8 12 ♕e2 ♗a6

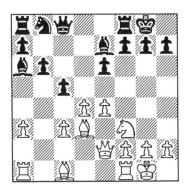

13 ♖d1

Others:

a) 13 a4 ♗xd3 14 ♕xd3 ♖d8 15 ♗f4 (15 a5 bxa5 16 ♖xa5 ♘c6 17 ♖a4 cxd4 18 cxd4 ♕d7 with equality – Dautov) 15...♕b7 16 a5 ♘c6 (16...cxd4!? 17 cxd4 bxa5 18 ♖xa5 ♘c6 would probably be fine) 17 axb6 cxd4 18 cxd4 axb6 19 ♖xa8 ♖xa8 20 ♖d1 ♖d8 with equality, Azmaiparashvili-Epishin, Reggio Emilia 1995/96. Dautov has suggested the following alternatives: 14...♕a6 15 ♕b5 ♕b7 16 ♖e1 a6 17 ♕e2 ♖d8 18 d5 with good prospects for White, and 14...cxd4!? 15 cxd4 ♘c6, which possibly equalises. I am not completely sure on this one, although it looks natural.

b) 13 ♗f4 gives White the advantage according to ECO, but I will remain sceptical on that one, too. Black should be fine after 13...♗xd3 14 ♕xd3 ♖d8 (more careful is 14...♘d7 15 a4 ♖d8 16 ♖fe1 cxd4 17 cxd4 ♕b7 18 ♖ab1 ♖ac8 19 a5, when White might have a slight positional edge but it will be very difficult to prove, and he was nowhere even close in Piket-Polugaevsky, Aruba 1994) 15 ♕e3 (White has no advantage after 15

d5!? c4 16 ♕e2 exd5 17 exd5 ♗f6 18 d6 ♕f5 19 ♗g3 ♘d7 20 ♕xc4, when a draw was agreed in Piket-Van der Wiel, Holland 1996) 15...♘c6 16 ♖fd1 ♘a5!?, Arbakov-Levin, Berlin 1994. Now White had sufficient compensation for the pawn after 17 h4 ♘c4 18 ♕e2 cxd4 19 cxd4 ♗xa3 20 ♘d2 ♘xd2 21 ♖xa3! ♘c4 22 ♖g3, but nothing has been decided. Personally I would not like to be Black here, but I think it is more a question of style than anything else..

13 ♗b2! leads to the note to White's 11th move.

13...cxd4 14 cxd4 ♗xd3 15 ♕xd3

White has no chance for an advantage here, it seems. The alternative looks a little clumsy and Black equalises easily: 15 ♖xd3 ♘d7 16 ♗b2 (16 ♗g5?! ♗xg5 17 ♘xg5 h6 18 ♘h3 ♕c4, as in Peshina-Gurevich, Eger 1987, is already better for Black; White's forces are misplaced) 16...♕a6 17 ♖ad1 ♖fe8 18 ♕e3 ♖ac8 19 d5 exd5 20 ♖xd5 ♘f8 21 h4 ♕a4 22 ♖1d4 and a draw was agreed in Bareev-Rodriguez, Sochi 1988.

15...♕a6 16 ♗b2

16 d5 ♕xd3! 17 ♖xd3 exd5 18 exd5 ♗d6 19 ♗e3 ♖c8 20 ♖e1 ♘d7 is equal according to Knaak. 16 ♕e3!? ♘d7 17 ♗b2 ♖ac8 is more adventurous, but Black should be able to gain sufficient counterplay on the c-file.

16...♕xd3 17 ♖xd3 ♘d7 18 ♖c1

White gains the c-file but Black has the possibility of a distant passed pawn and of creating a good square for the knight on c4. Also equal is 18 d5 ♘c5 19 ♖e3 ♖fd8 20 ♖d1 ♖ac8.

18...♖fc8 19 ♖dc3 ♖xc3 20 ♖xc3 ♘f6 21 ♘d2

21 e5? ♘d5 helps only Black.

21...b5!

Black would never allow 22 a4, where the pawn is less weak and when he would not have c4 waiting for the knight.

22 ♖c6

22 ♖c7 ♔f8 23 ♖b7 a6 has been assessed as unclear. I think White should be very care-

ful here that ...⟂c8 does not suddenly win something. All in all it seems that improving the king should be a priority.

22...♔f8 23 f3 ♔e8 24 ♘b3

24 ♔f2 ♔d7 shows that White somehow gained nothing by 22 ⟂c6, only to have to waste time keeping it there.

24...♘d7

24...♔d7 25 ⟂c1 ⟂c8 26 ♘c5+ and White maintains the balance.

25 ♔f1?

Creating problems later. Actually it is difficult to why 25 ♔f2! was not played.

25...♘b6 26 ♘c5?

White is drifting. The knight does less here than it seems to while the knight on c4 is really annoying. 26 ♘a5 ♔d7 27 ⟂c2 ⟂c8 28 ⟂xc8 ♘xc8 29 ♔e2 results in an endgame where Black has very slightly better chances due to the prospects of creating a passed pawn and the weakness of the a3-pawn. However, this should be a drawable option for White.

26...♘c4! 27 ♗c1 ⟂d8

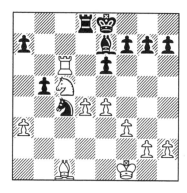

Now White just loses something. If the king had been on f2 the game continuation would have worked better because there would be no check on d1.

28 a4

28 d5 ♘e5 29 ⟂c7 ♗d6 and Black should win.

28...⟂xd4! 29 ♘b3 ⟂d3 30 axb5 ♘e5 31 ⟂c8+ ♔d7 32 ⟂a8 ⟂xb3 33 ⟂xa7+ ♔e8

0-1

┌─────────────────────────────┐
│ *Game 19* │
│ **Kasparov-van der Wiel** │
│ *Amsterdam 1988* │
└─────────────────────────────┘

1 d4 ♘f6 2 c4 e6 3 ♘f3 b6 4 a3 ♗b7 5 ♘c3 d5 6 ♕c2 c5 7 cxd5 ♘xd5

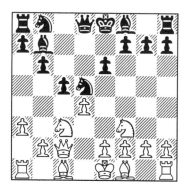

8 dxc5!

This is the only move that is dangerous for Black. The alternatives both promise Black equality.

a) 8 e4 ♘xc3 9 bxc3 and now:

a1) After 9...♘d7 White reaches another crossroads.

a11) In reply to 10 ♗d3 the best move is 10...♕c7! according to Kasparov, a draw being agreed in Kasparov-Sosonko, Lucerne 1982 after 11 ♕d2 g6 12 0-0 ♗g7. Kasparov was, in fact, so uncomfortable with his position here that he claimed in Chess Informant that Black already has a slight advantage. Whether or not this is too strong an assessment I shall not say, but the fact that Black is not unhappy with the outcome of the opening is quite clear to me. Black is also fine after the alternatives, e.g. 11 ♕b1 g6 12 0-0 ♗g7 13 ⟂a2 0-0 14 ⟂e1 a6 15 a4 ⟂fc8 16 h3 ♗c6 17 ♗e3 c4 18 ♗c2 b5 with equality, as in Ostermeyer-Sosonko, Hannover 1983. Meanwhile 11 ♗b2 cxd4 12 cxd4 ♕xc2 13 ♗xc2 ♗a6 led to a carefree endgame for Black in Yusupov-Miles, Linares 1983, and

11 0-0 cxd4 12 cxd4 ♕xc2 13 ♗xc2 ♖c8 even gave Black some initiative in Franco Ocampos-Van der Sterren, Wijk aan Zee 1983.

a12) 10 ♗f4. This bishop needs to be developed immediately. 10...cxd4 11 cxd4 ♖c8 12 ♕b3 ♕f6!? 13 ♗g3 ♕g6 (13...♗xe4 14 ♗b5 is very dangerous for Black) 14 ♗d3 ♗e7 15 0-0 0-0 16 ♖fe1 ♖fd8 and Black was well placed in Van der Sterren-Van der Wiel, Wijk aan Zee 1986. There are both good things and bad things to say about the queen on g6. The rather futuristic 12...♕f6!? seems to be the best, while more solid is 12...♗e7 13 ♗d3 ♘f6 14 ♕b5+ (the only serious move – after 14 ♕b1 0-0 15 ♗d2 ♘e8 16 0-0 ♘d6 17 e5 ♘f5 18 ♗xf5 exf5 19 ♕xf5 ♗xf3 20 ♕xf3 ♕xd4 Black was already slightly better in Cramling-Karpov, Oropesa del Mar 1996, and 14 d5?! exd5 15 ♖d1 0-0 16 0-0 dxe4! was better for Black in Miles-Polugaevsky, Sarajevo 1987) 14...♕d7 (14...♗c6! 15 ♕b1 0-0, with good play for Black, is probably what Karpov would have played against Cramling) 15 ♘e5 ♕xb5 16 ♗xb5+ ♔f8 17 f3 ♘e8! 18 ♗d7 ♖d8 19 ♗c6 ♗c8! and Black was only slightly worse in Timman-Karpov, Jakarta 1993. Also possible is 10...♗e7, when 11 d5?! is too early: 11...exd5 12 exd5 0-0 13 ♖d1?! g5! 14 ♗c1 g4 15 ♘d2 ♗xd5 and Black is close to winning. Instead White should develop first with 11 ♗d3, e.g. 11...♖c8 12 ♕e2 0-0 13 0-0 cxd4 14 cxd4 ♘f6 (not 14...♖c3? 15 ♖fc1! ♖xc1+ 16 ♖xc1, Gulko-Timman, Amsterdam 1987, when White had the advantage due to the threat of ♖c7) 15 a4 ♖c3! 16 e5 ♘d5 17 ♗d2 ♖c7 18 ♖fc1 with equality in Bareev-Chernin, Lvov 1987.

a2) Black can also try 9...♗e7 10 ♗b5+! ♗c6 11 ♗d3 and the bishop is badly placed on c6. No need for further variations...

a3) Or 9...♘c6, which also puts Black in trouble after 10 ♗b2!, e.g. 10...♗e7 11 d5! exd5 12 ♖d1 0-0 (worse is 12...♗f6 13 exd5 ♘e5 14 ♘xe5 ♗xe5 15 ♗b5+ ♔f8 16 0-0 ♕d6 17 f4 ♗f6 18 c4 a6 19 ♗e5 and White is already winning, Tukmakov-Oll, Kujbyshev 1986 continuing 19...♗xe5 20 fxe5 ♕xe5 21 ♕f2 f6 22 ♖fe1 ♕h5 23 ♗d7 ♕f7 24 ♗e6 ♕c7 25 d6 ♕d8 26 ♗h3 ♗c6 27 ♖e7 1-0) 13 exd5 ♘a5 14 ♗d3 ♗f6 15 ♗xh7+?! (15 0-0! gives White the advantage due to 15...g6 16 c4) 15...♔h8 16 ♗e4 (16 0-0 g6 17 ♗xg6 fxg6 18 ♕xg6 ♕e7 and White's queen is alone in attack) 16...♗a6 17 ♗d3 ♖e8+ 18 ♔f1 ♘c4 19 ♗xc4 ♗xc4+ 20 ♔g1 ♖e2 and Black had enough for the pawn (to put it mildly) in Portisch-Sosonko, Tilburg 1982. 10...g6 11 ♖d1 ♗g7 12 d5 exd5 13 exd5 ♕e7+ 14 ♗e2 ♘e5 15 ♕a4+ ♘d7 16 0-0 0-0 17 ♖fe1 left White better developed in Petrosian-Sosonko, Tilburg 1982, while 10...♖c8? 11 d5!? exd5 12 exd5 ♕xd5 13 ♗d3 ♘e5 14 0-0-0 was just a killer in Agdestein-Lau, Dortmund 1987. I would say that Black's king is not completely safe...

b) 8 ♗g5 is also not so dangerous. After 8...♗e7 9 ♗xe7 ♕xe7 10 ♘xd5 exd5 11 e3 0-0 12 ♗d3 g6 (taking control over the kingside light squares) 13 dxc5 bxc5 14 0-0 ♘d7, as in Seirawan-Timman, Amsterdam 1992, Black secured equality. Vilela-Rodriguez, Cienfuegos 1985 seemed okay for Black after 11 g3 0-0 12 ♗g2 ♘d7 13 0-0 ♖ac8.

8...♗xc5 9 ♗g5!

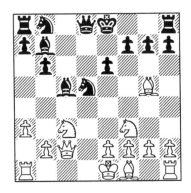

The most energetic. There are two differences between this and 8 ♗g5 – Black no longer has a c-pawn, so the d4-square is available to White, and Black has already moved his bishop. Now there are three different paths to choose from. I would recommend 9...f6, although none of them promises equality.

9...♕c8

Others:

a) 9...f6 10 ♗d2 0-0 (Black should not hesitate over this logical move – after 10...♘d7 11 e4 ♘xc3 12 ♗xc3 ♕c8 13 0-0-0 0-0 14 b4 ♗e7 15 ♕b3 ♖f7 16 ♗c4 ♘f8 17 ♘d4 White had strong pressure [his king will be fine on b1] in Plaskett-Short, Plovdiv 1984) and now White should play 11 e3! (intending to use the b1-h7 diagonal), e.g. 11...♔h8?! 12 ♗c4! ♕e7 (12...♘xc3?! 13 ♗xc3 ♕e7 14 h4! with the idea of h4-h5 with a very dangerous attack) 13 ♖d1!? and White has the better prospects (Piket). An improvement is 11...a5! – there is no need to go to the h-file before being forced to do so. Gelfand-Lautier, Manila 1990 continued 12 ♗d3 ♔h8! 13 ♖d1 (13 h4!? ♕e8 14 ♘g5 f5 15 e4 ♘f6 16 0-0-0 ♘c6! offers Black counterplay according to Gelfand, while 13 ♗xh7?! f5 14 ♗g6 ♕f6 15 ♗h5 ♕h6 benefits only Black) 13...♘d7 14 0-0 ♕e7 15 ♗e4! ♘xc3 16 ♗xc3 (16 ♗xb7? ♘xd1 17 ♗xa8 ♘xe3 and Black wins) 16...♖a7 17 ♘d4?! (17 ♖d2!? and White is perhaps a little bit better – Gelfand) 17...♗xd4 18 exd4 ♖d8! 19 ♖fe1 ♗xe4 20 ♕xe4 ♘f8 21 d5 ♕d6! with equality. Note that after 11 e4 there is no good place for the light-squared bishop, e.g. 11...♘xc3 12 ♗xc3 a5 13 ♖d1 ♕c8 14 ♗d3 ♘a6 15 0-0 ♔h8 16 ♖fe1 e5 with equality in Vyzmanavin-Lautier, Sochi 1989, or 13 ♗c4 ♕c8 14 ♕e2 ♗a6 15 ♗xa6 ♕xa6 16 ♕xa6 ♘xa6 17 ♕e2 e5 18 ♖hd1 ♖fd8 with a good position for Black in Benjamin-Korchnoi, Jerusalem 1986.

b) 9...♗e7 is slightly passive. After 10 ♗xe7 ♕xe7 11 ♘xd5 exd5 12 e3 0-0 13 ♗d3 ♖c8 14 ♕e2 ♘d7 15 0-0 ♘c5 16 ♘d4 ♘xd3 17 ♕xd3 ♖c5 Black had the c-file to compensate for his structural deficiencies in Ehlvest-Korchnoi, Zagreb 1987. In Gurevich-Ionescu, Moscow 1987 White played 13 ♗b5! to be ready to remove Black's knight. Play continued 13...d4 14 ♘xd4 ♗xg2 15 ♖g1 ♗e4 16 ♘f5! ♗xf5 (16...♕e5? 17 ♘h6+ ♔h8 18 ♘xf7+! and White wins) 17 ♕xf5 a6 18 ♗d3 g6 19 ♕d5! with a clear advantage to White. Black's 13th move seems a bit too optimistic. White is just better developed for this kind of stuff. Best was 13...♖c8, when Black is still fighting to equalise.

10 ♖c1

10 e3 0-0 11 ♘xd5 ♗xd5 12 ♗d3 h6 13 ♗h4 ♘d7 14 0-0 a5 15 ♖ac1 a4 was harmless in Farago-Horvath, Hungary 1995.

10...h6 11 ♗h4!

The only serious move – the bishop must remain active. For example after 11 ♗d2 ♘f6! the bishop looks stupid on d2, e.g. 12 e3 0-0 13 ♗e2 ♘bd7 14 0-0 ♕b8 15 b4 ♗e7 16 ♘d4 ♖c8 17 ♕b3 a5 18 f3 axb4 19 axb4 ♗d6 and Black was clearly better in Chekhov-Timoshchenko, Berlin 1986, or 12 b4 ♗e7 13 ♘b5 ♘c6 14 ♕a4 a5 15 bxa5 0-0 with unclear play in Petursson-Arnason, Reykjavik 1985. Meanwhile 11 ♘xd5?! hxg5 12 b4 g4! 13 ♘e5 ♖h5 favoured Black in Petursson-C.Hansen, Borgarnes 1985, and Ligterink-Beliavsky, Wijk aan Zee 1985 went 11 ♘e4 ♘d7 (11...hxg5?? 12 ♘d6+!) 12 ♘xc5 ♘xc5 13 e4 (13 ♗d2 ♘f6!, to take control of e4, guarantees Black a good game) 13...hxg5 14 exd5 exd5 15 ♘xg5 ♔f8 16 ♗e2 d4! 17 0-0 d3 18 ♗xd3 ♕g4 19 ♘e4 ♗xe4 20 ♗xe4 ♕xe4 and White resigned.

11...a5

Perhaps the alternatives are better:

a) 11...♘c6 12 ♘xd5 exd5 13 e3 0-0 14 ♗d3 a5 15 0-0 d4 16 e4 ♖e8 17 ♗g3 with a slight advantage to White in Ftacnik-Hjartarson, Esbjerg 1985.

b) 11...0-0 12 ♘xd5 exd5 13 e3 ♘d7 14 ♗e2 ♗d6 15 ♕d1 ♕e8 16 0-0 ♘c5 17 ♘d4

♕e4 18 ♗g3 with only a tiny edge for White, Yusupov-Chernin, Tunis 1985.

12 ♘a4!

The only serious option. 12 ♘e4 ♘d7 13 ♕b1 0-0 14 ♘d6 ♕c6 15 ♘xb7 looks like White has never heard about development, but only about the two bishops (well, the king's bishop is yet to wake up). Ftacnik-C.Hansen, Esbjerg 1985 led to Black earning an enormous lead after 15...♕xb7 16 e4? (16 e3 was still equal) 16...♘f4 17 ♗g3 f5! etc.

12 e3 0-0 13 ♗e2 ♘xc3 14 ♕xc3 ♘c6 15 0-0 a4 was equal in Spraggett-Portisch, Montpellier 1985.

12...♘d7 13 e4!

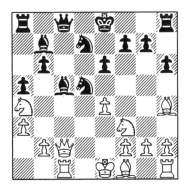

White needs to get going before Black finishes his development. After 13 e3- 0-0 14 ♗b5 ♗a6 15 ♗xa6 (15 ♕d3 ♗b4+ 16 ♔e2 ♘c5 17 ♗xa6 ♕xa6 18 ♕xa6 ♖xa6 19 ♘xc5 ♗xc5 with equality) 15...♕xa6 Black was no worse in Salov-Timman, Belgrade 1987.

13...♘c7

Black's position is beyond repair, e.g. 13...♘f4 14 ♗g3 ♘h5 15 ♘xc5! ♘xc5?!, while 15...bxc5 is horrible too in view of 16 b4! axb4 17 axb4 ♘xg3 18 hxg3 ♘b3 19 ♗b5+ ♔f8 20 ♕xc8+ ♖xc8 21 ♖xc8+ ♗xc8 22 ♗c4 and White wins. After 13...♘5f6 14 ♗xf6 ♘xf6 15 ♗b5+ ♔e7 16 e5 ♘e4 17 0-0 White has a powerful initiative.

14 ♘xc5 bxc5

14...♘xc5? 15 b4 and Black drops a piece.

15 ♗e2 ♗a6

15...e5 16 ♗c4! with a large lead.

16 0-0 0-0 17 ♖fd1 f6!

17...♖e8?! 18 ♗xa6 ♖xa6 19 ♕d2! and White wins.

18 ♗c4! ♗xc4 19 ♕xc4 ♖f7 20 ♗g3 e5 21 ♘h4!

With a clear advantage for White.

21...♕e8

21...♕a6? 22 ♕xf7+! ♔xf7 23 ♖xd7+ and White wins.

22 ♘f5 ♕e6 23 ♕e2! ♖b8 24 ♖d6 ♕e8

On 24...♕b3 Kasparov gives the following winning line: 25 ♕g4 ♔h7 26 ♘xg7 (26 ♘xh6!? gxh6 27 ♖xd7 ♔h8 28 ♖cd1 also looks good) 26...♕xb2 27 ♖f1 ♖xg7 28 ♖xd7 ♘e8 29 f4 and here Black has nothing better than 29...♕d4+ 30 ♖xd4 ♖xg4 31 ♖d7+ ♔g7 32 ♖xg7+ ♔xg7 33 fxe5 ♖b6 with a terrible endgame.

25 ♖cd1! ♘f8 26 f4! ♖b5

26...exf4 27 ♗xf4 ♘fe6 28 ♗g3 ♕b5 29 ♕g4 ♔h7 30 ♖xe6 ♘xe6 31 ♘d6 and White wins.

27 fxe5 ♘xd6?!

Apparently 27...fxe5 28 ♖6d5 ♘d7 29 ♕d2!, with a decisive advantage to White, is better.

28 ♘xd6 ♕a4 29 ♘xf7 ♖xb2! 30 ♘xh6+ ♔h7

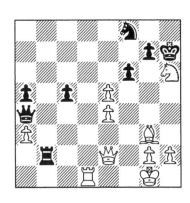

31 ♕h5

31 ♕f3! is even stronger.

31...g6 32 ♕f3 ♔xh6 33 ♖f1 ♕d4+ 34 ♔h1 ♘h7 35 exf6 ♘xf6 36 ♗f4+

36 e5 ♘h7 37 ♗f4+ ♔g7 38 ♗c1 and Black has nothing left to do but resign.

36...♔g7 37 ♗g5 ♖b6 38 ♕h3?!

Again 38 ♕f4! was simpler.

38...♔g8?!

38...♕xe4! 39 ♗h6+ ♔h7! 40 ♗f8+ ♔g8 41 ♗xc5 gives White a pawn but at least puts up some resistance.

39 ♕c8+ ♔g7 40 ♕c7+ ♘d7 41 ♕f4 ♕c4 42 h3 ♕e6 43 ♖d1! ♖c6 44 ♗d8! ♘b6 45 ♖f1 1-0

Game 20
Khalifman-Short
Paernu 1996

---

1 d4 ♘f6 2 c4 e6 3 ♘f3 b6 4 ♘c3 ♗b7 5 a3 d5 6 cxd5 ♘xd5 7 e3

This is the main move in *ECO*, but in recent times it has been less popular among those who know. This is due to 7...g6, and for this reason I will not consider other moves here, or give 7 e3 serious attention. Anyway, White plays the text with the idea of e3-e4. It does not seem to be so dangerous.

7...g6

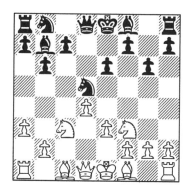

8 ♗b5+

Here there are other possibilities:

a) 8 h4 ♗g7 9 h5 ♘d7 10 ♗d3 0-0 11 e4 (this is just not very good!) 11...♘xc3 12 bxc3 ♘c5! 13 hxg6 hxg6 14 dxc5 (losing, but Black is already doing very well) 14...♗xc3+ 15 ♔e2 ♗xa1 16 ♕g1 ♕d7 17 ♕h2 ♖fd8 18

♕h7+ ♔f8 19 ♗h6+ ♔e8 and the attack never went further in Vokac-Sax, Lazne Bohdanec 1995. 10...♘xc3 11 bxc3 ♖c8 appears to be equally good, when White should start thinking of castling. After 12 e4?! ♘c5! 13 hxg6 ♘xd3+ 14 ♕xd3 hxg6 15 ♖xh8+ ♗xh8 16 ♗f4 ♗g7 17 ♔d2 c5 Black was better in Maksimovic-Groszpeter, Berlin 1988. 9...0-0 is also okay, although it seems natural to wait. Here after 10 hxg6 hxg6 11 ♘xd5 exd5 12 ♗d2 ♘d7 13 ♗d3 ♖e8 14 ♗c3 a5 15 ♕c2 ♖a6 16 ♗xa6 Black has no problems, Razuvaev-Rodriguez, Moscow 1985 already coming to a peaceful conclusion.

b) 8 ♘xd5 exd5 9 b4 is supposed to give White an advantage. But due to the plan illustrated in this game (...c7-c6 and ...a7-a5) nobody adopts this approach any more. Black is just fine. Shirov-Karpov, Monte Carlo 1995 went 9...♗g7 10 ♗b2 c6 11 ♗e2 0-0 12 0-0 ♘d7 13 ♕b3 ♖e8 14 ♖fc1 a5 15 bxa5 ♖xa5 16 a4 c5 with equality.

8...c6 9 ♗d3 ♗g7 10 ♘a4!?

Short wrote that this move was an invention of Lobron and his long-term companion Jack Daniels. Surely Mr. Daniels is an inventive guy. After 10 e4 ♘xc3 11 bxc3 c5! 12 ♗g5 ♕d6 13 e5 ♕d7 Black seems to do well as White's centre appears rather fragile. And after 14 dxc5?! 0-0! 15 cxb6 axb6 Black was even better in Kasparov-Korchnoi, London 1983. White has three weak pawns and is lacking in co-ordination and development..

10...♘d7 11 e4 ♘e7 12 0-0

Here (and on the next move) White has a serious alternative in 12 ♗f4 0-0 13 0-0. Then Black needs to accept a weak pawn and he will be okay: 13...c5! 14 dxc5 ♘xc5 15 ♘xc5 bxc5 16 ♕e2 (16 ♕c2 ♘c6! and Black is fine, while 16 ♖c1 c4! also equalises because after 17 ♖xc4? ♗a6 18 ♗c7 ♕d7 19 ♘e5 ♗xe5 20 ♗xe5 ♗xc4 21 ♗xc4 ♕xd1 22 ♖xd1 ♖fd8 Black has all the chances) 16...♘c6 17 ♖ac1 ♘d4 18 ♘xd4 ♗xd4 with equality in Yermolinsky-Ivanov, Parsippany

1996.

12...0-0 13 &g5

13 &f4–see the previous note..

13...h6!

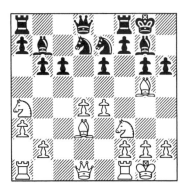

13...Ee8?! (Khalifman) 14 Ec1 Wb8 15 &h4! (going to the h2-b8 diagonal) 15...h6 16 b4 b5 17 ♘c5 ♘xc5 18 Exc5 with a strong positional advantage for White in Khalifman-Sivokho, St Petersburg 1996.

14 &e3 ♚h7 15 Ec1 f5!

Black has equalised (Short).

16 exf5 exf5

16...♘xf5 17 &e4 is just wrong.

17 &f4 ♘d5 18 &d6?!

18 &g3 improves.

18...Ee8 19 ♘c3 Wf6 20 &g3 ♘xc3 21 bxc3 c5

Here Black could have rewarded himself for his strong opening play with 21...f4! 22 &h4 Wf7, when all White's pieces are unprepared for ...c6-c5.

22 &b5 Ee7 23 ♘e5 ♘xe5 24 dxe5 Wf7 25 f4?!

Here White could have kept the balance with 25 Wd6! f4! 26 &xf4 &xg2 27 ♚xg2 Wxf4 28 Wxe7 Wg4+ with a perpetual.

25...a6 26 &e2 Ed7 27 We1 We6 28 &f3 &xf3 29 Exf3 &f8 30 &f2?!

30 &h4! is forced. Now Black will be able to play ...g6-g5 and prove a clear advantage.

30...&e7 31 c4 Ead8 32 Efc3 g5!

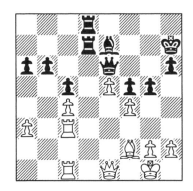

The e-pawn is now in trouble. From here Short's fantastic technique took over.

33 &e3 gxf4 34 &xf4 Ed4 35 Wf1 &g5 36 &xg5 hxg5 37 We2 ♚g6! 38 Ee3 Ed2 39 Wf3 g4 40 Wf1 E8d4 41 g3 Eb2 42 Ee2 Exe2 43 Wxe2 Ee4 44 Wd2 Wxe5 45 ♚f2 Ed4 46 We2 Wxe2+ 47 ♚xe2 f4! 48 gxf4 ♚f5 49 Eb1 Ed6 50 Ef1 Eh6 51 Ef2 Eh3 52 ♚f1 Eb3! 53 ♚g2 a5 54 Ee2 a4 55 Ee5+ ♚xf4 56 Ee6 Exa3 57 Ef6+ ♚e5 58 Exb6 Eb3 59 Ea6 a3 60 Ea5 ♚f4 0-1

Summary

The Petrosian system still holds great dangers for Black as it did 15 years ago when Kasparov was championing it. The move order with 4 a3 gives Black some extra lines to choose from, most notably 4...♗a6, therefore it can be a good idea for White players to play 4 ♘c3 with the idea of 4...♗b7 5 a3! with transposition to the 4 a3 ♗b7 lines. After 4 a3 then 4...d5 gives a typical d-pawn position, as discussed in the introduction. After 4...c5!? we get some interesting and unusual positions. Black has so far been able to keep the game level, but perhaps White can make his better structure count for something in the future. 4...c6 is just not very good, while 4...♗a6 leads to a whole series of variations which are basically okay for Black although precise play is needed. 4...♗b7 is still the main line, and after 5 ♘c3 Black only has one good plan: 5...d5 6 cxd5 ♘xd5 and now 7 ♕c2! is perhaps very slightly better for White.

1 d4 ♘f6 2 c4 e6 3 ♘f3 b6 4 a3 *(D)* **♗b7**

    4...d5 5 cxd5 exd5 6 ♘c3 ♗e7 – *Game 5*; 4...c6 – *Game 6*

    4...c5

        5 e3 – *Game 8*; 5 d5 ♗a6 6 ♕c2 – *Game 7*

    4...♗a6

        5 ♕b3 – *Game 9*

        5 ♕c2

            5...c5 6 d5 – 4...c5

            5...♗b7 6 ♘c3 c5

                7 d5 – *Game 10*

                7 e4 cxd4 8 ♘xd4

                    8...♗c5 – *Game 11*; 8...♘c6 9 ♘xc6 ♗xc6 10 ♗f4 *(D)*

          10...♘h5 – *Game 12*; 10...♗c5 – *Game 13*

5 ♘c3 d5

    5...g6 – *Game 14*

6 cxd5

    6 ♗g5 – *Game 15*; 6 ♕c2: 6...dxc4 – *Game 16*; 6...♗e7 – *Game 17*

6...♘xd5 *(D)* **7 ♕c2**

    7 e3 – *Game 20*

7...c5

    7...♘xc3 – *Game 18*

8 dxc5 – *Game 19*

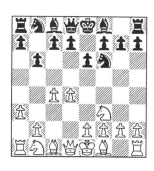

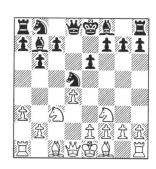

       4 a3   *10 ♗f4*   *6...♘xd5*

CHAPTER THREE

5 ♕c2 and 5 ♗g5

1 d4 ♘f6 2 c4 e6 3 ♘f3 b6 4 ♘c3 ♗b7/♗b4 5 ♕c2/5 ♗g5

In this chapter you will see White try to put Black under pressure and fight for the control of the e4-square – and you will see him fail. These lines do not offer White an advantage from the opening, yet they can nevertheless be difficult to play for Black, and if they suit you, as they used to suit Kamsky, there is a definite possibility that a level opening might later lead to a superior middlegame and, ultimately, a full point.

> *Game 21*
> **Tolnai-Adorjan**
> *Hungary 1992*

1 ♘f3 ♘f6 2 c4 b6 3 ♘c3 ♗b7 4 d4 e6 5 ♕c2

A rather harmless option, the game continuation demonstrating the easiest way to equalise.

5...c5! 6 dxc5 ♗xc5 7 ♗g5

7 e4 h6 8 ♗f4 ♗b4 9 ♗d3 0-0 10 0-0 ♗xc3 11 bxc3 d5 12 cxd5 exd5 gave Black at least equality in Szekely-Daroczy, Debrecen 1956.

7...h6 8 ♗h4 ♗e7 9 e3 0-0 10 ♗e2 ♘a6!

This move, aimed at planting a knight on

e4, is the best way to play with this structure. After the not so clever 10...d5 11 0-0 ♘bd7 (11...dxc4 12 ♖fd1 ♕c8 13 e4 gave White an initiative in Razuvaev-Kruszynski, Polanica Zdroj 1979) 12 ♖fd1 ♖c8 13 ♖ac1 White had an edge in Sokolov-Stohl, Burgas 1992.

11 0-0 ♘c5 12 ♖fd1 ♘fe4 13 ♗xe7

13 ♗g3 ♘xc3 14 ♕xc3 ♘e4 favours Black thanks to the two bishops.

13...♕xe7

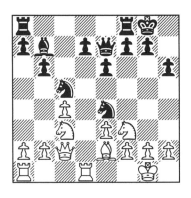

14 ♘d2?!

Presenting Black with the opportunity to take full control of the centre. 14 ♘xe4, with equality, improves.

14...♘xc3 15 ♕xc3 d5 16 ♗f3

16 b4 ♘d7 17 cxd5 ♖fc8 is nice for Black.

16...♖fd8 17 h3

17 b4!? ♘a6 18 a3 ♖ac8 19 ♕b3 dxc4 20 ♘xc4 ♗xf3 21 gxf3 ♘c7 is a shade preferable for Black.

17...dxc4! 18 ♗xb7 ♘xb7 19 ♘xc4 ♖ac8 20 ♕a3 ♕xa3 21 ♘xa3 ♘c5 22 ♘b5 a6

23 ♘c3?!

White could have equalised with 23 ♘d6 ♖c6 24 ♘c4 ♘d3 25 ♘e5 ♖cd6 26 ♘c4, with a repetition.

23...♘d3 24 ♖d2 ♘e5 25 ♖xd8+

25 ♖ad1 ♖xd2 26 ♖xd2 ♔f8 is only slightly better for Black. Now Adorjan's fantastic will to win comes into play

25...♖xd8 26 ♖d1 ♖c8 27 ♖d4 ♔f8 28 ♔f1 ♔e7 29 ♔e2 ♘c4 30 ♘d1 b5 31 ♖d3 b4 32 f4?

32 ♖b3 was forced.

32...a5 33 a3?

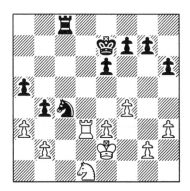

33 ♖d4, with problems but nothing more,

was necessary.

33...♘xb2! 34 ♘xb2 ♖c2+ 35 ♔f3 ♖xb2 36 axb4 ♖xb4 37 ♖c3 ♖b7 38 ♖a3 ♖a7 39 ♔e4 ♔d6 40 ♔d4 a4 41 ♔c4 f5 42 ♔b5 ♖b7+ 43 ♔c4 ♖a7 44 ♔b5 ♖b7+ 45 ♔c4 ♖b2 46 ♖xa4 ♖xg2 47 ♖a7 g5 48 ♖a6+ ♔e7 49 ♖a7+ ♔f6 50 ♖h7 ♔g6 51 ♖e7 ♔f6 52 ♖h7 gxf4 53 ♖xh6+ ♔g7! 54 ♖xe6 f3 0-1

Game 22
Kamsky-Yudasin
Biel 1993

---

1 d4 ♘f6 2 c4 e6 3 ♘f3 b6 4 ♘c3 ♗b7

4...♗b4 is treated below.

5 ♗g5

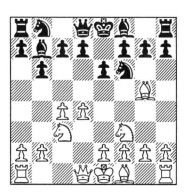

This variation is known to be quite harmless but, as this game clearly illustrates, it is a genuine struggle so long as the pieces remain on the board. The most normal move here must be 5 a3, transposing to the Petrosian System. Actually, this is the way I would play with White, as the lines with 4...♗b7 seem to be the most fragile for Black in the Petrosian.

5...h6 6 ♗h4 ♗e7

Now Black has this possibility, and therefore equalises easily.

7 e3

Standard. 7 ♕c2 has also been tried, when 7...c5! is another standard reaction, White having neglected the dark squares. Sokolov-Salov, Wijk aan Zee 1997 went 8 dxc5 bxc5 9

---

e3 d6 10 ♗e2 ♘bd7 11 ♖d1 0-0 12 0-0 a6 13 ♖d2 ♕c7 14 ♖fd1 ♖fd8 15 h3 ♘f8 16 ♘h2 ♖d7 17 ♗g3 ♖ad8 18 ♗f3 ♘g6 19 ♗xb7 ♕xb7 20 ♘f3 d5 and, if anyone is better, it is Black.

7...♘e4

This is a good way to equalise. Also possible is 7...0-0, and now:

a) 8 ♗d3 c5 9 0-0 cxd4 (9...d6 10 a3 ♘bd7 11 b4 d5 12 cxd5 ♘xd5 13 ♗xe7 ♕xe7 14 ♘xd5 ♗xd5 15 e4 and a draw was agreed in Onischuk-Dautov, Germany 2000) 10 exd4 d5 (also possible is 10...♗xf3!? 11 ♕xf3 ♘c6 12 ♘e2 d5 13 ♖ad1 ♘b4 14 ♗xf6 ♗xf6 15 cxd5 ♘xd5 16 ♗e4 with a draw in Seirawan-Schussler, New York 1985) and now the most testing is 11 ♗xf6!, unlike the harmless 11 cxd5 ♘xd5 12 ♗g3 ♘xc3 13 bxc3 ♘c6 14 ♖e1 ♗f6 15 ♖c1 ♖c8 16 ♕e2 ♘a5 17 ♘e5 ♕d5 18 f4 ♗xe5 19 fxe5 ♖c7 with complete equality in Spassky-Hjartarson, Reykjavik 1988. In Sokolov-Rivas Pastor, Leon 1995 the position after (11 ♗xf6) 11...♗xf6 12 cxd5 exd5 was reminiscent of the Tartakower where the bishop on b7 is somewhat silly, and where there might be a weakness on c6 occasionally. But the exchange of the dark-squared bishop does also influence White's position. After 13 ♖e1 ♘c6 14 ♗c2 ♕d6 15 ♕d3 g6 16 a3 ♖fe8 17 h3 ♗g7 the game was equal, Black having the manoeuvre ...♘a5-c4.

b) 8 ♗e2 c5 9 0-0 d6 (9...cxd4 10 exd4 d5 is, of course, also possible) 10 dxc5 bxc5 11 ♕c2 ♘bd7 12 ♖fd1 ♕b6 13 ♖d2 ♖fd8 with equality in Karpov-Polugaevsky, Bugojno 1980. 10 ♖c1 ♘bd7 11 a3 ♖c8 12 ♗g3 a6 13 b3 cxd4 14 ♘xd4 ♕c7, Groszpeter-Tal, Sochi 1984, was at least equal for Black. The move a2-a3 does not improve White's position.

8 ♘xe4!?

This should not be dangerous for Black at all, but neither is 8 ♗g3 ♗b4! 9 ♕c2 d6 10 ♗d3 ♗xc3+ 11 bxc3 f5 (11...♘xg3?! is too early: after 12 hxg3 ♘d7 13 e4 ♕e7 14 0-0

0-0 15 ♘h4! White had a space advantage in Korchnoi-Ligterink, Wijk aan Zee 1984) 12 h4 ♘d7 13 ♗h2 ♕e7 14 0-0-0 0-0-0 15 ♖df1 g5 with dynamic equality in Mikhalevski-Yudasin, Tel Aviv 1994.

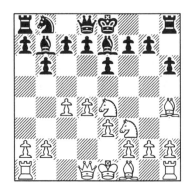

8...♗xh4?!

This is risky. A safe path to equality is 8...♗xe4 9 ♗g3 0-0, e.g. 10 ♘d2 ♗b7 11 ♗d3 c5! (standard when White weakens the dark squares) 12 dxc5 bxc5 13 0-0 d5 14 cxd5 exd5 15 e4 dxe4 16 ♗xe4 ♗xe4 17 ♘xe4 ♘c6 18 ♕a4 ♘d4 with complete equality in Uhlmann-Padevsky, Havana 1964, or 10 ♗d3 ♗xd3 11 ♕xd3 d6 12 0-0 ♘d7 13 b4 a5 14 b5 f5 15 ♕b3 a4 16 ♕c2 ♕e8 17 ♘e1 e5, Uhlmann-Antoshin, Leipzig 1965, also equal.

9 ♗d3 ♗e7 10 ♕b3!

White has a territorial advantage to add to his superior development, which he uses to generate an attack.

10...d6 11 h4!? ♘d7 12 0-0-0 c6?!

Slightly passive. After 12...c5!? 13 dxc5 dxc5 14 ♘c3 White has a small edge (Kamsky).

13 g4 ♕c7 14 ♔b1 a6 15 g5 c5 16 ♕c3!? ♖g8 17 ♖hg1 hxg5?!

Now the g5-square becomes available for White, with attacking possibilities on e6 and f7. Better is 17...0-0-0 with a messy position where anything could happen.

18 ♘exg5!

18 ♘fxg5?! allows 18...d5! etc.

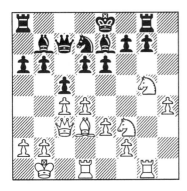

18...cxd4!? 19 exd4 ♗f6 20 ♕b3!

Shooting at e6 and f7 while taking control of the light squares on the queenside.

20...♗xf3?

From here on Black is defenceless on the light squares. A lesser evil is 20...♘f8 21 ♗e4!? 0-0-0 with a poor – but not losing – position.

21 ♘xf3 ♖h8 22 ♖g4!

A strong, active post.

22...♔e7 23 ♖e1 b5!? 24 cxb5 axb5 25 ♘g5! ♗xg5 26 hxg5 g6

White was considering g5-g6 himself.

27 ♖ge4 ♔d8 28 ♗xb5 d5 29 ♖4e3 ♖b8 30 ♖c1 ♕b6 31 a4 ♕xd4 32 ♕c2 ♕b6 33 ♖c3 ♖h4 34 ♖c6 1-0

Black resigned due to 34 ♖c6 ♕a7 35 ♖c8+ ♔e7 36 ♗xd7 etc.

Game 23
Portisch-Popovic
Ljubljana 1985

---

1 ♘f3 ♘f6 2 c4 e6 3 ♘c3 ♗b4 4 d4 b6 5 ♗g5 ♗b7

5...h6 6 ♗h4 ♗b7 and now 7 ♕c2, along with 7 ♘d2, is aimed at gaining control of e4. Both moves weaken the d4-square and should therefore be countered by ...c7-c5.

6 ♕c2

6 ♘d2 h6 7 ♗h4 c5! 8 a3 cxd4 9 axb4 dxc3 10 bxc3 0-0 11 f3 d5 12 e3 a5 13 bxa5 bxa5 14 ♗e2 ♘bd7 15 cxd5 exd5 16 0-0

♕e7 with a good position for Black in Moutousis-Nikolaidis, Glyfada 2001. Another suggestion for Black is 7...♗e7. Then, after 8 e4, 8...d6 is too passive – 9 ♗g3 ♘bd7 10 ♗e2 e5 11 d5 ♘f8 12 b4 ♘g6 13 ♘b3 h5 14 h3 h4 15 ♗h2 0-0 16 0-0 gave White the advantage in Ibragimov-Bischoff, Pulvermuehle 2000. Black's position is very solid but too passive, and White can hope to benefit from his space advantage on the queenside. Instead 8...♘xe4!? is another prospect altogether: 9 ♗xe7 ♘xc3 10 ♗xd8 ♘xd1 11 ♗xc7 ♘xb2 12 a4 d5 13 cxd5 exd5 14 ♖a2 ♘c4 15 ♘xc4 dxc4 16 ♗xc4 with equality. However, this position looks a little nasty for Black, so I would feel less inclined to test this line...

6...h6 7 ♗h4 g5 8 ♗g3 ♘e4

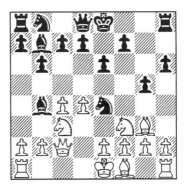

This is the simple way to equalise against this system. White now has no path to an advantage.

9 e3

White can also go for complications, but Black is okay after 9 ♗e5 f6 10 d5 exd5 11 cxd5 ♗xc3+ 12 ♗xc3 ♗xd5 13 0-0-0 ♘xc3 14 ♕xc3 ♗f7! 15 h4 g4 16 ♘e5 ♗h5 17 ♕c2 fxe5 18 ♕f5 ♕e7 19 ♕xh5+ ♔d8 with dynamic equality in Portisch-Timman, Hilversum 1984.

9...♗xc3+ 10 bxc3 d6

A natural move. Black can also choose to exchange the bishop immediately, which should lead to the same type of positions:

10...♘xg3 11 hxg3 ♘c6!? (Black decides that c4-c5 is the only White way to make sense of the position, so he avoids creating a 'hook' with d6 – 11...d6 12 c5 ♘d7 13 cxd6 cxd6 14 a4 ♔f8 15 ♗d3 ♖c8 16 a5 bxa5 17 e4 ♔g7 18 0-0 ended peacefully in Ehlvest-Adams, Pula 1997) 12 ♖b1 (in Langeweg-Karpov, Amsterdam 1981, the following manoeuvre did not favour White: 12 ♘d2 ♕e7 13 ♕b2 g4 14 ♘b3 ♕g5 15 c5 ♖b8 16 ♕a3 h5 17 ♖h4 ♗a8 18 ♗e2 f5 and Black is already better) 12...♕e7 13 c5 h5 14 ♗e2 ♘a5 15 ♘d2 ♗xg2 16 ♖xh5 0-0-0 17 cxb6 axb6 18 ♖xh8 ♖xh8 19 ♗f3 ♗xf3 20 ♘xf3 ♕f6 favoured Black in Gheorghiu-Miles, London 1980.

11 ♗d3 ♘xg3 12 fxg3!?

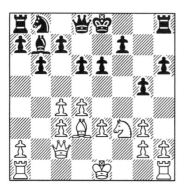

This decision is quite common in these positions. White wants to build up his artillery with the rooks on f1 and f2, aiming at f7. Black should be able to meet this plan without fear, but some attention is required, of course.

12...♘d7 13 0-0 ♕e7 14 ♗e4

Other, equally good, options are:

a) 14 ♘d2 0-0 15 g4!? seems rather exotic, and Black gets a good position after 15...♘f6 16 h3 h5! 17 gxh5 ♘xh5 18 g4 ♘g3 19 ♖f2 f5 20 ♔h2 ♘e4!, the pawn sacrifice providing enough compensation to draw, but not more. Van Wely-Anand, Tilburg 1998 continued 21 ♘xe4 fxe4 22 ♖xf8+ ♖xf8 23 ♗xe4 ♗xe4 24 ♕xe4 ♖f2+ 25 ♔g1 ♕f7 26

♖e1 ♔g7 27 a4 ½-½.. And Black cannot use his activity for anything, as the rook must stay on f2 (otherwise White has ♖f1), while White cannot try to win as Black is too active to make a single pawn important.

b) 14 ♖f2 is the most natural. This does not mean that White immediately wants to play ♖af1, but that he can do so whenever he pleases, without spending time in preparation. Quite simply, his position becomes more flexible. We are following Zvjaginsev-Timman, Biel 1995, which continued 14...0-0-0 15 ♗e4 ♖hf8!? 16 ♖e1 (intending to meet 16...f5 with ♗xb7 and e3-e4 with a good game) 16...♗xe4 17 ♕xe4 ♔b8 18 ♕h7 ♖h8 19 ♕c2 h5 with unclear play. Now Black slightly misplayed his position with 20 e4 h4 21 gxh4 gxh4 (21...g4 22 ♘d2 ♕xh4 23 g3 ♕h6 is better, with chances for both sides) 22 e5 with a modest lead for White. 16 a4!? was suggested by Timman as a possible improvement. It is hard to say anything about that...

14...♗xe4 15 ♕xe4 0-0 16 ♘d2 c5 17 g4 ♖ac8 18 ♖f2 ♔g7 19 ♖af1 ♖ce8

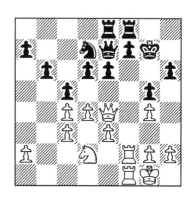

The position is more or less equal. Now the longest arms won the fight.

20 ♕b7 ♘b8 21 ♕f3 f5 22 ♕g3 ♘d7 23 ♔h1 fxg4 24 ♕xg4 ♖xf2 25 ♖xf2 ♖f8 26 ♖xf8 ♔xf8 27 ♔g1 ♘f6 28 ♕f3 ♔g7 29 e4 cxd4 30 cxd4 e5 31 ♕d3 exd4 32 ♕xd4 ♔f7 33 ♔f1 ♕e6 34 ♔e2 ♕g4+ 35 ♔d3 ♕xg2 36 e5 ♕h3+ 37 ♔c2

♕f5+ 38 ♔b3 dxe5 0-1

Game 24
Belozerov-Nikolenko
Moscow 1999

---

1 d4 e6 2 ♘f3 ♘f6 3 c4 b6 4 ♘c3 ♗b4 5 ♗g5 ♗b7 6 e3 h6 7 ♗h4 ♗xc3+ 8 bxc3 d6 9 ♗d3

This move is less good than the theory's favourite, 9 ♘d2!, for obvious reasons. After the bishop is developed White is forced to hurry with kingside castling as the knight cannot move, and White cannot build his usual impressive centre.

9...♕e7

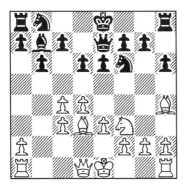

10 0-0

Practically the only alternative is 10 ♕c2, which does not pose Black problems after 10...g5 11 ♗g3 h5 12 h3 (now this is forced because 12 ♘xg5? drops a piece to 12...h4 13 ♗f4 e5, while 12 h4 g4 13 ♘d2 ♗xg2 drops a pawn) 12...h4 13 ♗h2 ♖g8 14 e4 ♘c6 15 ♘d2 e5 16 d5 and the bishop is now buried on h2, and White will have to do some manoeuvring to get it out. First the other bishop needs to get outside the pawn chain: 16...♘b8 17 ♗e2 ♘bd7 18 ♗g4 ♘xg4 19 hxg4 ♘c5 20 f3 ♗c8 and a draw was agreed in Beliavsky-Gulko, Munich 1990.

10...♘bd7 11 ♘d2 g5 12 ♗g3 h5 13 h4!

This is absolutely forced, otherwise White has no control over the dark squares on the queenside and is overrun completely. 13 f3? is how this happens: 13...h4 14 ♗f2 0-0-0 15 h3 ♖dg8 16 ♗e2 ♘h5 17 ♕a4 ♔b8 18 c5 dxc5 19 ♗a6 ♗a8 20 ♘b3 c4! 21 ♗xc4 f5 22 ♗e2 g4! (the final breakthrough; it is clear now that Black is the quicker) 23 fxg4 fxg4 24 ♗xg4 ♘hf6 25 ♘c5 ♘xc5 26 dxc5 ♘xg4 27 hxg4 ♕xc5 28 ♖fd1 h3 29 e4 h2+ and White resigned in Borik-Speelman, Dortmund 1981. The alternatives are no better, e.g. 15 a4 a5 16 ♖b1 g4 17 fxg4 h3 18 g3 ♖hg8 19 ♗e2 ♘e4 20 ♗f3 ♘xd2 21 ♗xb7+ ♔xb7 22 ♕xd2 ♖xg4 23 ♕e2 f5 with a clear advantage for Black in Rohde-Benjamin, USA 1986, or 15 e4 ♖dg8 (15...♘h5!? 16 c5!? dxc5 17 ♕a4 ♘f4! 18 ♗a6 ♘b8! gave Black a good position in Hjartarson-Stoica, Taflfelag-Politehnica 1987) 16 h3 ♘h5 17 ♖e1 ♘f4 18 ♗c2 c5 19 ♘f1 f5 20 exf5 g4!! 21 fxg4 ♗xg2 with an overwhelming attack in Nenashev-Tiviakov, Groningen 1997.

13...♖g8

13...♘g4 has also been tried, but it seems that White gets better control of the kingside after 14 ♘f3 gxh4 15 ♘xh4 0-0-0 16 e4 (Beckmann-Steil, Germany 1990) than he normally does.

14 f3 0-0-0 15 hxg5 ♖xg5 16 ♗h4 ♖g7

17 ♖f2

The alternative is very sharp, but perhaps the best way for White to place his pieces might be 17 ♘e4. If not Black has the following active continuation: 17...♖dg8 18 ♖f2

♘xe4! (Black will have to do something about the pin eventually, and this is a good way – a spectacular queen sacrifice) 19 ♗xe7 ♘xf2 20 ♔xf2 ♖xg2+ 21 ♔e1 ♖h2 22 ♗f1 ♖g1 23 e4 (White has nothing better since f3 must be protected; after 23 ♖c1 h4! 24 ♖c2 ♖xf1+ 25 ♔xf1 ♖h1+ 26 ♔e2 ♗xf3+ Black should win). Now Black should choose between three moves:

a) 23...f5? 24 exf5 exf5 25 ♕c1! (addressing the unwelcome rook on g1) 25...♗a6 26 ♕e3 ♖xf1+ (26...♖hg2 27 ♕e6! and Black cannot improve his position easily) 27 ♔xf1 ♖h1+ 28 ♔f2 ♖xa1 29 ♕e6! and White is winning. Black severely lacks co-ordination.

b) 23...d5!? seems to be the safest policy. After 24 exd5 (24 ♕d3 ♗a6 25 exd5 exd5 26 ♕e3 ♖gh1 and Black wins) 24...exd5 25 ♕a4 dxc4 26 ♖c1 b5! 27 ♕xb5 ♗xf3 28 ♕xc4 ♖g4 29 ♕a6+ ♔b8 30 ♗d3 ♖g1+ 31 ♗f1 ♖g4 a draw results.

c) 23...h4 24 ♗xh4 ♖xh4 25 ♔f2 ♖g5 with a complicated position in Barsov-Schoenthier, Germany 1996. I am a little sceptical about Black's position as I cannot find a good square for the knight, but perhaps most GMs would see great options in ...f7-f5 and ...♘f6.

17...♖dg8 18 ♕a4

18 ♘e4 transposes to the previous note.

18...♔b8

This seems more healthy than 18...e5, allowing 19 ♗f5 ♔b8 20 e4 when White looks good. After 20...♘f8?? 21 ♗xf6 he had already won(!) in Sideif Sade-Guedon, Cappelle 1995.

19 ♖e1!?

I have most faith in closing the long diagonal with 19 e4. Then Farago-Rechlis, Beersheba 1987 continued 19...♕e8! 20 c5 dxc5 21 ♗b5 ♕c8 22 e5 a6 23 exf6 axb5 24 ♕xb5 ♖g6 25 a4 e5 26 a5 exd4 27 axb6? ♘xb6 (now Black has a clear advantage) 28 ♔h2 dxc3 29 ♘f1 ♕f5 30 g3 ♖g4 31 ♕e2 ♖b4 32 ♘e3 ♕e5 33 f4 ♕e4 34 ♘c2 ♖b2 35 ♖e1 ♕xe2 and White resigned. Instead 27 a6! ♗d5 (27...♗a8 28 a7+ ♔b7 29 ♘e4 gives

White a winning attack) 28 cxd4 would have kept the struggle unclear.

19...♕e8 20 ♕c2 ♘g4!

A cute tactic that allows Black to break through to g2, albeit at a price.

21 ♖fe2

21 fxg4 ♖xg4 22 ♖f4 ♖xg2+ 23 ♔f1 e5 is inferior for White since Black's attack is even stronger and White's forces more exposed.

21...♘xe3! 22 ♖xe3 ♖xg2+ 23 ♔f1?

Losing by force. It is understandable that White did not want to go on to the long diagonal with 23 ♔h1, but at least this brings with it the possibility of putting something on e4. It is much harder to do something about g1. Anyway, Black is probably still better here, and it is not easy to recommend since the corner is no place to be during a raging attack. White does avoid having to worry about a rampaging h-pawn, though, and has slightly better piece co-ordination here than in the game. 23...♖2g4 24 ♗f2 ♕e7 25 ♘e4 ♖4g7! 26 ♗f1 h4 looks good, with the two pawns plus good co-ordination.

23...♖h2 24 ♗f2 ♕e7 25 ♘e4 ♖gg2 26 ♖1e2 ♗xe4!

Removing a defensive piece for one not taking part in the attack on White's second rank. Pure logic.

27 ♖xe4

There is nothing left to do. 27 fxe4 ♕g5 28 ♗g3 (28 ♖d2 ♖h1+ 29 ♔e2 ♖xf2+ 30 ♔xf2 ♕g1+ 31 ♔f3 ♖h3+ 32 ♔f4 ♕xe3 mate) 28...♖xe2! 29 ♗xe2 ♖h1+ 30 ♔f2 h4 and Black wins.

27...♕g5

...♖h1 is now a deadly threat.

28 ♖h4

The battle is over. 28 ♖d2 ♖h1+ 29 ♔e2 ♖xf2+ 30 ♔xf2 ♕g1+ 31 ♔e2 ♕e1 mate or 28 ♗g3 ♕xg3 29 ♖xg2 ♖h1+ and wins.

28...♖xf2+ 29 ♖xf2 ♖xh4 30 ♖g2 ♕e3 31 ♖g8+ ♔b7 32 ♔g2 ♘f6 33 ♖g7 ♕h6 34 ♖g3 ♖f4 35 c5 h4 36 ♗a6+! ♔b8 37 ♖g8+ ♘xg8 38 ♕a4 ♕g5+ 39 ♔h1 ♘f6 40 ♕c6 0-1

White resigned before Black could play 40...♕d5.

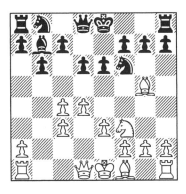

Game 25
Piket-Tiviakov
Wijk aan Zee 1994

1 d4 ♘f6 2 c4 e6 3 ♘c3 ♗b4 4 ♘f3 b6 5 ♗g5 ♗b7

Normally the moves 5...h6 6 ♗h4 ♗b7 are played here, but sometimes they are delayed. It does not really change anything, as long as they are played eventually.

6 e3 ♗xc3+ 7 bxc3 d6

This is the move I would recommend for Black. With sensible play from Black equality is possible.

8 ♘d2

This is the serious move here. After f2-f3 and e3-e4 White has a powerful centre.

8...♘bd7 9 f3 h6 10 ♗h4 ♕e7 11 ♗d3

There is no difference between this and 11 e4 in practice. After 11...e5 there are two alternatives to 12 ♗d3, which transposes to the game:

a) 12 ♗e2 ♘f8! (this is the right way to hit the bishop) with a further branch:

a1) 13 ♘f1 ♘g6 14 ♗f2 ♘f4 15 ♘e3 and now in Khalifman-Hulak, Bled, 1991 the natural 15...0-0 was, for some reason, new at the time. There followed 16 ♗f1?! (planning g2-g3 to chase away the knight, but this gives Black a chance to generate a substantial lead in development) 16...♖fe8 17 g3 (17 d5!? was probably becoming necessary) 17...♗xe4!!

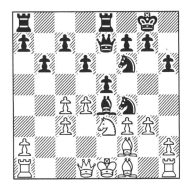

18 fxe4 (18 gxf4 exf4 19 fxe4 fxe3 20 ♗g3 ♘xe4 gives Black a completely winning attack; the e3-pawn is worth a piece) 18...exd4! (18...♘xe4 19 d5! keeps the position closed) 19 ♕xd4 (19 cxd4 ♘xe4 20 ♗g1 d5! with a powerful attack) 19...c5 20 ♕d2 ♘xe4 21 ♕c2 ♕f6!! (a brilliant quiet move) 22 ♗g1 (22 gxf4 ♘xf2 and White loses) 22...♘xc3 23 gxf4 d5! with a decisive attack.. According to Khalifman 16 0-0, with equality, is an improvement. After seeing the game one tends to agree.

a2) 13 ♕a4+ ♕d7 14 ♕b3 does not seem too smart. Now Black has 14...♘h5! 15 c5 ♘g6 16 ♗f2 dxc5 17 dxc5 ♘hf4 18 ♗f1 0-0 and White was on the way to trouble in Campos Moreno-Polugaevsky, Oviedo 1991.

a3) 13 ♗f2!? seems more to the point, but

after 13...♘g6 14 g3 0-0 15 ♘f1 c6!, with the idea of ...d6-d5, Black is able to use his lead in development constructively. In Dokhoian-Djuric, Philidelphia 1989, 16 d5 ♖ac8 17 ♕d2 b5! 18 dxc6 ♗xc6 19 ♘e3! bxc4 20 0-0 ♕d7! 21 ♗xc4 ♗b5! saw Black completely equalise.

Note that here 12...g5?! 13 ♗f2 ♘h5 14 g3! seems to guarntee White an opening advantage, e.g. 14...♘g7 15 0-0 0-0-0 (15...h5 16 c5 dxc5 17 ♗b5 0-0-0 18 ♕a4 ♔b8 19 ♘b3 with an attack – Epishin) 16 ♖e1 c5 17 a4 a5 18 ♖b1 ♖hf8 (18...f5 19 exf5 ♘xf5 20 ♗d3 ♖hf8 21 ♗e4 is also better for White – Epishin) 19 ♘f1! and White had a structural advantage in Epishin-Shneider, USSR 1990. When White's knight comes to d5 Black cannot really take it but, unfortunately, nor can he leave it!

b) 12 ♕a4 is not really dangerous. The only thing White has in this position is the pin from h4-e7, and Black can unravel without allowing ♘d2-f1-e3-f5, which at times is very annoying. Flear-Salov, Szirak 1987 continued 12...0-0 13 ♗e2 ♕e8! 14 ♖b1 ♘h5 with equality. After 15 0-0 ♘f4 16 ♖fe1 f5 17 ♗f1 ♔h8 Black's position looks like it is more pleasant to play...

11...e5 12 e4 g5(?!)

I am a little suspicious about this move. The hole on f5 is big enough to consume all the pieces I have blundered during the years. The alternatives are:

a) 12...0-0-0!? is quite a normal move that has been suggested in numerous places but never tried.

b) 12...♘f8! begins a logical manoeuvre. Piket-Ljubojevic, Monaco 1994 continued 13 ♘f1 ♘g6 14 ♗f2 (I think this is the best move because it keeps the option of g2-g3 open; in van der Wiel-Ljubojevic, Amsterdam 1986 Black was never really worse: 14 ♗g3 ♘h5 15 ♘e3 ♘gf4 16 ♕a4+ ♔f8 17 ♖d1 ♘xg3 18 hxg3 ♘e6 19 ♗e2 g6 20 ♔f2 ♔g7 21 ♕a3 ♕g5 22 ♕c1 ♖ad8 23 ♕d2 h5 24 ♘d5 ♕xd2 25 ♖xd2 f6 26 ♘e3 ♔f7 27

♗d1 c5) 14...♘f4 15 ♘e3 ♘xd3+!? (directed against ♗c2 and g2-g3) 16 ♕xd3 ♘h5! (not 16...♕d7 17 ♖d1 ♕a4 18 0-0 0-0 19 ♗g3 ♖fe8 20 ♖f2 ♘h5 21 ♖b2, when White had an enduring advantage in Sokolov-Govedarica, Belgrade 1987; 16...g6? runs into 17 ♗h4!) 17 0-0-0 g6 18 ♕c2 0-0-0 19 ♖d2 f6 and the position is unclear, with chances for both sides.

13 ♗f2 ♘h5 14 ♘f1 exd4?

Handing White a large advantage, but nothing leads to equality.

a) 14...f5 15 ♘e3 f4 16 ♘f5 ♕f6 17 g4 has been assessed as unclear, but I find that silly. With the knight on f5 and a strong structure in the centre White appears to be better.

b) 14...♘f4 does not work here. After 15 ♘e3 g4 16 0-0! White already has an enormous advantage: 16...gxf3 17 ♕xf3! exd4 (17...♘xd3 18 ♘f5! ♕g5 19 ♗h4 leads to a substantial plus due to 19...♕f4?! 20 ♘g7+ ♔f8 21 ♘e6+! fxe6 22 ♕xd3, when White wins) 18 ♘d5! ♘xd5 (18...♗xd5 19 ♕xf4 ♘c5 20 exd5 ♘xd3 21 ♕xd4 ♘e5 22 ♗h4 also wins for White) 19 exd5 and Black did not make it to move 30 in Khalifman-Yemelin, Russia 1996. The dark squares are simply too weak.

15 cxd4 f5 16 ♘e3! fxe4

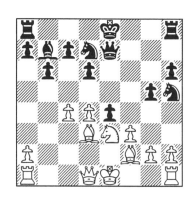

17 ♘f5!

An important trick to remember.

17...♕f7 18 fxe4

White has a very strong position. Now

♕xh5 is a threat.

18...♘f4 19 0-0 ♘xg2!?

Black is trying to create counterplay as the 'normal' 19...♘xd3 20 ♕xd3 0-0-0 21 ♗g3 ♕h7 looks very dangerous for Black. Here White can try 22 ♗xd6!? cxd6 23 ♘xd6+ ♔b8 24 ♕g3 ♔a8 25 ♖f7 ♕g6 26 ♖af1 with a strong attack against the king (Piket).

20 ♗g3 ♘f4 21 ♗xf4 gxf4 22 ♖xf4 ♕g6+ 23 ♖g4 ♕f6 24 ♘g7+ ♔d8 25 ♔h1?

This is unnecessary. Preferable is the logical 25 ♗c2! with an advantage after 25...h5 26 ♖g2 ♖g8 27 ♘xh5 ♖xg2+ 28 ♔xg2 ♕g5+ 29 ♘g3, when Black has nothing concrete for the pawn.

25...♔c8 26 ♗c2 ♗a6?

A terrible mistake, simply overlooking the reply. Better are 26...c5! and 26...♖f8!?, both with counterplay.

27 ♗a4!

Eyeing c6. This is much more important than the c-pawn.

27...♗b7 28 ♕d3 ♘c5

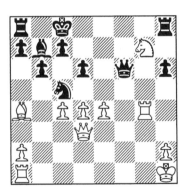

29 ♖f1! ♘xe4

29...♕xg7 30 ♕h3!.

30 ♖xf6 ♘f2+ 31 ♔g1 ♘xd3 32 ♘e6 ♘b2?

Losing immediately, but after 32...♔b8 33 ♖g7 ♖c8 34 ♖ff7 ♘b2 35 ♗b3 a5 36 ♘xc7 White also has a winning position.

33 ♖xh6!

No squares left for the pilgrim!

33...♘xa4 34 ♖xh8+ ♔d7 35 ♖xa8 ♗xa8 36 d5 1-0

Game 26
Miles-Timman
Tilburg 1986

1 d4 ♘f6 2 c4 e6 3 ♘c3 ♗b4 4 ♘f3 b6 5 ♗g5 ♗b7 6 e3 h6 7 ♗h4 g5!?

This used to be the main line, championed by Timman, but these days it is seen less and less.

8 ♗g3 ♘e4 9 ♕c2!

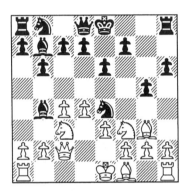

9 ♘d2 is dealt with in the following game.

9...♗xc3+ 10 bxc3 d6 11 ♗d3 f5

11...♘xg3 12 fxg3 leads to Game 23 by transposition. This variation is a good option for Black.

12 d5 ♘c5

This is the old move, and probably good enough for some kind of equality, but the new 12...♘d7!? is certainly more logical. Then 13 ♗xe4?! gives away all the light squares without any concessions. After 13...fxe4 14 ♕xe4 ♕f6 15 0-0 0-0-0 Black seems to have a good position despite the pawn deficit. 16 ♕xe6 ♕xe6 17 dxe6 ♘c5 18 ♘d4 ♖de8 saw Black enjoy a good ending in a few games, among them Hort-Bellon, Hastings 1975. The score so far is two wins for Black and one draw. Instead White should play 13 ♘d4 ♘dc5 14 dxe6 and now:

a) 14...♖f8 15 ♗e2 g4! 16 f3 ♘xg3 17

hxg3 ♕g5 18 0-0-0! 0-0-0 19 ♗d3 gxf3 20 gxf3 ♘xe6 21 ♗xf5 ♖xf5 22 ♕xf5 ♕xf5 23 ♘xf5 ♗xf3 24 ♖xh6 ♗xd1 25 ♔xd1 ♘g5 26 g4 ♖f8?! (26...♔b7! with compensation was better according to Tisdall, but it still feels as if Black is fighting for equality here) 27 ♔e2 with an advantage to White in Zvjaginsev-Hübner, Elista 1998.

b) 14...♕f6 appears to be the most natural move. After 15 f3 f4! 16 ♗xe4! (forced – 16 exf4? ♘xd3+ 17 ♕xd3 ♘c5 18 ♕e2 gxf4 was very dangerous for White in Komarov-Mantovani, Reggio Emilia 1996) 16...♗xe4 17 fxe4 fxg3 18 hxg3 0-0-0 the situation is unclear, although I feel a bit more comfortable about White's position. The pawns might look ugly, but they control many invasion squares.

13 h4 g4 14 ♘d4 ♕f6 15 0-0 ♘ba6

This is the only move these days since 15...♘xd3 16 ♕xd3 e5 17 ♘xf5 ♗c8

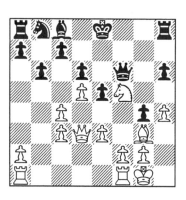

was met with 18 f4!! in Miles-Beliavsky, Tilburg 1986, practically winning on the spot. There followed 18...♕xf5 19 e4 ♕h5 20 fxe5 dxe5 21 c5 ♔d8 22 d6 ♕e8 23 dxc7+ ♔xc7 24 ♕d5 ♘c6 25 ♖f7+ ♗d7 26 ♖af1 ♖d8 27 ♖1f6 ♔c8 28 cxb6 axb6 29 ♕b5 1-0.

16 ♘xe6!?

This sacrifice is the only way for White to prevent his centre from collapsing. After 16 dxe6 Black's bishop would be a truly powerful piece and Black would rock n' roll on the light squares.

16...♘xe6 17 ♗xf5 ♘g7 18 ♗g6+ ♔d7 19 f3 ♖af8!

Preparing a possible getaway to the queenside for the king.

20 fxg4 ♕e7 21 e4 ♔c8

Also possible is 21...♘c5!? 22 ♕e2 ♔c8 23 e5 ♗a6 24 e6 c6 25 ♖xf8+ ♖xf8 26 ♖f1 ♖xf1+ 27 ♕xf1 ♔d8 28 ♕f4 ♗b7 29 ♕xh6 cxd5 30 ♗xd6 ♕xd6 31 ♕h8+ ♔c7 32 ♕g7+ ♔d8 33 ♕h8+, with a perpetual in Ivanchuk-Anand, Monaco 1993.

22 ♕d2

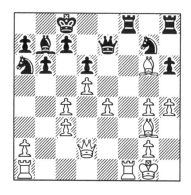

22...♘c5?!

This game was a sad episode for Black and, later, play was improved with 22...♔b8!, e.g. 23 ♖xf8+ ♖xf8 24 ♕xh6 ♗c8 (this is the idea behind ...♔b8 – the bishop is badly needed on the kingside to stop the pawns) 25 ♖e1 ♗xg4 26 c5 ♕f6 27 cxd6 ♘h5 28 e5 ♕xg6 29 ♕xg6 ♗xg6 30 e6 ♘c5 31 d7 ♘xd7 32 exd7 ♖d8 33 ♖e6 ♗h5 34 ♗e5 ♖xd7 35 ♖h6 ♗f7 36 ♗xg7 ♗xd5 37 ♗e5 ♗xa2 ½-½, Kasparov-Timman, Hilversum 1985, or 23 ♕d4 ♘e8 24 ♖f7 ♖xf7 25 ♕xh8 ♖f8! 26 ♕xh6 ♘c5 27 h5 ♘d7 28 ♗f5 ♗c8 29 ♖f1 ♘e5, which left Black okay in Salov-Timman, Saint John 1988.

23 ♖xf8+ ♖xf8 24 ♕xh6 ♕f6 25 ♗f5+ ♘xf5 26 ♕xf6 ♖xf6 27 exf5 ♗a6 28 ♗f2 ♗xc4 29 ♗d4 ♖f7 30 f6 ♖h7 31 ♗xc5 dxc5 32 ♖d1!

Keeping the bishop out of the game.

32...♗b5

32...♖xh4 33 f7 ♖h8 34 g5 and White wins.

33 g5 ♗e8 34 ♖e1!

And now the king.

34...♔d7 35 g3 b5 36 ♔g2 a5 37 ♔h3 b4 38 cxb4 axb4 39 g4 ♖h8 40 h5 ♔d6 41 ♖xe8! 1-0

Game 27
Crouch-Harikrishna
London 2001

1 d4 e6 2 c4 ♘f6 3 ♘f3 b6 4 ♘c3 ♗b7 5 ♗g5 h6 6 ♗h4 ♗b4 7 e3 g5 8 ♗g3 ♘e4 9 ♘d2?!

This is a gambit that might have been playable back in the days when people were afraid of taking the pawns and defending an awkward position. But these days – no.

9...♘xc3!

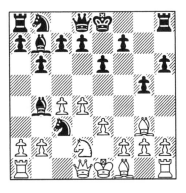

Take the money and run.

10 bxc3 ♗xc3 11 ♖c1 ♗a5

This appears to be the safest path here. It is doubtful that White has gained much for his pawn. But other moves have also brought good results.

a) 11...♗xd2+ 12 ♕xd2 d6 13 c5 (13 f3? is too slow: 13...♘d7 14 ♗d3 ♕e7 15 0-0 f5 16 c5 dxc5 17 ♗xc7 0-0 18 dxc5 ♘xc5 19 ♗e5 ♖ad8 and White resigned in Priehoda-Rozentalis, Trnava 1988) 13...dxc5 14 ♕b2!? (harmless is 14 dxc5 ♕xd2+ 15 ♔xd2 ♗a6 16 ♗xc7 ♗xf1 17 ♖hxf1 ♘a6 18 ♗d6 ♘xc5 19 ♗xc5 bxc5 20 ♖xc5 ♖d8+ 21 ♔e2 and a draw was agreed in Smirin-Rozentalis, New York 1997) 14...0-0 15 h4 g4 16 dxc5 ♕d5 17 ♗e2 and now Black was too careful with 17...♘c6? in Stocek-Cvek, Plzen 1997, after which the positional aspects of the position begin to count over material. Correct was 17...♕xg2! 18 ♖h2 ♕d5 to ruin White's set-up. After 19 ♕f6 ♘d7 20 ♕xh6 ♘xc5 21 ♕g5+ ♕xg5 22 hxg5 we have a big mess.

b) 11...♗b4 12 h4 and now the piece sacrifice 12...♘c6!? should be the reason to play this system. 12...gxh4? is still the main line given in ECO, but after 13 ♖xh4 ♗d6 14 ♕g4 ♕e7 15 ♗xd6 cxd6 16 ♕g3! they suggest to improve on 16...f5 with 16...d5!?. About 10 years ago I told Steffen Pedersen the refutation and he put it in his book *1 d4!*: 17 cxd5 exd5 (what else? 17...♘a6 is just plain bad) 18 ♖c7 ♗a6 19 ♖xa7 and White wins. But even stronger is 19 ♗c4!!, winning everything after 19...dxc4 (19...♕a3 20 ♗xa6 ♕xa6 21 ♕e5+ ♔d8 22 ♖c2! and White wins material or mates) 20 ♖xa7! ♖xa7 21 ♕xb8+ with a mate in 8 according to Junior. After 16...f5 White has 17 c5 d5 18 ♕e5! with a strong initiative, as in Agdestein-Hellers, Gausdal 1987. Returning to 13 d5, Schussler-Arnason, Reykjavik 1986 went 13...♕e7! 14 dxc6 dxc6 15 ♗e5 0-0-0 16 ♗c3 (16 ♖c2 ♖xd2 17 ♖xd2 ♖d8 and Black wins) 16...♗xc3 17 ♖xc3 c5 18 hxg5 hxg5 19 ♖xh8 ♖xh8 20 e4 f5 21 ♖h3 ♖d8 22 ♖d3 ♖f8 23

♕c2 ♕f7 and Black actually won this position. Here I will just say that White has no easy way to co-ordinate his pieces, and Black's bishop does look terribly strong. Still, my choice would be 11...♗a5.

12 h4 ♖g8 13 ♕c2 ♕e7!

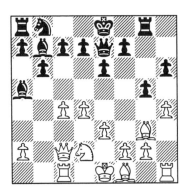

Black lives with the knowledge that c7 falls. So what? White is still trapped in a terrible pin and g2 is still exposed. All in all it looks as if White does not have any chances to gain an advantage in this line, as he does not have the fluent development you usually get when you sacrifice a pawn.

14 hxg5 hxg5 15 ♗xc7 ♘a6 16 ♗e5

♕a3 **17 ♖d1 ♘b4 18 ♕b3 ♕xa2 19 ♕xa2 ♘xa2 20 f3 ♗b4 21 ♖a1 ♘c3 22 ♔f2 a5 23 ♗f6 g4 24 ♗d3 g3+ 25 ♔e1 b5 26 ♗h7 ♖f8 27 ♗g7 bxc4 28 ♗xf8 ♔xf8 29 ♘xc4 f5 30 ♗g6 ♔g7 31 ♘e5 ♘e4+ 32 ♔f1 ♗a6+ 33 ♔g1 ♘g5 34 f4**

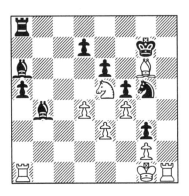

34...♗d2!

The winning move. Once the e3-square caves in the game is up.

35 ♖h4 ♗xe3+ 36 ♔h1 ♗xd4 37 ♖d1 ♗xe5 38 ♗h5 ♗xf4 39 ♖xd7+ ♔f6 40 ♖xf4 ♖h8 41 ♖h4 ♗e2 42 ♖a7 ♖xh5 43 ♖xh5 ♗xh5 44 ♖xa5 f4 45 ♔g1 ♗e2 46 ♖a8 f3 47 gxf3 ♗xf3 0-1

Summary

5 ♕c2 is not ambitious and Black equalises without trouble. 4 ♘c3 ♗b4 5 ♗g5 ♗b7 6 e3 h6 7 ♗h4 ♗xc3 8 bxc3 d6 is a good reliable system for Black. Now 9 ♘d2 is the only good move, but 9 ♗d3, which has led to disaster for many White players, is still seen occasionally. 7...g5 8 ♗g3 ♘e4 is also seen at the top level, and after 9 ♕c2 the game seems to be more or less equal, even though this is a complex line. The gambit after 9 ♘d2 is simply not to be recommended.

1 d4 ♘f6 2 c4 e6 3 ♘f3 b6 4 ♘c3 *(D)* ♗b4

    4...♗b7

        5 ♕c2 – *Game 21*; 5 ♗g5 – *Game 22*

5 ♗g5

    5 ♕b3 – Chapter 4

5...♗b7 6 e3

    6 ♕c2 – *Game 23*

6...h6 7 ♗h4 ♗xc3+

    7...g5 8 ♗g3 ♘e4 *(D)*

        9 ♕c2 – *Game 26*; 9 ♘d2 – *Game 27*

8 bxc3 d6 *(D)*

    9 ♗d3 – *Game 24*; 9 ♘d2 – *Game 25*

    4 ♘c3   *8...♘e4*   *8...d6*

CHAPTER FOUR

5 ♕b3

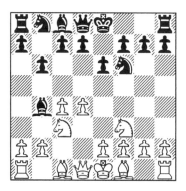

1 d4 ♘f6 2 c4 e6 3 ♘f3 b6 4 ♘c3 ♗b4 5 ♕b3

In this chapter we will investigate Seira-wan's pet line which, in my opinion, is one of the most difficult for Black to face. Look out particularly for Alterman's nice strategic idea in the first main game, and that of Miles in one of the sub-variations.

> ### Game 28
> ### Alterman-Liss
> *Israel 1999*

1 d4 ♘f6 2 c4 e6 3 ♘f3 b6 4 ♘c3 ♗b4

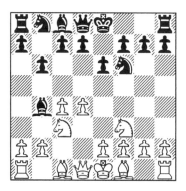

5 ♕b3!

I give this move an exclamation mark not because it is better than 5 e3, leading to the Nimzo-Indian, or 5 ♗g5, but because this is what I would play myself with White in this position, as it is clearly the most problematic line for Black to face.

5...a5

This is one of three ways to protect the bishop. 5...♕e7 is considered in the following game and 5...c5 in Game 30.

6 ♗g5

The main line. Black has no problems after the alternatives:

a) In reply to 6 g3, 6...♗b7 7 ♗g2 0-0 8 0-0 ♗xc3 9 ♕xc3 d6 10 b3 ♘bd7 11 ♗b2 leads us to a standard position where White seems to have a tiny edge thanks to the potential pressure on the long diagonal, as in Dreev-Kiselev, Podolsk 1992. Instead 6...♘c6! is the aggressive approach, e.g. 7 ♗g2 a4! (now this is possible) 8 ♕c2 ♗a6 9 a3 (9 0-0 ♗xc4 10 ♘e5 ♘xe5 11 dxe5 ♘d5 12 ♘xa4 b5 13 ♘c3 ♗xc3 14 bxc3 ♖a4 was fine for Black in Labunsky-Tsesarsky, USSR 1986) 9...♗xc3+ 10 ♕xc3 ♘a5 11 ♘e5?! (11 ♘d2 d5 12 cxd5 ♘xd5 13 ♕c2 is unclear according to Giplis) 11...d5! 12 cxd5 ♘xd5 and it is already clear that Black has considerable power in his pieces. That he used it to win a superb game in Polugaevsky-Ljubojevic, Linares 1985, is no surprise: 13 ♕c2 ♘b3 14 ♕c6+ ♔f8 15 ♗g5 ♕e8 16

♘d7+ ♔g8 17 e4 ♘xd4 18 ♕xa4 c5 19 exd5
♗b5 20 ♕d1 ♕xd7 21 ♗e3 ♗e2 22 dxe6
♕xe6 23 ♕xe2 ♘xe2 24 ♗xa8 ♕c4 25 ♖d1
♘d4 26 ♗xd4 cxd4 27 ♗e4 g6 28 ♗d3 ♕a2
29 ♖b1 ♕b3 30 ♔d2 ♔g7 and Black went
on to win.

b) 6 a3 ♗xc3+ (6...a4 7 ♕c2 ♗xc3+ 8
bxc3! reminds me of the main game. 8 bxc3
has never been played before) 7 ♕xc3 ♗b7 8
g3 0-0 9 ♗g2 a4! and Black had at least
equalised in Ahner-Bischoff, Germany 1997
(c4 is a potential problem for White and the
queen's bishop has no good squares).

6...♗b7 7 e3

White is developing. 7 a3 ♗xc3+ 8 ♕xc3
d6 9 e3 ♘bd7 10 ♗d2 ♕e7 11 f3 e5 12 ♗e2
exd4 13 ♕xd4 a4 was good enough for
equality in Zaja-Baklan, New Delhi 2000.

7...h6

There is only one really independent way
to play this position, namely 7...♕e7 8 ♕c2
a4!? 9 a3 ♗xc3+, and now 10 ♕xc3 ♘e4! 11
♗xe7 ♘xc3 12 ♗h4 ♘e4 seems to give
Black equality due to the weakness of c4.
Instead 10 bxc3! is best, the idea being that
Black will have some commitment to the a4-
pawn and that White will benefit from a
strong centre, as is the case in the 5 ♗g5
lines. Miles-Arkhipov, Münster 1993 continued 10...♗e4 (it is not easy to decide where
this bishop belongs, as White will certainly
play f2-f3 and e3-e4 soon) 11 ♕b2 h6 12
♗h4 0-0 13 ♘d2 ♗h7 14 f3 e5 15 e4 ♘c6
16 ♗e2 (planning to re-route the knight to
d5) 16...d6 17 ♘f1 g5 18 ♗f2 ♘h5 19 ♘e3
♘f4 20 ♘d5! ♕d8 21 g4! and White had a
very promising position.

8 ♗h4

The only serious move. After 8 ♗xf6
♕xf6 9 ♗e2 0-0 10 0-0 ♗xc3 11 ♕xc3 d6 12
♘d2 ♘d7 the position was even in Ivanov-
Farago, Philadelphia 1984.

8...d6

Black should develop smoothly. After
8...g5 9 ♗g3 ♘e4 10 ♗d3 d6 11 ♗xe4!
♗xe4 12 0-0-0 ♗xc3 (12...♗b7 13 d5! gives

White the advantage due to his influence in
the centre) 13 ♕xc3 ♘d7 14 ♘e1 ♗b7 15 c5
White seemed to have some initiative in
Miles-Budnikov, Beijing 1991, although
Black might be fine.

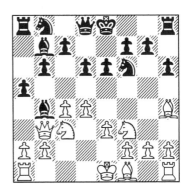

9 a3!?

This builds on a very interesting concept,
similar to the one Miles used in the note to
Black's 7th move. Others:

a) 9 ♗e2?! – it is not easy to see what the
bishop is doing here. Black is doing well after
9...g5 10 ♗g3 ♘e4, e.g. 11 0-0-0 ♗xc3 12
bxc3 ♘d7 13 ♘e1 h5 14 h4 g4 15 ♘d3
♘xg3 16 fxg3 ♗xg2 17 ♖h2 ♗e4, and White
did not have enough compensation for the
pawn in Conquest-Onischuk, Germany 1997,
or 11 d5 ♘d7 12 ♘d4 ♘dc5 13 ♕c2 ♗xc3+
14 bxc3 e5, and Black was satisfied in Stohl-
Polak, Olomouc 1998.

b) 9 ♗d3 is the main line here. After
9...♘bd7 10 0-0-0 ♗xc3 11 ♕xc3 Black has
a variety of valid options:

b1) 11...a4!? 12 ♕c2 ♖a5 13 ♘d2 g5 14
♗g3 ♗xg2 15 ♖hg1 ♗b7 16 f3 ♕a8 17
♖df1 ♕e7 18 ♗e1 c5 19 ♘e4 ♖a7 20 ♘c3
♗a6 21 f4, Miles-Bischoff, Havana 1998, and
White had compensation for the pawn but it
was still a battle.

b2) 11...♕c8?! 12 ♕c2! c5 13 d5 e5 14
♘d2 g5 15 ♗g3 ♕c7 16 f4 and Black experi-
enced serious problems on the light squares
in Khalifman-Tunik, Maikop 1998.

b3) 11...♕e7 12 ♘e1 e5?! 13 ♗f5 0-0-0 14

c5! put Black under fire in Miles-Singh, Calcutta 1994. After 14...exd4 15 cxd6 ♕xd6 16 ♖xd4 ♘d5 17 ♕c2 c5 18 ♘d3 ♗c6 19 ♗g3 ♕f6 20 ♘e5 cxd4 21 ♘xc6 he was ready to resign.

b4) 11...g5 12 ♗g3 ♘e4 13 ♕c2 ♘df6 14 ♖he1 ♕e7 with an even position in Khalifman-Granda Zuniga, Ulcinj 1998.

9...a4

9...♗xc3+!, with the idea of 10 ♕xc3 a4! with equality, is probably a better line. Now White gets something.

10 ♕c2 ♗xc3+ 11 bxc3!

I would like to quote Alterman on this position because he says it all: 'This was my idea. It looks as if Black gets a tempo with ...a5-a4 but, as I understand it, the pawn on a4 only presents problems for Black because it requires constant protection.'

11...♘bd7 12 ♘d2 ♕e7 13 f3 e5 14 e4 0-0 15 ♗e2

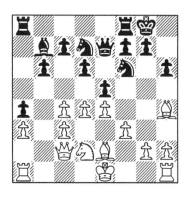

Here Black should find a way to organise his pieces so that he gets out of the pin and activates his forces. I have a feeling that Liss does not find the appropriate route.

15...♕e6?!

15...♕e8! improves, with indirect protection of a4 and the manoeuvre ...♘h5-f4 coming up, perhaps even ...c7-c6 and ...d6-d5 in some situations. Liss leaves the e8-square free for a rook, which seems sensible enough, but the queen appears to be slightly awkward on e6 and he still has problems

with the a4-pawn.

16 0-0 ♘h5 17 ♖fe1 ♘f4 18 ♗f1 ♕g6 19 ♖ad1 f5 20 exf5 ♖xf5 21 ♗g3!

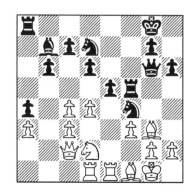

All White's pieces are well organised here and Black has managed to do nothing other than open up the position for them. White is clearly better.

21...♕f7 22 ♘e4! ♔h8 23 ♘f2 ♖f8!?

Leaving the pawn to its own devices seems a rational thing to do. The pieces need to play before everything goes wrong.

24 ♕xa4 ♘f6 25 ♗xf4 ♖xf4 26 dxe5 dxe5 27 ♘d3 ♖f5 28 ♖xe5 ♘h5

Here Black has only one minute left with which to reach the 40th move, but White completely overlooks his threat, and the game takes a sudden turn.

29 ♖de1?? ♖xf3!

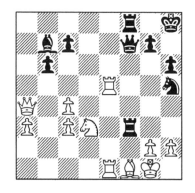

This rook is obviously taboo.

30 ♕d1 ♕g6 31 ♕d2?!

31 ♕e2! is better according to Alterman.
31...♘f4 32 ♘xf4 ♖3xf4 33 g3 ♖4f6 34 ♗d3 ♕f7 35 ♖e7 ♕h5 36 ♕e2 ♕c5+ 37 ♕e3 ♖f2 38 ♗f1?

Presenting Black with the opportunity to finish the game with a nice tactical blow. After 38 ♕xc5 ♖g2+ 39 ♔h1 bxc5 40 ♗e4 ♗xe4 41 ♖1xe4 ♖ff2 42 ♖h4 ♖a2 43 a4 ♖gc2 44 ♖e1 ♖xc3 Black is close to winning, but White retains some drawing chances.
38...♕c6!

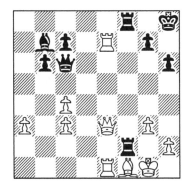

0-1
Now the control of h1 is deadly.

Game 29
Timman-Karpov
Hoogeveen 1999

---

1 d4 ♘f6 2 c4 e6 3 ♘f3 b6 4 ♘c3 ♗b4 5 ♕b3 ♕e7

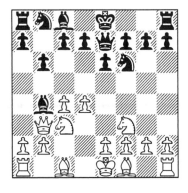

I like this move quite a lot. The next note demonstrates the main reason why (...♘e4).
6 a3!

The most challenging set-up. At least it earns the bishop pair. Others:

a) After 6 ♗g5 ♗b7 7 e3 a5 8 a3 ♗xc3+ 9 ♕xc3 ♘e4! Black steers the game to an ending where c4 is a slight weakness. Seirewan-Sokolov, Candidates 1985, went 10 ♗xe7 ♘xc3 11 ♗h4 ♘e4 12 ♘d2 ♘xd2 13 ♔xd2 a4! 14 f3 ♘c6 15 ♗d3 ♘a5 16 ♔c3 ♗a6 17 e4 0-0 18 ♗c2 ♘xc4 19 ♗xa4 c6 20 ♗b3 d5 21 ♗xc4 ♗xc4 22 b3 with complete equality.

b) 6 g3 ♗b7 7 ♗g2 c5 8 a3 ♗xc3+ 9 ♕xc3 cxd4 10 ♕xd4 ♘c6 11 ♕h4 ♘a5 12 ♗g5 h6 13 0-0 0-0 14 ♗xf6 ♕xf6 15 ♕xf6 gxf6 16 ♘d2 ♖fc8 and Black was completely fine in Dreev-Karpov, Dortmund 1994. However, I think White might be slightly better after 7...0-0 8 0-0 ♗xc3 9 ♕xc3 d6 10 b3 ♘bd7 11 ♗b2 ♗e4 12 ♖fe1. At least Black was in trouble after 12...c5 13 ♖ad1 ♖fd8 14 d5! exd5 15 cxd5 b5 16 ♘h4! ♗xg2 17 ♔xg2 b4 18 ♕f3 g6 19 e4 in Van Wely-Psakhis, Internet 1995, the bishop making its presence felt.

c) 6 ♗f4. The bishop is nice here, but not very useful. 6...d5 7 e3 0-0 8 a3 ♗xc3+ 9 ♕xc3 ♗a6! 10 ♗g5 ♖c8 11 cxd5 ♗xf1 12 ♖xf1 exd5 13 ♖c1 ♕e6 left Black no worse in Alterman-Hracek, Bad Homburg 1997.
6...♗xc3+ 7 ♕xc3 ♗b7 8 e3

Here I prefer 8 g3 0-0 9 ♗g2 as it puts less restraint on the queen's bishop. Now 9...d6 10 0-0 ♘bd7 11 b4 is perhaps a touch better for White, but this is difficult to prove, e.g. 11...a5 12 ♗b2 axb4 13 axb4 ♖fc8 14 ♖fd1, Gurevich-Karpov, Reggio Emilia 1991, when 14...♕f8!, with the intention of ...♖xa1 and ...♖a8, puts Black as close to equality as he can possibly come in positions like this (without a mistake from White). Indeed he should not fear such positions. Gurevich calls it equal, but this is because White's advantage is so minor that, at his level, it is insignificant. 11...♘e4 12 ♕c2 f5 is less good for Black. Smyslov-Chandler, Hastings 1988, went 13 ♗b2 ♘df6 14 a4 a5 15 b5 ♖ae8 16 ♘e1 c6 17 bxc6 ♗xc6 18 f3 ♘g5 19 ♘d3, and White was better. Look at all the weak pawns on the dark squares!

8 ♗g5 ♘e4! sees Black equalise immediately.

8...0-0

8...d6 9 ♗e2 ♘e4 10 ♕c2 ♘d7 11 0-0 0-0 12 ♘d2 f5 13 f3 ♘g5 14 ♖f2 e5 15 ♘f1 exd4 16 exd4 ♘e6 gave Black sufficient counterplay in Seirawan-Karpov, Roquebrune 1992, but there is still a lot of play in the position for White, and the bishop might later become strong on b2, so I would not recommend playing like this.

9 ♗e2 d6

I think this is the most natural way to play the position, but also possible is 9...c5!? 10 0-0 ♖c8 11 dxc5 ♕xc5 (11...bxc5 12 b3 followed by 13 ♗b2 is slightly better for White) 12 b4 ♕e7 13 ♗b2 d5 14 ♕d4 dxc4 15 ♗xc4 a5! (15...♘c6?! 16 ♕h4 and Black needs to be careful) 16 ♘e5 ♘c6 17 ♘xc6 ♖xc6 18 bxa5 (18 b5 ♖d6 19 ♕h4 e5 20 a4 ♖d2 21 ♗a3 ♕d8 22 ♕g3 ♗d5 is no worse for Black at all) 18...e5! 19 ♕h4 ♖xa5?! was Sokolov-Karpov, Groningen 1995. Better is 19...bxa5, when Black is not worse in any way.

10 0-0 ♘bd7 11 b4 c5!

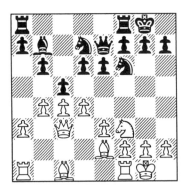

Black should seek counterplay, and the only way to do so is to put pressure on a

weakness on the light squares, namely the c4-pawn. 11...♘e4 12 ♕d3 f5 tries to put pressure on g2, but Black is not in position to justify this: 13 ♘d2 ♕h4 14 f3 ♘g5 15 d5! gave White a slight advantage in Van Wely-Lobron, London 1995. The point is, of course, 15...e5 16 f4!, with a fight for a giant bishop on b2.

12 ♗b2 a5

Here Black has a great range of alternatives.

a) 12...♖ac8 13 dxc5 dxc5 14 b5 ♖fd8 15 a4, Becker-Pitschak, Bad Liebenwerda 1934. This kind of position is typical for the line. White has a very minor plus due to the bishop's superiority over the knight.

b) 12...♘e4 13 ♕c2 and now 13...f5?! does not sit well with ...c7-c5. Now White's dark-squared bishop assumes great influence that could otherwise be neutralised later with ...f7-f6 if necessary. Moreover Black's second rank is slightly more exposed, and this is felt on g7. In Shamkovich-Kholmov, Baku 1972, 14 dxc5 bxc5 15 b5 ♘df6 16 ♘d2 ♖ad8 17 f3 ♘g5 18 ♖fd1 gave White the advantage. Better is 13...♖ac8, e.g. 14 dxc5 dxc5 15 b5 h6 16 ♖fd1 ♖fd8 17 a4 ♘g5 18 ♕c3 ♘xf3+ 19 ♗xf3 ♘f6 20 ♗xb7 ♕xb7 with an edge for White in Cebalo-Hohler, Saint Vincent 1998. Often Black should not fear such positions as White's bishop tends to have difficulties causing any harm all by itself.

c) 12...♖fd8 13 ♖fd1 ♖ac8 14 ♕b3 ♗e4 15 ♘d2 ♗a8 16 dxc5 dxc5 17 b5 ♘e4 18 ♘xe4 ♗xe4 19 a4 f6 20 a5 ♘f8 21 f3 ♗g6 and, because Black's bishop looks so good and the a1-h8 diagonal is limited, Black had equalised in Gurevich-Rozentalis, Belfort 1997.

d) 12...♖fe8 13 ♘d2 ♖ac8 14 dxc5 dxc5 15 b5 e5 16 f3 ♘f8 17 a4 was slightly better for White in Burmakin-Zayac, St. Petersburg 1998. White's set-up here is probably the most promising.

13 ♖fd1

13 dxc5 dxc5 14 b5 ♖fe8 15 ♖fd1 ♖ad8

16 ♘d2 e5 equalises. Perhaps 16 ♘e5!? Might offer some kind of an advantage.

13...axb4 14 axb4 ♖fb8!

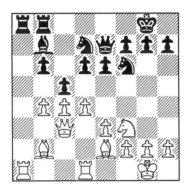

Clearing space for the queen in order to trade major pieces on the a-file.

15 ♘d2 ♕d8 16 f3 ♖xa1 17 ♗xa1 ♖a8 18 ♗d3 ♕c7 19 ♗c2 ♖c8?!

A slight positional mistake. After 19...e5! Black has neutralised the pressure on the long diagonal and thus limited the scope of the bishop. Now White has a chance to establish a small edge.

20 dxc5 dxc5 21 b5!

The pawn structure is now clearly favourable for White. His bishops enjoy open diagonals, but Black's knights have no good squares.

21...♘e8

21...e5 22 ♗f5! is uncomfortable for White. Thanks to the misplacement of Black's pieces, e3-e4 followed by ♘f1-e3 will soon be a relevant option.

22 ♘e4 f6 23 ♕d3! ♗xe4

This move is based on the following tactics: 23...♘f8 24 ♘d6! ♕xd6 (24...♖d8 25 ♘xe8 ♖xe8 26 ♕d6 gives White a great advantage; b6 falls) 25 ♕xd6 (with the threat of ♕xc7 and ♖d6) 25...♕xd6 26 ♖xd6 ♖a8 27 ♗c3 ♖a2 28 ♗d3 ♗c8 29 ♗f1 ♖a3 30 ♗e1 and White wins b6 for e3, which gives him a passed pawn on the queenside and establishes c5 as a weakness.

24 ♕xe4 ♘f8 25 ♕d3 ♔f7 26 ♗c3 ♔e7

26...♖a8 27 ♗e1! shows the strength the bishops have even in this semi-closed position.

27 ♖a1 ♖d8 28 ♕e2 ♘d6

28...e5 29 f4! and the black king's defences crack.

29 f4 ♔f7 30 e4 ♘c8 31 e5!

White is trying to open the position.

31...f5

31...♘e7 32 ♕h5+ ♘eg6 33 exf6 gxf6 34 ♖f1! and White is ready to launch a direct assault on f6 with f4-f5.

32 ♕f3 ♘e7 33 h3 ♔g8 34 ♔h2!

Improving the king before the attack.

34...♘fg6 35 g3 ♔f7 36 h4! ♔g8 37 h5 ♘h8

37...♘f8 38 g4! – now this is possible as Black cannot organise counterplay against f4.

38 g4 ♖f8

38...fxg4 39 ♕xg4 ♕c8 40 ♖a7 ♖e8 41 h6 with a winning attack.

39 gxf5 ♘xf5

39...exf5 40 e6 and the bishop comes to life.

40 ♗xf5 ♖xf5 41 ♖a8+ ♖f8 42 ♖xf8+ ♔xf8 43 ♕a8+ ♔f7 44 ♕xh8 ♕b7 45 h6! 1-0

Game 30

Seirawan-Timman

Hilversum Match (5th game) 1990

1 d4 ♘f6 2 ♘f3 e6 3 c4 b6 4 ♘c3 ♗b4

5 ♕b3 c5

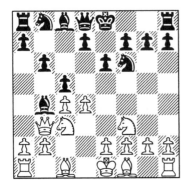

This is the main line. Actually it was this match between Timman and Seirawan that put the 5 ♕b3 line on the map as a serious main line, instead of a decent sub-variation. Seirawan used it in all three of his games with White – all of which he won.

6 a3

This is the most serious move. Alternatives:

a) 6 ♗f4 0-0 and here White has two ways he can go:

a1) 7 a3 ♗a5 8 ♖d1 (8 dxc5 ♘e4 9 cxb6 axb6 10 g3 ♘c6 11 ♗g2 ♗xc3+ 12 bxc3 ♗a6 13 0-0 ♘c5 14 ♕c2 ♗xc4 15 ♘e5 ♗b3 16 ♕d2 ♘xe5 17 ♗xe5 d5 was nice for Black in Dreev-Timman, Moscow 1993, until he blundered a few moves later...) 8...♗a6! and the bishop is much better placed here than on b7. In Garcia Palermo-Eingorn, Cienfuegos 1986 Black organised a quick attack on White's centre: 9 e3 cxd4 10 ♘xd4 d5 11 ♗e2 ♗xc4 12 ♗xc4 dxc4 13 ♕xc4 ♕d5 and Black had equalised, if not more...

a2) 7 e3. This must be the way to play with ♗f4 but it fails to earn White an advantage. Dreev-Ivanchuk, Linares 1995 continued 7...d5 8 ♖d1 ♘bd7 9 cxd5? (9 dxc5 bxc5 10 ♗d3, with an unclear position, is better, while 9 ♗d6 ♖e8 10 ♗d3 ♗a6 seems dangerous for White – what is the bishop really doing on d6?) 9...♘xd5 10 ♗g5 (10 ♗d6? c4! might have been what Dreev overlooked)

10...♕c7 11 ♗c4 cxd4 12 ♗xd5 ♗xc3+! 13 bxc3 exd5 14 cxd4 ♗a6 and Black had the advantage.

b) 6 ♗g5 with a further branch:

b1) Now after 6...♘c6 there has been much debate as to whether 7 d5 gives White an advantage. But the basic fact that the knight looks misplaced is possibly best illustrated by the less ambitious, but smooth 7 e3!? h6 8 ♗h4 g5 9 ♗g3 ♘e4 10 ♗d3 ♗xc3+ 11 bxc3 ♘xg3 12 hxg3 d6 13 ♗e4 ♗d7 14 ♗xc6 ♗xc6 15 d5, when White had an advantage in Condie-Cullip, Edinburgh 1989.

b2) 6...♗b7

b21) 7 0-0-0 ♗xc3! 8 ♕xc3 ♘e4 9 ♗xd8 ♘xc3 10 bxc3 ♗xd8 11 d5 ♔e7 gives Black an even endgame.

b22) 7 e3 0-0 (7...♗xf3? 8 gxf3 ♘c6 9 d5! exd5?! 10 cxd5 ♘e5 11 f4! ♘f3+ 12 ♔e2 ♘xg5 13 fxg5 ♗xc3 14 ♕xc3 ♘h5 15 ♕e5+ ♕e7 16 ♕xe7+ ♔xe7 17 ♗g2 ♔d6 18 ♗f3 gave White a strategically won position in Van Wely-Miles, London (rapid) 1995) 8 ♗e2 cxd4 9 exd4 ♘c6 10 0-0 ♗xc3! 11 ♗xf6 (11 ♕xc3 ♘e4 and Black appears to have an edge after 12 ♗xd8 ♘xc3 13 bxc3 ♖fxd8, when c4 is exposed) 11...♗xf6 12 ♕xc3 ♖ac8 13 ♕d2 ♘e7! 14 ♖ac1 ♘g6 15 ♖c3 ♘f4 and Black was doing fine in Timoscenko-Pelletier, Leon 2001. Actually it might be White who should be careful here.

b23) 7 ♖d1!? 0-0 8 e3 cxd4 9 exd4 and now 9...♗xc3+! is a strong theoretical novelty of Boris Gelfand which gives Black equality. 10 bxc3 ♕c7! 11 ♗xf6 ♗xf3! 12 gxf3 gxf6 13 ♕c2 ♕f4 14 ♕e4 ♕xe4+ led to a draw in Alterman-Gelfand, Tel Aviv 1999. This ending is equal.

c) 6 e3!? ♗a6 (6...♘c6!? looks so natural here that one wonders why it has not been played – when there is no ♗g5, then d4-d5 also becomes less of a real threat) 7 a3 ♗a5 8 ♗d2 0-0 and now:

c1) 9 ♖d1 cxd4 10 ♘xd4 d5 11 ♘db5 ♗b7! 12 cxd5 a6! 13 ♘d4 ♘xd5 14 ♘xd5

♕xd5 15 ♕xd5 ♗xd2+ 16 ♖xd2 ♗xd5 17 f3 ♖a7! 18 e4 ♗a8! was even in Seirawan-Browne, USA 1987. A decent alternative is 9...d5!? with the following idea: 10 dxc5 bxc5 11 cxd5 exd5 12 ♗xa6 ♘xa6 13 0-0 ♖b8 14 ♕a2 c4! and Black has good play on the light squares.

c2) 9 0-0-0 and now after 9...♕e7 10 d5 exd5 11 ♘xd5 ♘xd5 12 cxd5 ♗xf1 13 ♖hxf1 ♗xd2+ 14 ♘xd2 d6 15 e4 ♘d7 16 ♖fe1 ♘e5, Browne-Korchnoi, Chicago 1982, I prefer White (slightly). 9...d5!? looks like an obvious improvement. White has no way of turning the tension in the centre to his advantage: 10 dxc5?! ♘bd7! 11 cxb6 ♘c5 12 ♕a2 axb6 13 cxd5 ♗xf1 14 ♖hxf1 ♗xc3 15 ♗xc3 ♘xd5 and Black is a pawn down but certainly has the advantage!

6...♗a5!?

Also possible is 6...♗xc3+ 7 ♕xc3 0-0, when 8 dxc5 is the best try for an advantage, e.g. 8...bxc5 9 ♗g5 ♘c6 10 e3 h6 11 ♗h4 g5 12 ♗g3 ♘e4 13 ♕c2 f5 14 0-0-0 ♕f6 15 ♗d3 ♘xg3 16 hxg3 ♗b7, and now in Seirawan-Arnason, Manila 1992, White played 17 ♗e2?. Instead 17 g4! gives White a powerful attack. When the kings are castled on opposite flanks and there are lots of open files, time is an important aspect of the game. The alternatives are 8 ♗g5 ♗b7 9 e3 d6 10 dxc5 bxc5 11 ♖d1 ♕e7 12 ♗d3 ♘bd7 13 0-0 ♖fd8, which appeared to secure Black equality in Malaniuk-Lerner, Donetsk 1998, 8 e3 ♗b7 9 b4 d6 10 ♗b2 ♘e4 11 ♕c2 f5 12 ♖d1 ♘d7 13 ♗e2 a5 14 bxc5 bxc5 15 0-0 ♖f7 16 ♗a1 ♘b6 17 dxc5 ♘xc5 18 ♘d4 ♕g5 19 ♗f3 ♗xf3 20 ♘xf3 with equality in Seirawan-Arnason, Reykjavik 1986 (although this set-up might be more dangerous than it appeared here) and, finally, 8 g3? cxd4! 9 ♕xd4 ♘c6 10 ♕h4 ♗b7 11 ♗g2 ♖c8 12 ♗d2 ♘a5! 13 ♗xa5 bxa5, when Black had a lead in development and very active pieces in Gurevich-Kasparov, Linares 1991.

7 ♗g5

The aggressive move. After 7 e3 0-0 8 ♗e2 ♘e4! 9 d5! ♗xc3+! 10 bxc3 ♗a6!? 11 ♗b2 ♕e7 12 ♖d1 ♖e8! 13 ♗d3 (13 0-0? exd5 14 ♖xd5 ♘c6 with ...♘a5 to follow) 13...♘d6!? Black was doing very well in Seirawan-Timman, Hilversum 1990. 7 ♗f4 ♗b7 8 ♖d1 0-0 9 e3 cxd4 10 ♘xd4 ♘e4 11 ♕c2 ♗xc3+ 12 bxc3 was fine for Black in Portisch-Polugaevsky, Linares 1985. It seems that the bishop is rather harmlessly placed on f4 in these lines, as the attack on d6 and c7 is not supported by other pieces.

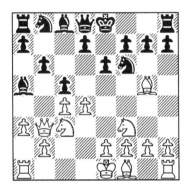

7...♘c6?

This move is refuted in the meanest possible way. Others:

a) 7...h6?! 8 ♗h4 g5 (8...♘c6? 9 0-0-0! ♗xc3 10 ♕xc3 cxd4 [10...g5 11 d5! and Black is clearly not developed to meet this] 11 ♘xd4 ♘e4 12 ♕h3! and White won a quick victory in Seirawan-Timman, Hilversum (3) 1990, while 8...♗b7 is, of course, best here, but because the bishop is now on h4 Black will have less effect with the ...♗xc3+ and ...♘e4 trick than without ...h7-h6). After 8...g5 9 ♗g3 Black has played:

a1) 9...♘c6 10 0-0-0 ♗xc3 11 d5! exd5 12 cxd5 ♘xd5 13 ♖xd5 ♗g7 14 h4 and White had a powerful initiative in Nielsen-Hracek, Germany 2000.

a2) 9...♘e4 10 e3 ♘c6 11 ♗d3 ♘xg3 (11...♗xc3+ 12 bxc3 ♘xg3 13 fxg3! gives White some prospects on the f-file) 12 hxg3 g4 13 d5! gxf3 14 dxc6 fxg2 15 ♖g1 with a powerful initiative for White in Psakhis-

Gruenfeld, Israel 1991.

a3) 9...g4 10 ♘d2 cxd4 11 ♘b5 ♗xd2+ 12 ♔xd2 ♘e4+ 13 ♔e1 with a clear advantage for White in Malaniuk-Lendwai, Kesckement 1991.

b) 7...♗b7! and now White has a flood of different opportunities:

b1) 8 0-0-0!? ♗xc3! 9 ♕xc3 ♘e4 10 ♗xd8 ♘xc3 11 bxc3 ♔xd8 12 d5 ♔e7 13 e4 d6 14 ♗d3 ♘d7 15 ♖he1 ♖ad8 with an equal ending in Gretarsson-Hjartarson, Leeuwarden 1995.

b2) There is no time for 8 dxc5?!. Black now develops a lot of threats quickly: 8...♘a6! 9 cxb6 (9 ♕c2 ♗xc3+ 10 ♕xc3 ♘xc5 11 ♘d2 a5 12 b4 axb4 13 axb4 ♖xa1+ 14 ♕xa1 ♘a6 15 ♕b2 ♕e7 gave Black a development advantage in Campos Moreno-Adams, Cala Galdana 2001 –who cares about two bishops when the rook is still on h1 with no immediate prospects?) 9...♘c5 10 ♕c2 ♗e4 11 ♕d1 ♗xc3+ 12 bxc3 ♕xb6 and Black has a strong initiative, Van Wely-Seirawan, Wijk an Zee 1995.

b3) 8 ♖d1 ♗xc3+! 9 bxc3 ♕e7 10 d5 d6 11 e3 ♘bd7 12 ♗e2 h6 13 ♗h4 e5 with a good position for Black in Gunawan-Timman, Bali 2000.

b4) 8 e3 and now:

b41) 8...0-0 is the most normal. 9 ♖d1 d5 (again the most logical, but also possible is 9...♗xc3+ 10 bxc3 ♕e7 11 ♗e2 d6 12 0-0 ♘bd7 13 ♘d2 ♖fc8 14 f3 h6 15 ♗h4 with a complicated struggle ahead in Seirawan-Adams, Bermuda 1999) 10 ♗e2 ♘bd7 11 0-0 cxd4 12 ♘b5!? (although neither of the players could have foreseen it, this move practically leads to a forced draw; anyway, Black appears to be doing well) 12...h6 13 ♗h4 ♘c5 14 ♕c2 d3! 15 ♗xd3 ♘xd3 16 ♖xd3 a6 17 cxd5 axb5 18 dxe6 ♕e8 19 ♗xf6 fxe6 20 ♗e5 ♗e4 21 ♖d7! (21 b4?? ♖xf3 22 gxf3 ♕g6+) 21...♗xc2 (21...♖xd7 22 ♕xe4 gives White powerful compensation for the exchange as his minor pieces are very strongly placed in the centre) 22 ♖xg7+ ♔h8

and a draw was agreed in Bareev-Adams, Wijk aan Zee 2002. Note that 9...cxd4?! quickly leads to trouble: 10 ♖xd4! ♘c6 11 ♖f4! ♘e7 12 ♖xf6! and White had an initiative in Seirawan-Adams, Bermuda 1999.

b42) 8...cxd4!? 9 ♘xd4 0-0 10 ♕c2 ♗xc3+ 11 ♕xc3 d5 looked fine for Black in Sokolov-Adams, Dortmund 1999.

b43) 8...h6?! 9 ♗h4 g5 (9...0-0 10 ♖d1 cxd4 11 ♖xd4 ♗xf3 12 gxf3 ♘c6 13 ♖d2 ♘e5 14 ♗e2 ♘g6 15 ♗g3 ♘e8 16 ♕c2 ♗xc3 17 ♕xc3 f5 18 ♕d3 left White in a strong attacking position in Sokolov-Janssen, Netherlands 1999) 10 ♗g3 ♘e4 11 ♗d3 ♗xc3+ 12 bxc3 ♘xg3 13 hxg3 d6 14 ♕c2 ♘d7 and a draw was soon agreed in Nielsen-C.Hansen, Aars 1995, but the position does not feel completely safe for Black.

b44) 8...♗xf3? 9 gxf3 cxd4 10 exd4 ♘c6 11 0-0-0 ♗xc3 12 ♕xc3 ♖c8 13 ♔b1 gave White a storming advantage in Korchnoi-Polugaevsky, Reykjavik 1987.

b45) 8...♕e7 9 ♗e2 d6 10 dxc5 dxc5 11 0-0-0 ♘bd7?! (11...♗xc3 12 ♕xc3 is a little better for White due to 12...♘e4 13 ♕xg7! with advantage) 12 ♘b5 0-0 13 ♘d6 ♗c6 14 e4 was critical for Black in Shabalov-Yemelin, Moscow 2002.

8 0-0-0 ♗xc3

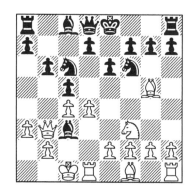

9 d5!!

This is the main point of the fight against ...♘c6 in this system, and why I suggest that Black should avoid ...♘c6 altogether. 9 d5 is available to White because the lead in development over-rides a possible loss of a pawn.

9...exd5?

Opening up the position when behind in development tends to be a poor idea. 9...♗e5! 10 dxc6 ♗c7! is the correct defence (weaker is 10...♕c7?, e.g. 11 g3! ♗d6 12 ♗g2 dxc6 13 ♖xd6!! ♕xd6 14 ♖d1 ♕c7 15 ♗f4 ♕b7 16 ♘e5 ♗d7 17 ♖xd7! ♘xd7 18 ♗xc6, which led to a swift victory in Seirawan-Zarnicki, Buenos Aires 1993). Then with 11 e3! White maintains a lead in development for as long as possible in order to create the greatest possible disharmony in the opponent's camp. Soppe-Debarnot, Buenos Aires 1991 continued 11...h6 12 ♗h4 ♕e7 13 ♕a4 d6 14 ♗d3 (14 ♗e2!? appears logical) 14...g5 15 ♗g3 ♘h5 16 ♗e2 f5 17 ♘d2 ♘f6 18 h4 g4 19 f3 h5 20 ♘b1! a6 21 ♘c3 0-0 22 ♗f4 ♖b8 23 ♗h6 ♖f7 24 ♗g5 ♕f8 25 e4 with excellent prospects for White. Note that the bishop is yet to be of use on c8 and, therefore, the c6-pawn remains a constant source of discomfort for Black.

10 cxd5 ♗e5 11 dxc6 ♕e7

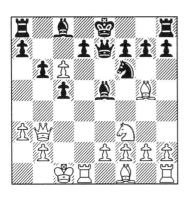

12 cxd7+?

This move wins the game but, as a pupil of mine illustrated when given this game as an exercise, 12 ♗xf6! is more straightforward: 12...♗xf6 (12...♕xf6 13 cxd7+ ♗xd7 14 ♕e3) 13 ♕d5 0-0 14 cxd7 ♗a6 15 e4 and White wins.

12...♗xd7 13 e3!

With the idea of ♖xd7 and ♗b5+. Note that Black cannot get the king into safety as he will lose instantly.

13...♖d8

13...0-0? 14 ♘xe5 ♕xe5 15 ♗xf6 ♕xf6 16 ♖xd7 and White wins a piece, or 13...0-0-0 14 ♗a6+ ♔b8 15 ♘xe5 and Black can only resign.

14 ♖xd7! ♖xd7

14...♔xd7 15 ♕a4+! ♔e6 16 ♗c4+ ♔f5 17 ♕c2+ ♔g4 18 h3+ ♔h5 19 g4+ and White wins.

15 ♗b5 ♗d6 16 ♖d1 0-0 17 ♗xd7 ♕xd7 18 ♗f4!

And Black has no defence.

18...c4

18...♘e4 19 ♕d5 ♕a4 20 ♗xd6 ♖d8 21 ♘e5 ♘xd6 22 ♘c4 and White wins a piece.

19 ♕c2! ♘e8 20 ♘g5! f5 21 ♕xc4+ ♔h8 22 ♗xd6 ♘xd6 23 ♕d5 ♖d8 24 ♘e6! ♕c8+ 25 ♔b1 ♖d7 26 ♕xd6! 1-0

Summary

The positions after 5 ♕b3 are less well known than other lines in the QID, and that is already a good reason for playing it. Furthermore it can give White some good pressure. After 5...a5 and 5...♕e7 Black is probably always going to be very slightly worse, while after the more active 5...c5 – with the idea of 6 a3 ♗a5! keeping the bishop – Black should be able to find a path to equality. This latter line is particularly worthy of experimentation.

1 d4 ♘f6 2 c4 e6 3 ♘f3 b6 4 ♘c3 ♗b4 5 ♕b3 *(D)*

     5...a5 – *Game 28*

     5...♕e7 – *Game 29*

5...c5 *(D)* **6 a3 ♗a5 7 ♗g5** *(D)* – *Game 30*

5 ♕b3

5...c5

7 ♗g5

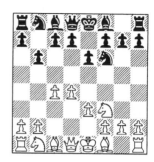

CHAPTER FIVE

4 e3

1 d4 ♘f6 2 c4 e6 3 ♘f3 b6 4 e3

The 4 e3 line is often favoured by players who do not like to study a lot of theory. Not because knowledge of the line is limited but because it has a tendency not to change. Consequently in the books (as in this one) Black is completely equal and the lines are rather harmless, but some older GMs (who might prefer playing with their kids) choose this line over others that they feel will demand more study. A large number of draws should be anticipated.

In fact the e3-line is rather harmless for Black and I simply cannot recommend it for White, despite strong players such as Yusupov and Gelfand having found it useful for their purposes occasionally. The system simply does not put Black under any pressure and therefore he should be able to equalise without too great an effort. Of course, that is if he is prepared. I just think that playing a more aggressive system will benefit your game generally, no matter who you are.

Game 31
Gelfand-Karpov
Sanghi Nagar (7) 1995

1 c4 ♘f6 2 d4 e6 3 ♘f3 b6 4 e3 ♗b7 5 ♘c3 d5

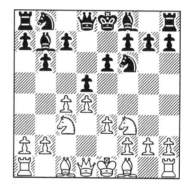

Black should play this for safety. After 5...♗e7!? 6 d5! White is playing against the bishop on b7. Nevertheless this is still playable for Black; only the main line is safer.

6 cxd5 exd5 7 ♗b5+!

Played in order to limit Black's influence on e4.

7...c6 8 ♗d3 ♗e7!?

8...♗d6 appears equally but we are following the path of the great masters here.

9 0-0 0-0 10 b3

White is taking it slowly. 10 e4 dxe4 11 ♘xe4 ♘bd7 12 ♖e1 ♖e8 13 ♘eg5 h6 14 ♘e4 ♘xe4 15 ♗xe4 ♗b4 was fine for Black in Kurajica-Dizdar, Zagreb 1993.

10...♘bd7

This is where the knight belongs. After

10...♘a6 11 ♗b2 c5 12 ♖c1 ♘c7 13 dxc5 bxc5 14 ♘a4 ♘e4 (14...♗e6 15 ♗xf6! would be uncomfortable for Black), 15 ♗xe4 was played in Langeweg-Schneider, Plovdiv 1983, but 15 ♘e5! is stronger, securing White an advantage. The main threat is f2-f3, but ♗xe4 followed by ♘d7 is also in the air.

11 ♗b2

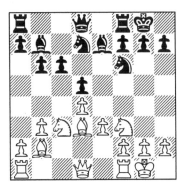

11...♗d6

This move order is actually not so exact. As we shall see ♘f3-f5 is a relevant manoeuvre, and therefore Black should start with 11...♖e8!, securing equality and ensuring that dropping back to f8 with the bishop no longer wastes time.

12 ♖c1

Others:

a) 12 ♕c2 ♖e8 13 ♖fe1 ♖c8 14 e4 (14 ♖ac1 c5 15 ♕e2 ♘e4 16 ♗a6 ♗xa6 17 ♕xa6 ♘df6 18 dxc5 ♖xc5 19 h3 ♕d7 20 ♕d3 ♖ec8 was equal in Portisch-Hübner, Manila 1990) 14...dxe4 15 ♘xe4 ♘xe4 16 ♗xe4 ♘f6 17 ♗f5 ♗c7 18 ♖xe8+ ♕xe8 19 ♘e5 c5 20 ♕d3 ♖e7 with equality, Polugaevsky-Karpov, Roqueburne 1992.

b) 12 ♘h4! ♖e8 13 ♘f5 ♗f8 14 ♖c1 was a little better for White in Petrosian-Taimanov, Zurich 1953.

12...♖e8 13 ♘e2 ♕e7 14 ♘g3 g6 15 ♕e2 ♗a3!

Apparently exchanging the 'good' bishop, but in reality preventing any problems on the long diagonal after ...c6-c5, and creating a

possible weak square on c3.

16 ♖fe1 ♕d6

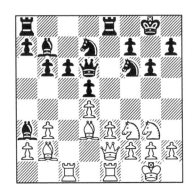

Black has equalised.

17 ♕c2 ♗xb2

17...a5!? is also possible.

18 ♕xb2 c5 19 ♖ed1 ♖ac8 20 ♘e2 ♖ed8

20...a6 21 ♖c2 cxd4 22 ♘exd4 gave White a little something in Gelfand-Karpov, Sanghi Nagar 1995.

21 ♖c2 cxd4 22 ♘exd4 ♖xc2 23 ♗xc2 ♖c8 24 ♖c1 ♘e4 25 ♗d3 ♖xc1+ 26 ♕xc1 ♕c5 27 ♕d1 b5 28 ♘e2 b4 29 ♕a1 ♕d6 30 ♕d4 ♕c5 31 ♕a1 ♕d6 32 h3 ♘dc5 33 ♗c2 ♕f6 34 ♕e5 ♕xe5 35 ♘xe5 f6 36 ♘f3 ♘e6 37 ♘e1 ♔f7 38 f3 ♘4c5 39 g4 a5 40 ♔f2 ♗a6 41 h4 h6 42 h5 gxh5 43 gxh5 ♔e7 44 ♘g3 ♘g7 45 ♗g6 ♔d6 46 ♔g2 ♗b5 47 ♘c2 ♘ce6 48 f4

White has played well and Black is still defending. Now Karpov's superior technique pays dividends.

48...♗d7 49 ♔f2 ♘c7 50 ♘d4 ♘b5 51 ♘xb5+?! ♗xb5 52 ♔e1 ♗d7 53 ♗d3 ♗g4 54 ♗e2 ♘f5!

Suddenly White has a difficult bishop endgame on his hands.

55 ♘xf5+

55 ♗xg4 ♘xg3 56 ♗f3 ♘f5 and White has problems.

55...♗xf5 56 ♔d2 ♔c5 57 ♗d3 ♗d7 58 ♗c2 ♗e8 59 ♗g6 ♗c6 60 ♗c2 ♗d7 61

♗d1 ♗h3 62 ♗f3 ♗f5 63 ♔c1 ♗d7 64 ♔d2 a4 65 bxa4

65 ♔d3 a3! and tricks like ...♗a4 will always be in the air.

65...♗xa4 66 ♗e2 ♗c6 67 ♗f3

67 ♗d3 d4 68 e4 ♗e8 69 ♗e2 ♗f7 and Black wins.

67...♗e8 68 ♗d1 d4 69 ♔d3 ♗b5+ 70 ♔d2 dxe3+ 71 ♔xe3 ♗e8 72 ♔e4 ♔d6 73 ♔f5

73 ♔d4 ♗f7 74 ♗b3 ♗xh5 75 ♔c4 ♗f7+ and the pawn ending is winning for Black.

73...♔e7 74 ♗e2 ♗f7 75 ♗d1 ♗xa2 76 ♔g6 b3 77 ♔xh6 b2 78 ♗c2 ♔f7!

Prevents all counterplay. After 78...b1♕ 79 ♗xb1 ♗xb1 80 ♔g7 the position is drawn.

79 ♗g6+ ♔f8! 80 ♗d3 b1♕ 81 ♗xb1 ♗xb1 82 f5 ♔f7 0-1

Game 32
Danner-Yu Shaoteng
Gyula 2000

---

1 d4 ♘f6 2 c4 e6 3 ♘f3 b6 4 e3 ♗b7 5 ♗d3 d5 6 0-0 ♗e7 7 b3

As this game shows Black has no problems in this line.

7...0-0 8 ♘c3 c5 9 ♗b2 cxd4 10 exd4 ♘c6

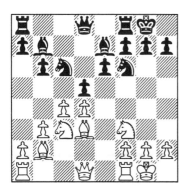

11 ♖c1

The main line. The alternatives are:

a) 11 ♕e2?! is not so good because the rook now gets stuck on a1 – 11...♘b4! 12 ♗b1 dxc4 13 bxc4 ♗xf3 14 gxf3 ♕xd4 15 ♘e4 ♕d8 16 ♖d1 ♕c7 17 ♘xf6+ ♗xf6 18 ♗xf6 gxf6 19 ♗xh7+ ♔g7! (19...♔xh7 20 ♕e4+! is not something Black allows) 20 ♖d4 ♖h8 21 ♖g4+ ♔f8 22 ♕b2 ♖xh7 23 ♕xb4+ ♕c5 and Black had a positional advantage in Grigorian-Karpov, Moscow 1976.

b) 11 ♖e1!? dxc4 (this does not look quite right; after 11...♖c8! White has nothing better than 12 ♖c1, transposing to the main line) 12 bxc4 ♖c8 13 ♖c1 ♖e8 14 d5! (suddenly this is possible) 14...♘b4 15 ♗b1 exd5 16 a3 d4 17 ♘xd4 ♘c6 18 ♘f5 ♕xd1 19 ♖cxd1 ♗f8 20 ♘d5 ♘d7 21 h3 ♖xe1+ 22 ♖xe1 ♖d8 and Black kept his stuff together in Portisch-Hjartarson, Szirak 1987, although the line looks shaky.

11...♖c8

This is the most natural move. Black is improving his position before taking action.

11...♘b4 12 ♗b1 ♖c8 13 ♘e5 ♘c6 14 ♘xc6 ♖xc6 15 ♕e2 ♖e8 16 ♘d1 ♗f8 17 ♘e3 was agreed drawn in Gelfand-Kramnik, Novgorod, 1997. It seems to me that White has more freedom to manoeuvre than is usual in this line.

11...♕d6?!, as in Portisch-Adorjan, Szirak 1987, is probably best met with 12 cxd5! exd5 13 ♖e1 ♖fe8 14 ♘b5 ♕f4 15 g3 ♕b8 16 ♘e5 and White has the advantage.

12 ♖e1!

The rook belongs here. After 12 ♕e2 ♖e8 13 ♖fd1 ♗f8 14 h3 g6 15 ♗b1 ♗h6! 16 ♘d2 dxc4 17 bxc4 ♘xd4 18 ♕e1 e5 Black was much better in Polgar-Hansen, Aabenraa 1989.

12...♘b4!

With this move Black takes control of the centre. Others seem to be inferior.

a) Now 12...♖e8!? comes out okay here, but I do not trust it completely: 13 cxd5 ♘xd5 14 ♘xd5 ♕xd5 (14...exd5 15 ♗f5 ♖c7 16 ♕e2 gave White an edge in Yusupov-Renet, Kaufbeuren 1993) 15 ♗e4 ♕h5 (15...♕d7? 16 ♖xc6! ♗xc6 17 ♘e5 ♕b7 18

♗xh7+! was winning in Portisch-de Firmian, Reggio Emilia 1989; while 15...♕d6 16 d5! led to White assuming the initiative in Yusupov-Rodriguez, Novi Sad 1990). Then 16 ♘e5 (certainly not forced...) 16...♕xd1 17 ♖exd1 ♘xe5 18 ♗xb7 ♖xc1 19 ♗xc1 ♖d8 20 ♔f1 ♖d7 21 ♗c8 ♖d8 22 ♗b7 ♖d7 23 ♗c8 ♖d8 24 ♗b7 was agreed drawn in Petrosian-Peters, Lone Pine 1978.

b) 12...♗b4 13 a3 ♗xc3 14 ♗xc3 ♘e7 15 ♘e5 looked better for White in Ambarcumjan-Shabalov, Seattle 2002, but I am sure that Shabalov only wanted to depart from the normal paths and somehow unbalance the situation.

13 ♗f1 ♘e4

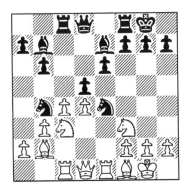

Clearly the most active move. Also possible is 13...♖e8 14 a3 ♘c6 15 cxd5 exd5 with equality in Nogueiras-Farago, Aosta 1990.

14 a3 ♘xc3 15 ♖xc3 ♘c6 16 ♕c2?!

White wants to prepare d4-d5, but this is too slow and Black is excellently placed to meet it. Better was 16 cxd5 ♕xd5 17 ♗c4 (17 ♗d3? ♘xd4 18 ♗xh7+ ♔xh7 19 ♕xd4 ♕xd4 20 ♘xd4 ♗f6 21 ♖d3 ♖fd8 was better for Black in Van der Werf-Van den Doel, Holland 1994) and now 17...♕d6?! 18 d5 ♘a5 (18...exd5 19 ♖d3! gives White the initiative) 19 ♖d3 ♘xc4 20 bxc4 ♖fd8 21 ♘d2? (21 ♗e5! ♕d7 [21...♕c5! 22 d6! with an advantage to White] 22 ♗xg7!! ♔xg7 23 ♘e5 and White has a winning attack on the way) 21...exd5 (now Black holds the lead) 22 cxd5

♗xd5 23 ♘f1 ♗f8 24 ♘e3 ♖c5 25 ♕d2 ♕h6 26 ♖d1 ♗d6 27 g3 ♗e4 28 ♘g4 ♕h3 29 f3 ♗xd3 30 ♕xd3 ♖d5 and White resigned in Lukacs-Atalik, Budapest 1991.

17...♕h5 heads for the safe spot. 18 d5 exd5 19 ♕xd5 ♕xd5 20 ♗xd5 ♗f6 21 ♖c2 ♖fd8 22 ♗xf6 ♖xd5 23 ♗b2 ♖cd8 was equal in Shariyazdanov-Chernyshov, Djakovo 1994.

16...♗f6 17 ♖d1 ♕d6 18 cxd5

18 ♖e3 dxc4 19 bxc4 ♘a5! and Black's pieces are much the better placed.

18...♕xd5 19 ♗c4 ♕h5 20 d5 ♘a5!

Black sacrifices a pawn for the two bishops and to open up the position in order to exploit White's uncoordinated pieces.

21 dxe6 ♘xc4

21...♗xc3? 22 ♕xc3 ♕g6 23 exf7+ ♔h8 24 ♖d6 is given by Gershon as winning. After 24...♖xc4 25 bxc4 ♕xf7 it is, presumably, not bad at all, but still – why should Black want this position in the first place if he does not win the exchange?

22 exf7+ ♕xf7 23 ♖xc4 ♖xc4 24 bxc4 ♗xb2 25 ♕xb2 ♗xf3 26 gxf3 ♕xf3

The number of weaknesses in White's camp spells the end.

27 ♖d4 h6

Creating an escape square for the king so the rook can be activated.

28 a4 ♖f6 29 ♕c2 ♖e6 30 ♕d2 ♖g6+ 31 ♔f1 ♕g2+ 32 ♔e2 ♖e6+ 33 ♔d1 ♕f1+ 34 ♔c2 ♖e2 35 ♖d8+ ♔h7 0-1

Game 33
Yusupov-Beliavsky
Austria 1998

This game is an illustration of one line that Black should try to avoid, and into which White players have occasionally had luck in tricking their opponents.

1 d4 ♘f6 2 ♘f3 e6 3 e3 b6 4 ♗d3 ♗b7 5 0-0 c5

Already the problems begin. After 5...d5! Black can play 6 ♘bd2 c5! and return to these solid positions against the Colle or, in the event of 6 c4 ♗e7, employ a transposition to the previous game.

6 c4 ♗e7 7 ♘c3 cxd4?!

7...d5! is still good enough for Black. 7...h6!? has also been tried (to avoid ♗xh7+ and thereby d4-d5, as in the following example) and now 7...0-0?! 8 d5! exd5 9 cxd5 d6 10 e4 ♘a6 11 ♖e1 ♘c7 12 ♖b1 ♖e8 13 a3 ♘d7 14 ♗f4 ♖c8 15 ♕d2 gave White an enormous advantage in Bukic-Ljubojevic, Bugojno 1978. The bishop is not well on b7.

8 exd4 d5

Seems forced. After 8...d6 9 d5! White has a better version of: 8...0-0 9 d5! ♘a6 10 ♗f4! d6 11 dxe6 fxe6 12 ♗g3, which gave White an edge in Malaniuk-Tiviakov, Moscow 1992.

9 cxd5 ♘xd5 10 ♘e5 0-0 11 ♕g4

Also possible is 11 ♕h5 g6!? (11...f5?! 12 ♗c4! secures White a strong position) 12 ♕h3 ♘xc3! 13 bxc3 ♘c6 14 ♕g4! with menacing play.

11...♘f6

Perhaps it was better to play 11...♘xc3 12 bxc3 ♘d7 13 ♗h6 ♗f6 14 ♖ad1, although White retains the initiative.

12 ♕h4?

This move gives Black a chance to fight. After 12 ♕g3! ♔h8 (12...♕xd4 13 ♗e3 ♕b4 14 a3! is clearly favourable to White according to L.Hansen) 13 ♗g5 h6 14 ♕h3 ♘g8 15 ♕h5! Black was in serious trouble in Dizdar-Hansen, West Berlin 1988.

12...♘bd7?!

Necessary is 12...♘e4! 13 ♕h5 ♘f6 14 ♕h4 ♘e4 15 ♕h5 ♘f6 16 ♕h4 ♘e4 17 ♕h5 ♘f6 18 ♕h4 ♘e4 19 ♕h3?! ♕xd4 20 ♗f4 ♘f6 21 ♘e2 ♕a4 22 ♖fc1 ♗a6 23 ♗c2 ♕e8 and Black held out in Kishnev-Schlosser, Budapest 1991.

12...♘c6? 13 ♗g5 g6 (13...h6 14 ♗xf6 ♗xf6 15 ♕e4 g6 16 ♘xc6 ♕c7 17 ♕f3 ♗g7 18 ♗e4 f5 19 ♘e7+ and wins) 14 ♗a6! and White was winning in Plaskett-Arkell, London 1991.

13 ♖d1 ♘e4?

After this it seems that Black is in dire straits. Imperative is 13...♖e8 14 ♗b5! a6 15 ♘c6 ♗xc6 16 ♗xc6 ♖a7 17 ♗f3, where White is simply better (Yudasin).

14 ♕h3 ♘df6

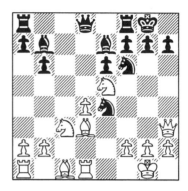

15 d5!!

Opening the d-file and thereby undermining e4 as a strongpoint.

15...♘xc3 16 bxc3 ♗xd5 17 ♗g5 h6

17...g6 18 ♕h4! h6 demonstrates how bad things are. In Polgar-Christiansen, San Francisco 1991, White was in the driving seat after 19 ♗xg6! fxg6 20 ♕xh6 ♘h7 21 ♕xg6+ ♔h8 22 ♗xe7 ♕xe7 23 c4 ♕h4 24 cxd5 ♕xf2+ 25 ♔h1 ♖f6 26 ♕e4 exd5 27 ♕xd5 ♖g8 28 h3 etc.

18 ♗xh6! gxh6 19 ♕xh6 ♕c7 20 ♕g5+ ♔h8 21 ♕h4+ 1-0

The moves ♕g3+ and ♘g6+ will soon win the queen.

Summary

The variation with e2-e3 is not really theoretical, but it can still be a minefield for Black. The right way to meet it has been presented in this chapter. If you play like Black in Danner – Yu Shaoteng, or the sidelines, you should not end up in any trouble. The most important lesson is not to play like Beliavsky against Yusupov. Many grandmasters have suffered in this line.

1 d4 ♘f6 2 c4 e6 3 ♘f3 b6 4 e3 ♗b7 *(D)* 5 ♗d3

    5 ♘c3 d5 6 cxd5 exd5 7 ♗b5+ *(D)* – *Game 31*

5...d5

    5...c5 6 0-0 ♗e7 7 ♘c3 cxd4 8 exd4 d5 – *Game 33*

6 0-0 ♗e7 7 b3 0-0 8 ♘c3 c5 *(D)* – *Game 32*

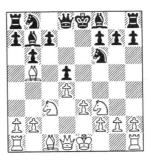
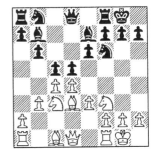

4...♗b7   *7 ♗b5+*   *8...c5*

CHAPTER SIX

4 g3 ♝b4+ and 4...♝a6 without 5 b3

1 d4 ♘f6 2 c4 e6 3 ♘f3 b6 4 g3 ♝b4+

In this chapter we are considering the lines arising after 4...♝b4+ and also those that occur after 4...♝a6 when White tries any move other than 5 b3. 4...♝a6 is the modern way of playing these Queen's Indian positions, and usually generates more lively play than 4...♝b7, which will be considered in Chapter 8. After 4...♝a6, White has several replies besides 5 b3. They include 5 ♕c2 and 5 ♕b3, which are not really dangerous for Black. Korchnoi has tried to come up with some ideas after 5 ♕c2, but I find it hard to believe in them. 5 ♕a4 has been played for a long time now. It was originally made popular by Michael Rohde in the 1980's, and has ever since been a serious alternative. 5 ♘bd2 is also a popular alternative, but as this chapter illustrates, Black can always find a safe path for equality in these lines.

Game 34
Magerramov-Makarichev
Moscow 1991

1 d4 ♘f6 2 c4 e6 3 ♘f3 b6 4 g3 ♝b4+!?

This is rather off-beat but does offer a chance for transposition to standard lines.

5 ♝d2 a5

The alternative is 5...♝xd2+ 6 ♕xd2 ♝a6 7 ♘a3!? (the knight is not so impressive out here; 7 b3 transposes to 5 b3 ♝b4+ 6 ♝d2 ♝xd2 7 ♕xd2 and Game 47) 7...0-0 8 ♝g2 ♝b7 9 0-0 d6 10 ♖fd1 ♘bd7 11 ♖ac1 ♕e7 12 ♘b5 a6 13 ♘c3 ♘e4 14 ♕d3 f5 15 ♘e1 ♘df6 16 d5 ♖ae8 17 e3 b5 18 b3 ♘c5 19 ♕c2 b4 20 ♘e2 e5 with an unclear game in Beliavsky-Miles, Tilburg 1986. Garcia Palermo-Groszpeter, Zenica 1987 went 10 ♘h4 ♝xg2 11 ♘xg2 c5 12 d5 exd5 13 cxd5 ♖e8 14 f3 a6 15 ♘c4 b5 16 ♘ce3 ♖e5 with equality, while 10 ♘b5 ♘bd7 11 ♖fd1 a6 12 ♘c3 ♘e4 13 ♘xe4 ♝xe4 14 ♖ac1 ♘f6 15 ♕e3 ♕b8 16 ♘e1 ♝xg2 17 ♘xg2 ♕b7 was equal in Yusupov-Kuzmin, Minsk 1982. White's space advantage is not so important because so many pieces have been exchanged.

6 ♝g2 0-0

Here White has a very slight advantage after 6...♝a6 7 ♝xb4 axb4 8 ♘e5 ♖a7! 9 a3 ♝c8 10 ♘d3 bxa3 11 ♖xa3 ♖xa3 12 ♘xa3 0-0 13 0-0, as in Browne-Spassky, Manila 1976.

7 0-0 ♝a6

7...♝b7 8 ♝g5 (8 ♕c2 h6 9 ♝f4 ♝e4 10 ♕d1 ♘c6 11 a3 ♝d6 12 ♝xd6 cxd6 13 ♘c3 d5 14 cxd5 exd5 15 e3 ♘e7 16 ♘e5 ♝xg2 17 ♔xg2 d6 18 ♘d3 was also better for White in Ivanchuk -Speelman, Roquebrune 1992) 8...♗e7 9 ♘c3 ♘e4 10 ♘xe4 ♗xe4 11 ♗xe7 ♕xe7 12 ♕d2 d6 13 ♕e3 ♗xf3 14 ♗xf3 ♖a7 15 ♖ac1 with advantage to White in Karpov-Van der Wiel, Brussels 1987.

8 b3

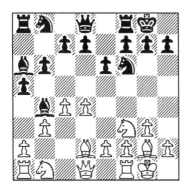

8...d5

This is the main move here, but there are some important alternatives:

a) 8...♖a7 9 ♗f4 a4 (9...d5!? 10 c5 ♘e4 11 a3 ♗c3 12 cxb6 cxb6 13 ♖a2 b5 14 ♘g5! ♘xg5 15 ♘xc3 b4 16 axb4 axb4 17 ♘b5 ♖d7 18 ♕c1 with an edge for White) 10 ♕c2 d5 11 ♖d1 ♕c8 12 ♘e5 c5 13 dxc5 ♗xc5 14 ♘c3 and now, instead of 14...b5?, which was played in Avrukh-Mikhalevski, Beersheba 1997, Black should play 14...axb3 15 axb3 dxc4, although White is better after 16 ♘xc4.

b) 8...c6 9 ♕c2 d5 10 ♗xb4 axb4 11 a3 ♗b7 12 ♘bd2 bxa3 13 b4 ♘a6 14 ♕b3 dxc4 15 ♘xc4 ♘d5 16 ♖xa3 ♘dxb4 17 ♘fe5 ♕c7 18 ♖b1 gave White excellent compensation for the pawn in Zimmerman-Letreguilly, Budapest 1994.

c) 8...♗b7 transposes to Games 48-50 with 4...♗a6 5 b3 ♗b7 6 ♗g2 ♗b4+ 7 ♗d2 a5 8 0-0 0-0.

9 cxd5 ♘xd5

9...exd5 10 ♘e5 is a structural advantage for White.

10 ♖e1 c5 11 e4 ♘f6 12 a3! ♗xd2 13 ♘bxd2 ♘bd7 14 e5 ♘d5 15 ♘e4

White has won the opening battle. The

d6-square secures him a slight pull.

15...♕b8?!

15...♕e7! (Magarramov) 16 ♘d6 ♖ad8! 17 ♖c1 cxd4 18 ♘xd4 ♘xe5 19 ♘c4!? ♘xc4 20 bxc4 ♘f6 21 ♘c6 ♕c7 22 ♘xd8 ♖xd8 with just about enough compensation, although it is still White who is trying for a win.

16 ♘d6 cxd4?!

Now White gets the chance to start an attack. Necessary was 16...h6.

17 ♕xd4 ♘c5

17...♖d8? 18 ♘xf7! ♔xf7 19 ♘g5+ ♔e7 20 ♘xe6! would eliminate Black completely.

18 ♘g5! ♕d8

18...h6? 19 ♘gxf7! ♖xf7 20 ♗xd5 exd5 21 ♘xf7 ♔xf7 22 e6+! ♘xe6 23 ♕xd5 ♗c8 24 ♖ac1 and White wins.

19 ♕g4 ♖a7

Black is trying very hard to defend. 19...h6? 20 ♘gxf7 ♖xf7 21 b4! and White wins.

20 b4 ♘d3 21 ♗e4! g6 22 ♘xe6 ♘xe5

Black is running out of defensive resources. After 22...♕d7? White wins with 23 ♗xd5 ♘xe1 24 ♖xe1 ♗c8 25 h3! fxe6 26 ♘xc8 exd5 27 ♘xa7.

23 ♘xd8 ♘xg4

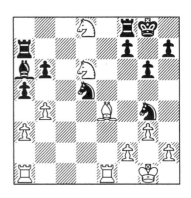

24 ♘8xf7!

A nice combination that in practice wins the game.

24...♘df6 25 ♗c2 ♖axf7 26 ♗b3! ♘h6 27 ♘xf7 ♘xf7 28 ♖e6 ♔g7 29 ♖xb6 ♗c8 30 bxa5 ♘g5 31 f4 ♘h3+ 32 ♔g2

♖e8 33 ♖c1 ♖e2+ 34 ♔f1 ♖f2+?! 35 ♔e1 ♘e4 36 ♖c2 1-0

Game 35
Anastasian-Brodsky
Moscow 1992

---

1 d4 ♘f6 2 c4 e6 3 ♘f3 b6 4 g3 ♗a6 5 ♕c2!?

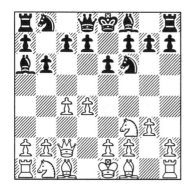

This idea is not particularly popular. The main reason is probably 5...d5, which appears to be a very easy route to equality.

5...c5

ECO suggests this move but does not include 6 e4 in its world view.

a) After 5...d5! we have:

a1) 6 b3 ♗b4+ 7 ♗d2 ♗xd2+ 8 ♘bxd2 0-0 9 ♗g2 c5 promises Black equality, and 10 e3 ♘c6 11 dxc5 dxc4 12 bxc4 ♘b4 13 ♕b1 ♘d3+ much more than that in Vacek-Hausner, Brno 1969.

a2) 6 ♘bd2 ♗e7 7 ♗g2 0-0 8 0-0 c5 9 dxc5 (9 ♖d1 ♘c6 10 ♕a4 ♕c8 11 dxc5 dxc4 12 ♘e5 ♘xe5 13 ♗xa8 b5 14 ♕a5 ♖d8 15 ♗g2 ♗xc5 was crushing in Udovcic-Rakic, Sombor 1957) 9...♗xc5 10 a3 ♘bd7 11 ♕a4 ♗b7 12 cxd5 exd5 13 b4 ♗d6 14 ♗b2 a5 15 b5 ♖e8 16 e3 ♘e4 and Black had sufficient counterplay in Blom-Johannessen, Marianske Lazne 1961.

a2) 6 cxd5 is the most logical move: 6...exd5 7 ♗g2 ♗b4+ 8 ♘c3 0-0 9 0-0 ♖e8! and Black is ready to give up the dark-

squared bishop to concentrate on the light squares. To be successful in this strategy he needs to keep the bishop outside the pawn chain, meaning on the b1-h7 diagonal. Lilloni-Gereben, San Benedetto 1957 continued 10 ♖e1 c5 11 a3 ♗xc3 12 bxc3 ♘bd7 13 e3 ♕c7 14 ♕a4?! (doing nothing about solving the most important problem – where does the queen's bishop belong?) 14...♗d3 15 ♗b2 (hardly a dream spot for the bishop) 15...b5 16 ♕d1 ♗e4 17 ♗f1 c4 18 ♘d2 ♗g6 19 ♗g2 ♘b6 20 f3 ♘a4 and Black was better.

b) 5...♘c6!? tries to exploit White's lack of development. I am not sure Black equalises with this line, but it does result in an interesting position, e.g. 6 a3?! (6 ♗g2! must be the right move – after 6...♘b4 7 ♕b3 d5 8 ♘e5 [8 cxd5 ♕xd5 is already equal] 8...dxc4 9 ♕d1! [9 ♘xc4 ♕xd4 10 ♗xa8 ♗xc4 11 ♕d1 ♕xd1+ 12 ♔xd1 ♗c5 is terrible for White] 9...b5 10 a4 c6 11 axb5 ♗xb5 12 ♘c3 ♘bd5 13 e4 ♘xc3 14 bxc3 and White has a strong centre to compensate for his pawn deficit). Returning to 6 a3, play might continue 6...♗b7 7 ♕d3 e5! 8 dxe5 ♘xe5 9 ♘xe5 ♗xh1 10 f3 ♗d6 11 ♕c3 ♕e7 12 ♘g4 ♘xg4 13 ♕xg7 0-0-0 14 ♕xg4 h5 15 ♕f5 ♖dg8 16 ♗f4 ♗xf4 17 ♕xf4 h4 18 g4 f5 19 gxf5 ♗g2 20 f6 ♕d6 21 ♕e4 c6 22 f7 ♖f8 23 ♗xg2 ♕xh2 24 ♕g4 h3 25 ♗f1 ♖xf7 26 ♘d2 ♕e5 27 ♗xh3 ♖g7 28 ♕e4 ♕g3+ 29 ♔d1 ♕xh3 30 ♔c2 ♖g2 31 ♕d3, and Black had great winning chances in Korchnoi-Kachiani Gersinska, Willingen 1999.

6 ♗g2

After this move Black can equalise. I am less sure about 6 e4!, although it has been played only once – 6...cxd4 7 ♘xd4 ♗b7 8 ♗g2 a6 9 0-0 ♕c7 10 ♖e1 ♘c6 11 ♘xc6 ♕xc6 12 b3 ♗e7 13 ♘d2 d6 14 ♗b2 0-0 15 ♕c3 appears to be very slightly better for White. After 15...♖fc8 16 g4 ♘e8 17 ♕g3 ♗f6 18 ♗xf6 ♘xf6 19 g5 ♘d7 20 ♖ad1 ♕c5 21 ♘f1 White is better, and in Korchnoi-Lau, Hessen 1999, Korchnoi more or less outplayed his opponent by advancing the h-pawn.

6...♘c6 7 dxc5 ♗xc5 8 0-0 0-0 9 ♗g5!? ♖c8 10 ♕a4 ♗b7 11 ♘c3 h6 12 ♗f4! ♕e7 13 a3 a5?

13...♗d6 would have kept the position more or less equal. Now Black has problems.

14 ♖ad1 ♖fd8 15 ♘e5

The b-file is a terrible source of weakness for Black.

15...♗a8 16 ♘d3!

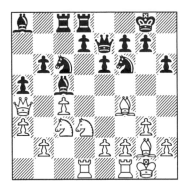

White has a clear advantage.

16...♘h5 17 ♗c1 ♗d4

17...♘d4 18 ♗xa8 ♖xa8 19 ♗e3!? ♘f5 20 ♗xc5 bxc5 21 ♘e4, with the idea g3-g4 is given by Dautov. White is close to winning.

18 ♘b5 ♘f6 19 ♗f4 ♘e8 20 ♖d2 ♗f6 21 ♖fd1 d5 22 cxd5 exd5 23 ♖c2 ♘a7 24 ♘xa7 ♕xa7 25 ♖dc1 ♖xc2 26 ♖xc2 ♕e7 27 ♕b5 ♕e6 28 h4 g5!? 29 hxg5 hxg5 30 ♗c1 ♖b8 31 ♘e1! ♘d6 32 ♕d3 ♘e4 33 ♘f3 ♘c5 34 ♕d1 ♕f5 35 ♗e3 ♗c6 36 ♖d2

Entering some complicated tactics. 36 ♗xc5? ♗a4 37 e4 ♗xc2 38 ♕xc2 ♕xe4 would turn the tables, but 36 b3!?, as suggested by Dautov, might improve.

36...♗a4 37 ♖xd5 ♕xf3 38 ♗xf3 ♗xd1 39 ♖xd1 ♗xb2 40 ♗xg5 ♗xa3 41 ♗f6!

Now White also has an attack on the kingside to make him happy.

41...♘e6?! 42 ♖d7! ♘f8 43 ♖a7 ♘h7 44 ♗e5 ♖d8 45 ♗h5 f6 46 ♗f7+ ♔h8 47 ♗c3 ♖c8 48 ♗d2 ♗c1 49 ♗e6 ♖d8 50

♗c3 ♗h6 51 ♗f5 ♗g7 52 ♗xh7 ♔xh7 53 ♗xf6 ♖g8 54 ♔f1 1-0

Game 36
Barlov-Beliavsky
Yugoslavia 1992

1 d4 ♘f6 2 c4 e6 3 ♘f3 b6 4 g3 ♗a6 5 ♕b3

This line can at best be described as completely harmless. After...

5...♘c6!

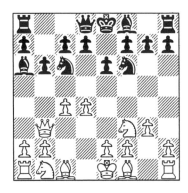

...White is forced to protect e4 an additional time.

6 ♘bd2 d5!

Black's forces are quickly finding a way into the game.

7 ♕a4

Perhaps it is better to simply play 7 cxd5 exd5 (7...♕xd5!? must also equalise) 8 ♕a4 ♗b7 9 ♗g2 ♗d6 10 0-0 0-0, e.g. 11 ♘b1 ♘e4 12 ♗f4 ♖e8 13 ♖c1 ♗xf4 14 gxf4 ♘e7 15 ♘c3 ♘f5 and Black had equalised in Gelfand-Leko, Monaco 2002.

7...♗b7 8 ♗g2 ♗d6 9 0-0

9 ♘e5 looks good, but after 9...0-0! 10 ♘xc6 ♕d7 Black retains his piece with no minuses whatsoever, and complete equality. Chekhov-Bareev, Germany 1992 continued 11 0-0 ♖fe8 12 ♕c2 ♗xc6 13 b3 (13 ♖d1 ♖ad8 with equality, as in Grivas-Delchev, Varna 1994, is probably better) 13...e5! 14 ♗b2 dxc4 15 ♗xc6 ♕xc6 16 ♕xc4 ♕b7 17

♖ac1?! (17 dxe5 ♗xe5 18 ♗xe5 ♖xe5 is active and quite pleasant for Black) 17...b5! 18 ♕c2 exd4 19 ♘f3 c5 20 b4 cxb4 21 ♗xd4 ♘e4 22 ♖fd1 a5 23 ♘h4 ♗f8 24 f3 ♘c3 25 ♗xc3 bxc3 26 e4 b4 27 ♖d5 ♖ed8 28 ♖cd1 ♖xd5 29 exd5 ♖d8 30 ♕d3 ♖xd5 and White resigned.

9...0-0 10 a3 a5!? 11 ♕c2 a4 12 ♖e1 ♗e7?

This move makes very little sense at all. Correct is 12...e5 13 dxe5 ♘xe5 14 ♘xe5 ♗xe5 15 ♘f3 ♗d6 16 ♘d4 ♗c5 17 ♘f5 ♖e8! with an unclear game. White is not very well co-ordinated to exploit the well placed knight.

13 e3 ♕d7 14 cxd5 exd5 15 ♘b1!

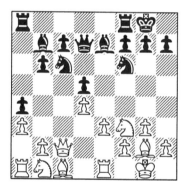

The knight belongs on c3.

15...♘a5!?

An interesting pawn sacrifice.

16 ♘e5 ♕e8 17 ♕xc7 ♗d8 18 ♕c2 ♘b3 19 ♖a2 ♖c8 20 ♘c3 ♘e4 21 ♘d3 ♗f6

More accurate is 21...f5!, with the idea of 22 ♖d1 g5 followed by ...f5-f4 etc.

22 ♖d1 h5 23 ♗d2!

White has the advantage.

23...♗g5 24 ♗e1 h4 25 ♖aa1!?

As the a4-pawn also falls, this makes good sense.

25...♘xa1 26 ♖xa1 ♕e6 27 ♕d1 ♖fe8 28 ♘xa4 ♕h6 29 ♘c3 ♖cd8 30 f4!

Black is strategically lost. His rooks have no play.

30...♗f6 31 ♘xe4 dxe4 32 ♘f2 ♕g6 33

♕g4?!

33 g4! is simpler.

33...♕h7 34 ♖c1 ♗c8 35 ♕e2 hxg3 36 hxg3 ♕g6 37 g4?

Allowing a strong combination. After 37 ♖c6, planning g3-g4, Black is busted.

37...♗xd4! 38 exd4?

38 ♖xc8 ♖xc8 39 exd4 retains the better chances. Now Black takes over.

38...e3 39 ♘d3 ♗xg4 40 ♕c2 ♗f5 41 ♕c6 ♗xd3 42 ♕xg6 ♗xg6 43 ♗c3 ♖d6 44 ♔h2 ♗f5 45 ♖e1 ♖h6+ 46 ♔g3 ♖g6+ 47 ♔h2 ♖g4 48 d5 ♖xf4-+ 49 ♔g3 ♖g4+ 50 ♔f3 ♖g6 51 ♗h1 ♗e4+ 52 ♔e2 ♗xh1 53 ♖xh1 f5 54 ♗b4 ♖g2+ 55 ♔d3 ♖xb2 56 d6 e2 57 ♖e1 f4 58 ♔c3 ♖xb4 0-1

Game 37
Barbero-Cebalo
Caorle 1987

1 d4 ♘f6 2 c4 e6 3 ♘f3 b6 4 g3 ♗a6 5 ♘bd2

This is one of the main systems and should offer White a modest chance for an advantage.

5...♗b4!? 6 ♕b3

6 ♕c2 ♗b7 7 ♗g2 a5 8 0-0 d5 9 ♘e5 0-0 10 cxd5 exd5 11 ♘df3 ♘e4 12 ♗e3 ♖e8 led to equality in Portisch-Bronstein, Las Palmas 1972, as did 6 ♕a4 c5 7 a3 ♗xd2+ 8 ♗xd2 cxd4 9 ♗g2 ♗b7 10 0-0 ♗c6! 11 ♕d1 ♗xf3 12 ♗xf3 ♘c6 13 ♗f4 0-0 14 ♗d6 ♖e8 15 ♗xc6 dxc6 16 ♕xd4 c5 17 ♕f4 ♘h5 18 ♕e5 f6 19 ♕xh5 ♕xd6, Dizdar-Palac, Medulin 1997.

6...c5

Best. 6...♘c6 7 d5 ♗xd2+ 8 ♗xd2 ♘e7 (8...♘a5 9 ♕a4! ♘e4 10 ♗xa5 bxa5 11 dxe6 fxe6 12 ♗g2 0-0 13 0-0 gave White a clear advantage in Vaganian-Nogueiras, Montpellier 1985) 9 ♗c3 ♘f5 10 ♘d2 favours White. Kasparov-Speelman, La Valetta 1980 continued 10...♘d6?! 11 f3! 0-0 12 e4 and White was now clearly better. After 12...exd5 13 cxd5 ♗xf1 14 ♖xf1 a5 15 e5 a4 16 ♕c2 ♕e8 17 ♔f2 ♘xd5 18 ♕d3 ♕e6 19 exd6 the lead had grown to being technically winning. An improvement is 10...♕e7 11 0-0-0 exd5 12 cxd5 ♘e4 13 ♘xe4 ♕xe4 14 f3 ♕e3+ 15 ♗d2 ♕xb3 16 axb3 ♘d4 17 b4 with a plus for White (Kasparov).

6...♕e7 7 ♗g2 ♗b7 8 0-0 ♗xd2 9 ♗xd2 0-0 10 ♖ad1 gave White a slight edge in Alexandria-Chiburdanidze, Tbilisi 1981.

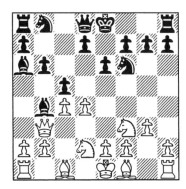

7 ♗g2!

7 a3 ♗xd2+ 8 ♗xd2 ♘c6 9 d5 (9 ♗g2 cxd4 10 ♕a4 ♕c8 11 0-0 ♗b7 12 b4 ♘e4 was a pawn in Nesis-Sanakoev, corr. 1986, while 9 dxc5 bxc5 10 ♕c2 looks best, but White has no chance of an advantage) 9...♘a5 10 ♗xa5 bxa5 11 dxe6 fxe6 12 ♕c2 ♖b8 13 ♗h3 ♕b6 and Black has the better prospects, Fedorowicz-Seirawan, South Bend 1981.

7...♘c6

7...♗b7 8 dxc5 ♗xc5 9 0-0 0-0 10 ♕c2 ♗e7 11 b3 d6 12 ♗b2 ♘bd7 was equal in Oll-Andersson, Tallinn 1998. But the simple 8 0-0 looks enough for an edge.

8 dxc5

8 a3 transposes to the note to White's 7th move.

8...bxc5!?

8...♗xc5 9 0-0 0-0 seems to equalise, e.g. 10 a3 ♗e7 11 ♕a4 ♗b7 12 e4 ♕c7 13 ♕c2 ♘e5! 14 b3 ♘xf3+ 15 ♗xf3 ♗d6 16 ♗g2 ♖ac8 17 ♗b2 ♗e5 with equality, Tibensky-

Hracek, Slovakia 2000, or 10 ♕a4 ♗b7 11 ♘b3 ♗e7 12 ♖d1 ♕c8 13 ♗f4 ♘b4 14 ♘e5 ♗xg2 15 ♔xg2 ♕b7+ 16 ♔g1 d5, Redzepagic-Popovic, Novi Sad 1985.

9 0-0

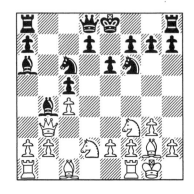

9...♖b8?

The rook is misplaced here due to a future ♗f4. Both alternatives are better.

a) 9...♖c8 10 ♕c2 0-0 is interesting. We don't know much about it because 11 ♘b3 ♘d4 12 ♘bxd4 cxd4 13 b3 d5 14 ♘xd4 e5 15 a3 ♗c5 16 ♘f5 dxc4 17 bxc4 ♗xc4 was a display of poor opening play that left Black in front in Dlugy-Ehlvest, Mazatlan 1988. But this looks like the route that Black should pursue.

b) 9...0-0 10 a3 ♗xd2 11 ♗xd2 d5 12 cxd5 exd5 13 ♖fc1 was, potentially, slightly better for White in Kempinski-Hansen, Hamburg 1999.

10 ♕c2 0-0 11 ♘b3! ♕e7?!

11...♘a5 12 ♗f4! d6 13 ♘fd2 gives White the advantage but is nonetheless preferable.

12 ♗f4

12 a3! ♗a5 13 ♘xa5 ♘xa5 14 ♕a4 ♘b3 15 ♕xa6 ♘xa1 16 ♗f4 ♖b6 17 ♕xa7 ♖xb2 18 ♖xa1 has been suggested as giving White an advantage.

12...e5

Forced. After 12...d6? 13 ♖fd1 ♖fd8 14 a3 ♗a5 15 ♘g5 White wins a piece.

13 ♗g5 ♖fc8?!

Imperative is 13...♘d4 14 ♘bxd4 cxd4 15

♕a4 ♖b6 16 a3 ♗d6 17 ♘d2! ♗b8 18 b4 d6 19 b5 ♗c8 20 ♗c6!, when White has some positional pluses. Now he is winning.

14 a3 ♗a5 15 ♘xa5 ♘xa5 16 ♕a4!
♗xc4 17 ♕xa5 ♗xe2 18 ♖fe1 ♗xf3 19
♗xf3 h6 20 ♗xf6 ♕xf6 21 ♕c3 d6 22
♗d5 c4 23 ♖e3 ♖b3 24 ♕d2 ♖xe3 25
fxe3 ♕g5 26 ♖c1 ♕g4 27 ♕f2 ♔h8 28
♕xf7 ♕e2 29 ♕f2 ♕d3 30 e4 a5 31
♖xc4 ♖xc4 32 ♕f8+ ♔h7 33 ♗g8+ 1-0

Game 38
Salov-Karpov
Wijk aan Zee 1998

---

1 d4 ♘f6 2 c4 e6 3 ♘f3 b6 4 g3 ♗a6 5 ♘bd2 ♗b7

5...c5 6 ♗g2 ♗b7 is just a transposition, but 6...♘c6! is much stronger, as can be seen in the next game.

6 ♗g2 c5

6...♗e7 7 0-0 0-0 8 b3 normally leads to transposition after 8...d5.

7 e4!

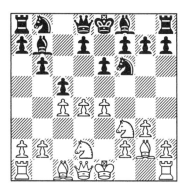

Time has given this move the stamp of approval. 7 d5!? exd5 8 ♘h4 g6! 9 cxd5 ♗g7 10 ♘c4 0-0 11 ♘d6 (11 0-0 d6 12 ♗f4 ♗a6! 13 ♖c1 ♗xc4 14 ♖xc4 b5 is fine for Black) 11...♗a6 12 a4 ♘e8 13 ♘e4 d6 14 0-0 ♘d7 15 ♖b1 ♘df6 led to equality in van Wely-Psakhis, Leeuwarden 1993.

7...cxd4

Black cannot exploit the e-pawn's mo-

mentarily weakness: 7...♘xe4?! 8 ♘e5! d5 (8...♘c3?? 9 ♕h5 g6 10 ♕h3) 9 ♕a4+ ♘d7 10 cxd5 ♘xd2 11 ♗xd2 ♗xd5 12 ♗xd5 exd5 13 0-0 f6 14 ♖fe1 fxe5 15 ♖xe5+ ♗e7 16 ♗g5?! b5! with a quick draw in Goldin-Smirin, Moscow (GMA) 1989, but Avrukh recommends 16 ♖ae1! (with the threat of ♗g5), when 16...♔f7 17 ♖xd5! appears to be decisive.

After 7...d6 8 d5 exd5 9 cxd5 ♗a6 10 ♗f1 ♕c8 11 ♕a4+ ♘fd7 12 ♗xa6 ♕xa6 13 ♕xa6 ♘xa6 14 0-0 ♘b4 15 ♘c4 f5 16 exf5 ♘f6 17 ♗g5 ♘bxd5 18 ♖ad1 White was clearly better in Sosonko-Miles, Wijk aan Zee 1981.

8 0-0!

The modern treatment – Black cannot cling on to the pawn. Other options promise nothing:

a) 8 e5 ♘e4! 9 0-0 ♘xd2 10 ♗xd2 ♗xf3 11 ♕xf3 ♘c6 12 ♕xc6 dxc6 13 ♗xc6+ ♕d7 14 ♗xd7+ ♔xd7 was completely equal in Salov-Karpov, Wijk aan Zee 1993.

b) 8 ♘xd4 ♗c5! and now:

b1) 9 ♘4b3 ♗e7 10 0-0 ♕c7 11 ♖e1 d6 12 ♘d4 0-0 13 b3 a6 14 ♗b2 ♘bd7 was equal in Piket-Salov, Wijk An Zee 1992.

b2) 9 ♘c2 ♕c7 10 0-0 ♗e7 and now in Agdestein-Hjartarson, Belgrade 1989, White should have maintained the balance with 11 b3. Instead 11 e5?! was too optimistic. After 11...♗xg2 12 exf6 ♗xf1 13 fxe7 ♗d3 14 ♕f3 ♗xc2 15 ♕xa8 ♔xe7 16 b3 ♖d8! 17 ♗a3+ ♔e8 18 ♕f3 ♕e5! 19 ♖c1 ♗g6 Black had a clear lead.

b3) 9 ♘b5 a6 10 ♘c3 ♕c7 11 ♕e2 ♗e7 with complete equality in Welin-Chernin, Lugano 1989.

8...d6

The alternatives favour White:

a) 8...♘xe4?! has never been played but has been analysed by Cifuentes, among others. After 9 ♘e5 d5 10 cxd5 exd5 11 ♕a4+ ♘d7 12 ♘xe4! dxe4 13 ♗h3 b5 (13...♗c8 14 ♕c6 ♖b8 15 ♘xf7! ♕f6 16 ♗e6! ♖g8 17 ♗g5 and White wins) 14 ♕xb5 ♗c8 15 ♕c6 ♖b8 16 ♘xf7! White wins. Black's best option seems to be 9...♗d6 10 ♘xf7 ♚xf7 11 ♘xe4 ♗xe4 12 ♗xe4 ♘c6 13 ♕f3+ ♚g8 14 ♗xc6 dxc6 15 ♕xc6 ♖c8 16 ♕e4, although White still has a pleasant structural advantage, while 9...♘d6 10 ♗xb7 ♘xb7 11 ♕f3 does not work out well...

b) 8...♘c6?! 9 e5 ♘g4 10 h3 ♘h6 11 ♘e4 gives White a clear advantage.

c) 8...♗c5?! 9 e5 ♘e4 10 ♘g5! ♘c3 11 bxc3 ♗xg2 12 ♚xg2 ♕xg5 13 ♘f3 is given as clearly better for White by Ftacnik. In fact 13 cxd4! looks even stronger...

9 ♘xd4 a6!?

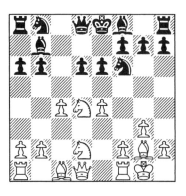

Here there are a number of alternatives but it would seem to be an enormous waste of energy trying to memorise them all. White has a simple plan in a2-a4-a5 followed by a knight transfer to a5. That is really all you need to know, and that ...♘bd7 often runs into e4-e5 after ♖e1, as we shall see. 9...♘bd7 10 ♖e1 (10 a4 ♘c5 is premature) 10...♕c8 11 a4! a6 12 a5 e5 13 ♘f5 g6 14 ♘e3 ♗e7 15 axb6 0-0 16 b4 was poor for Black in Oll-Kengis, Riga 1995. 12...♖b8 has been suggested as an improvement, but to me it still looks as if White is a whole lot better. 10...♗e7?! has also been investigated, 11 e5 ♗xg2 12 exf6 ♗xf6 13 ♘xe6 fxe6 14 ♚xg2 ♘c5 15 ♘e4 giving White a clear advantage according to Avrukh. Browne-Bradford, Dallas 1996 continued 10...♕c7?! 11 ♘b5 ♕b8 12 c5! (freeing the c4-square for the knight) 12...dxc5 13 ♘c4 e5 14 f4

♗c6 15 ♘c3! b5 16 fxe5 and White had a powerful initiative. Finally 10...e5!? 11 ♘b5 a6 12 ♘c3 ♗e7 13 ♘f1 ♖c8 14 ♘e3 0-0 15 a4 was slightly worse for Black in Cramling-Chiburdanidze, Groningen 1997, although Black's position remains solid.

10 ♖e1 ♕c7

10...♘bd7 11 e5! ♗xg2 12 exf6 ♗b7 (12...♗xf6 13 ♘xe6 fxe6 14 ♚xg2 ♘c5 15 ♘e4 ♘xe4 16 ♖xe4 was clearly better for White in Browne-Burger, Philadelphia 1990) 13 fxg7 ♗xg7 14 ♘e4 0-0? (14...♗xe4 15 ♖xe4 0-0 16 ♖g4 gives White an edge) 15 ♘xd6 ♘e5 16 ♘xb7 ♕xd4 17 ♕xd4 ♘f3+ 18 ♚f1 ♘xd4 19 ♖d1 ♖ab8 20 ♘d6 ♖fd8 21 ♘e4 f5 22 ♘c3 and White was winning in Tregubov-Grooten, Amsterdam 2001.

11 a4!

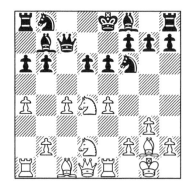

The reason why this is possible here and not in other hedgehog positions is the knight on d2 and the excellent support it adds to the c-pawn. White is also more flexibly placed to push with b2-b4.

11...♘c6

11...♘bd7 12 a5 ♗e7 13 ♘2b3 ♖d8 14 axb6 ♘xb6 15 ♘a5 was better for White in Bönsch-Chuchelov, Berlin 1996.

12 ♘xc6 ♗xc6 13 a5 ♖b8?!

This is probably because Karpov overlooked White's 15th move. Now Black is in trouble. 13...♗e7, developing, is necessary.

14 axb6 ♕xb6

14...♖xb6 leaves the rook awkwardly

placed without solving the problem of the a6-pawn. After 15 b3, with the idea &b2-d4, Black has problems and is still not developed.

15 &e3! &d7

Now Black is in trouble as developing is not possible. Note that 15...&e7? 16 &b3 &c7 17 &xb8+ &xb8 18 e5 &xg2 19 exf6 wins for White.

16 &b3 &a7

Or 16...&c7 17 &xa6 &xb3 18 &xb3 &b7 19 &a1 &xe4 20 &a5 &a8 21 &xe4 &xe4 22 &f4 and the lead in development is again a key factor.

17 &ba3

White exerts maximum pressure on the primary weakness.

17...&b7

17...&c5 18 &b3! &xb3 19 &xb3 &xb3 20 &xb3 &e7 21 &a2 and the a-pawn is difficult to protect without allowing &a4+.

18 b4 &b6?!

Black is wasting time. 18...&e7 has to be tried, although White has many strong opportunities.

19 &a4! &e7 20 &b2 &f6?

The lesser evil 20...e5 is tantamount to positional resignation.

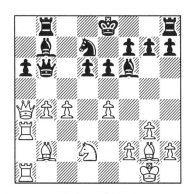

21 e5!!

Fully exploiting the lead in development.

21...&xe5

21...dxe5 22 &d3! and Black will never escape as c4-c5 is coming.

22 c5 &c7

22...&b5 23 &xb5 axb5 24 &xe5 and White wins.

23 &xe5 dxe5 24 &xb7 &xb7 25 c6 &b6 26 &xa6 &xc6 27 &c4!

Winning a piece and the game. The threat is &a5.

27...&b8 28 &xb6 0-0

28...&xb6 29 &a8+ and White wins a rook.

29 &c4 &e4 30 &e3 &d5 31 &xe5 &fc8 32 &d3 1-0

Game 39
Tregubov-Shaposhnikov
Samara 2000

1 d4 &f6 2 c4 e6 3 &f3 b6 4 g3 &a6 5 &bd2 c5

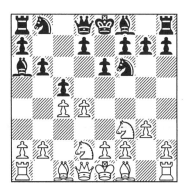

In my opinion this line is unnecessarily

risky for Black.

6 e4

The only serious option. 6 ♗g2 ♘c6 7 ♘e5!? (White can also play safe, but he will gain no advantage) 7...♘xd4 8 e3 ♘f5 9 ♕a4 ♕c8 10 ♗xa8 ♕xa8 11 ♖g1 ♗c8 12 b3 ♘e4 13 ♗b2 ♘xd2 14 ♔xd2 ♗e7 15 ♖ad1 f6 16 ♘d3 ♗b7 gave Black the better chances in Timman-Dautov, Forchheim 2000.

6...cxd4 7 e5!

White needs to act now to gain an advantage. 7 ♗g2?! is a waste of time. Remember that White has sacrificed the d4-pawn! von Herman-Hübner, Altenkirchen 1999 went 7...♘c6 8 e5 ♘g4 9 0-0 ♖b8 10 ♖e1 ♗c5 11 h3 ♘e3, and White resigned.

7...♘g4 8 h3 ♘h6

Now the knight is worse off and White can take time to develop.

9 ♗g2 ♘c6 10 0-0 ♘f5

10...♗e7 11 a3 0-0 12 b4 ♗b7 13 ♘e4 ♘xb4? (13...♘f5!? is better, but White appears to be well placed) 14 ♘f6+! ♗xf6 15 exf6 ♘c6 16 ♗g5 ♕c7 17 ♗xh6 gxh6 18 ♕d2 ♔h8 19 ♕xh6 ♖g8 20 ♘g5! ♖xg5 21 ♗e4 ♖xg3+ 22 fxg3 ♕xg3+ 23 ♔h1 and Black resigned in Hellsten-Aström, Ronneby 1998.

11 a3!

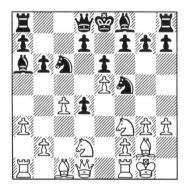

Menacing. 11 ♕a4 has also been played (Hellsten-Shipov, Gistrup 1997 being one example) but never with much success. White has to realised that he is well placed

and that the pawn on d4 is very difficult for Black to hang on to, so he should just play around it.

11...♗e7

This move has been given a ?! by one commentator but no improvement has been suggested. The following lines demonstrate the problems faced by Black:

a) 11...♖c8?! 12 ♖e1 ♗e7 13 b4 ♗b7 14 ♘e4! and Black is in trouble as he cannot develop freely. After 14...0-0 comes 15 g4! ♘h4 16 ♘xh4 ♗xh4 17 ♘d6 ♖c7 18 ♘xb7 ♖xb7 19 b5 ♘a5 20 ♗xb7 ♘xb7 21 ♕xd4 f6 22 ♖a2 and the compensation for the exchange is not apparent.

b) 11...♕c7 12 b4 ♗b7 13 ♘e4 h5 14 ♗f4 a5 15 b5 ♘d8 16 ♘xd4 ♕xc4 17 ♘xf5 exf5 18 ♖c1 ♕e6 19 ♘g5 gave White a clear advantage in Sherbakov-Galliamova, Cheliabinsk 1989.

c) 11...b5 12 g4 ♘h4 13 ♘xh4 ♕xh4 14 ♘f3 ♕d8 15 ♘xd4 ♘xd4 16 ♕xd4 looks good for White (Gershon).

12 b4 ♗b7 13 ♘e4!

This is the most logical move. Before White takes any action he improves his pieces to the maximum. 13 g4 has proved to be less dangerous.

13...d5

Here Black has a serious alternative in 13...0-0!? 14 g4 d5 (only move) 15 cxd5! exd5 16 ♘ed2 (16 ♘eg5 ♘h4! is only in Black's interest; the knight is misplaced on g5) 16...♘h4 17 b5 ♘a5 18 ♘xh4 ♗xh4 19 ♘f3 ♗e7 20 ♘xd4 and White has an appealing position, but Black has some good things going for him, too. The c4-square is a strongpoint for the knight and the c-file will also come in handy. However, I believe that the potential storm on the kingside is very serious, and White should be optimistic.

14 cxd5 ♕xd5

After this White gets time to irritate Black. Preferable is 14...exd5 15 ♘ed2 a6! (directed against b4-b5) 16 ♘b3 ♖c8!, and now 17 g4?! ♘h4 18 ♘xh4 ♗xh4 19 ♘xd4 ♘xd4 20

♕xd4 ♖c4 gives Black a strong initiative. Instead after 17 ♗b2 17...0-0 18 g4 ♘h4 19 ♘xh4 ♗xh4 White has only a slight edge.

15 ♖e1 d3?!

Black is in trouble and now self-destructs. After 15...0-0 16 g4! ♘e3 (16...♘h6 17 ♗xh6 gxh6 18 ♕d2 looks very dangerous for Black) 17 fxe3 ♕xe4 18 exd4 ♕d5 19 ♗e3 White is slightly better.

16 ♗b2 0-0-0?

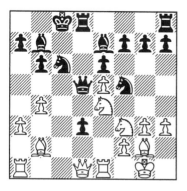

This seems completely ridiculous.

17 g4 ♘h6 18 ♘fd2 ♕b5??

Losing. After the necessary 18...♕d7 19 ♘c4 ♔b8 20 ♘ed6 Black is still in trouble.

19 ♘c3! 1-0

White wins material.

Game 40
Lautier-Karpov
Monte Carlo (rapid) 2000

---

1 d4 ♘f6 2 c4 e6 3 ♘f3 b6 4 g3 ♗a6 5 ♘bd2 d5

This is the main reason why 5 ♘bd2 is not such a popular choice.

6 ♗g2 ♗e7 7 0-0 0-0 8 ♘e5

Here White could transpose with 8 cxd5! exd5 9 ♘e5. Other options causes no problems for Black. With the move order in the game Black has some additional options.

In Aagaard-Gavrikov, Gothenburg 1998 I discovered that the queen is not well placed after 8 ♕c2: 8...♗b7 9 b3 a5 10 ♗b2 ♘a6 11

♖ac1 a4 and Black was already doing fine.

8 b3 c5 9 dxc5 ♗xc5 10 ♗b2 ♘bd7 11 ♖c1 ♗b7 12 ♘d4 ♖c8 13 ♘b5 ♕e7 led to equality in Piket-Karpov, Wijk aan Zee 1998.

8...♗b7!

This move, followed by ...a7-a5 and ...♘a6, is the main option for a good reason. With the knight on d2 White has to play b2-b3 and ♗b2 to develop his dark-squared bishop, but cannot meet ...a5-a4 very well. However, there is another way to go, namely 8...c5!?, e.g. 9 cxd5 exd5 10 b3 ♖e8 (10...♗b7! followed by ...♘a6 is the right path; Black does not play the opening altogether well here) 11 ♗b2 cxd4?! 12 ♘df3! (standard in these lines) 12...♗c5 13 a3 ♘bd7 14 ♘d3! and White has a very clear advantage, Polugaevsky-Rodriguez, Sochi 1988. 10 dxc5!? is interesting. Black should probably not play 10...bxc5, when White was better in Romanishin-Psakhis, Moscow 1983 after 11 b3 ♗b7 12 ♗b2 a5 13 e4! d4 14 ♘ec4 ♘fd7 15 ♖e1 ♘b6 16 ♘xb6 ♕xb6 17 ♘c4. Instead 10...♗xc5! 11 ♘d3 (heading for f4) 11...♖e8 12 ♘f3 ♘c6 secures equality. Earlier 9 ♘b3 is possible, e.g. 9...♗b7 10 dxc5 bxc5 11 cxd5 ♗xd5 12 ♗f4 ♕b6 13 ♕c2 ♗xg2 14 ♔xg2 ♘c6 15 ♘xc6 ♕xc6+ 16 ♔g1 ♘d5, which was perhaps slightly preferable for White in Jusupov-Polugaevsky, Toluca 1982.

9 cxd5!

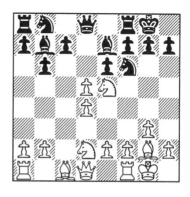

Clearly the most dangerous option. Alternatives:

a) 9 ♕a4. What the queen is supposed to do out here is not altogether clear. Kempinski-Nisipeanu, Krynica 1998 continued 9...♗d6 10 cxd5 ♗xd5 11 e4 ♗b7 12 ♘ec4 ♗e7 with a good opening for Black, although it was about to get even better: 13 e5?! ♗xg2 14 exf6 ♗xf6 15 ♔xg2 ♕d5+ 16 ♘f3 b5 and Black had a clear advantage.

b) 9 b3 c5! 10 dxc5 bxc5 11 ♗b2 ♘bd7 12 ♘xd7 ♕xd7 with equality, Oll-Khalifman, Parnu 1996. After 10 ♗b2 cxd4! a difference from positions where cxd5 exd5 has been played is that White cannot delay the recapture – 11 ♗xd4 ♘c6 was equal in Uhlmann-Stahlberg, Prague 1954. Note that 10 cxd5 does not transpose to the main lines because after 10...♗xd5! Black has already equalised.

c) 9 ♕c2 c5 10 cxd5 exd5 11 dxc5 ♗xc5 12 ♘df3 ♘bd7 13 ♗f4 ♖e8 was also level in Sutter-Kindermann, Bern 1995.

9...exd5

The interesting 9...♗xd5!? 10 e4 ♗b7 11 ♕c2 (11 ♕a4 ♕e8 12 ♕c2 ♘c6!, with an even game, is better) 11...♘a6 12 ♖d1 ♕e8? was seen in Dizdar-Granda Zuniga, New York 1997. After 12...♕xd4! 13 ♘dc4 ♕c5 14 ♗e3 ♕b5 it is clear that White has genuine compensation for the pawn. A GM once told me that the most important thing he had learned from Fritz was that you should take pawns when it seems dangerous but you cannot actually see any real danger. If you look through Tal's old games you will find that he bluffed half his way to the World Championship title.

10 b3 a5

Here Black can also try 10...c5 11 ♗b2 ♘c6!? 12 ♘xc6 ♗xc6 13 ♖c1 ♗b7 with counterplay according to Dolmatov. Instead 11...♘bd7 12 ♘xd7 ♕xd7 13 dxc5 bxc5 14 e4 seemed slightly better for White in Topalov-Gelfand, Monte Carlo 1999, while 11...♘a6 12 ♖c1 ♘c7 13 dxc5 ♗xc5 14 ♘d3 ♗d6 15 ♘f3 ♘e4 16 ♘d4 was a good deal better for White in Goldin-Ulibin, Kazan 1995.

11 ♕c2

Again I do not like this move at all. White should concentrate on developing his minor soldiers first before sending the queen into battle. 11 ♗b2 ♘a6 12 ♖c1 c5 13 ♘d3! (another standard manoeuvre in such positions) 13...♖e8 14 ♘f4 was played in Khalifman-Leko, New Delhi 2000. Such situations are what the main lines of the Queen's Indian Defence are all about. White might have a small plus and can manoeuvre around, trying to create something more, while Black will try to equalise or use any chance that might be given him to get some kind of an initiative.

11...♘a6 12 ♗b2 c5 13 dxc5 bxc5 14 ♖ad1?!

This move is rather careless. The only black piece that is not really well placed is the queen's knight, and now Black is allowed to bring it back into the game. 14 a3 ♕b6 15 ♖ad1 a4 16 bxa4 ♖fc8 17 ♖b1 ♕a7 results in a kind of dynamic equilibrium.

14...a4!

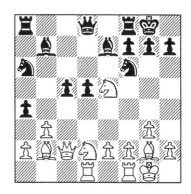

Black is activating all his pieces this way.

15 bxa4 ♘b4 16 ♕b1 ♕c7 17 e4

Black is about to advance his c-pawn and White uses the moment to claim squares for his knights. 17 a3 ♘c6 18 ♘xc6 ♗xc6 also gives Black the advantage.

17...d4 18 a3 ♘c6 19 ♘ec4 ♖xa4 20 ♖fe1?!

Inviting Black to exploit his more active

pieces. It was better to try to disturb Black with 20 ♕c2 ♖fa8 21 f4!?, when White's forces are not easily kept out.

20...♘a5!

Now this is possible. After this the defence of a3 is more difficult for White.

21 ♘xa5

21 ♕c2 ♘xc4 22 ♘xc4 ♖fa8, followed by ...♘d7-b6 with advantage.

21...♖xa5

White has no counterplay and Black has the c-pawn as a strong force and the a-pawn to put pressure on.

22 ♕c2 ♕c6 23 ♘c4 ♖a7 24 f4 ♘d7 25 ♕d2 ♘b6 26 ♖c1 ♘xc4 27 ♖xc4 ♖d8 28 ♖ec1 ♕b6 29 a4 ♗a6 30 a5 ♕b3 31 ♖xc5 ♗xc5 32 ♖xc5 ♖b7 33 ♗xd4 ♕a4 34 ♔f2 ♖b4 0-1

Game 41
Sakaev-Berzinsh
Duisburg 1992

---

1 d4 ♘f6 2 c4 e6 3 ♘f3 b6 4 g3 ♗a6 5 ♕a4

This line can easily be compared with 5 ♘bd2. It is by no means dangerous for Black from a theoretical point of view but there is still plenty of play in the position, allowing for innovations and improvements.

5...c6

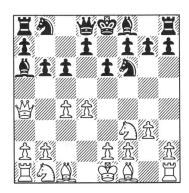

This line is somewhat dubious. The superior 5...c5 is considered in the following

games.

6 ♘c3 b5!?

The point. Passive play with 6...♗e7 7 ♗g2 0-0 8 0-0 d5 9 ♘e5 ♕c8 10 cxd5 cxd5 11 ♗f4 favoured White in Hübner-Bauer, Leon 2001.

7 cxb5 cxb5 8 ♘xb5 ♕b6 9 ♘c3 ♗b4

Black also fails to equalise after 9...♘c6 10 ♗g2 ♗b4, e.g. 11 0-0 ♗xc3 12 bxc3 ♗xe2 13 ♖e1 ♕a6 14 ♕xa6 ♗xa6 15 ♘e5 ♖c8 16 ♗xc6! dxc6 17 ♗a3, when White had a lasting advantage in Nikolic-Ljubojevic, Monte Carlo 1995.

10 ♗g2 0-0 11 ♕d1!

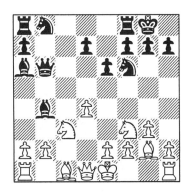

This is the dangerous move for Black. After 11 0-0 ♗xc3 12 bxc3 ♗xe2 13 ♖e1 ♗b5!? 14 ♕b3 d5 (Black must prevent c3-c4: White stood better in Skembris-Timman, Corfu 1993 after 14...♗c6?! 15 c4! ♘a6 16 ♗f4!) 15 ♘e5 ♖c8 16 ♗e3 ♘bd7 17 ♕b4 ♘f8 18 a4 ♗a6 19 ♕xb6 axb6 with equality in Vukic-Bronstein, Sarajevo 1971. Meanwhile in Tukmakov-Gulko, Leningrad 1977, 11 ♕c2 ♘c6 12 0-0 ♖fc8 13 a3 ♗xc3 14 bxc3 ♘d5 15 ♖d1 ♘ce7 16 ♗b2 ♖ab8 17 ♖ab1 ♕b3 gave Black enormous compensation for the pawn.

11...♖c8

11...♗xc3+ 12 bxc3 ♖c8 13 ♗d2 d5 14 0-0 ♘e4 15 ♖c1 leaves Black with compensation for the pawn, but perhaps not enough.

12 ♗d2 d5 13 0-0 ♗xc3 14 ♗xc3 ♘e4 15 ♖c1 ♘d7 16 ♖e1!

White is taking his time to untangle. After 16 ♘d2 ♘xc3 17 bxc3 ♖c7 Black will exert pressure on c3, and 18 c4 ♕xd4 19 cxd5 ♖xc1 20 ♕xc1 ♖c8! 21 ♕d1 exd5 is level.

16...♖ab8

16...♖c7 17 ♕a4! and Black will find it hard to improve his situation due to the threat of ♗a5.

17 ♕a4 ♗b5 18 ♕a3 ♕b7 19 ♗a5! ♖xc1 20 ♖xc1

White has more or less untangled.

20...♖c8

After 20...♗xe2 21 ♖c7! ♕b5 22 ♕b3!! ♕xb3 23 axb3 ♘f8 24 b4 a6 25 ♘e5 White loses his pawn but, suddenly, his pieces totally dominate Black and he can hope for a successful result.

21 ♖xc8+ ♕xc8 22 ♗f1 ♕c1 23 ♔g2 ♕d1 24 ♕b3 ♗xe2 25 ♕xd1 ♗xd1

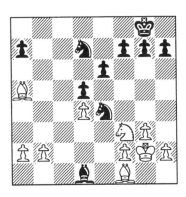

Again Black has won back his pawn, but at a price. White has the two bishops and an extra pawn on the queenside, so the ending is, in fact, dreadful for Black.

26 ♗b5 ♘b6 27 b3 ♗c2 28 ♘e5 ♘d6 29 ♗a6 ♗b1 30 ♘c6 ♗xa2 31 ♘xa7 ♘d7 32 b4 e5 33 ♗c7 ♘c4 34 ♘c6 exd4 35 ♘xd4 ♗b1 36 ♗b7 ♘db6 37 ♗c6 ♔f8 38 f3 ♗d3 39 ♔f2 ♔e7 40 ♗b5 ♘d7 41 ♗c6 ♘cb6 42 ♔e3 ♗b1 43 ♘b5 ♗a2 44 ♔d4 ♔e6 45 ♘c3 ♗b3 46 ♘e2 g5 47 ♔c3 ♗c4 48 ♘d4+ ♔e7 49 b5 ♘a4+ 50 ♔b4 ♘ac5 51 ♘f5+ ♔e6 52 ♘d4+ ♔e7 53 ♔a5 f6 54 ♘f5+ ♔e6 55 ♘d4+ ♔e7

56 b6 ♘a6 57 ♘f5+ ♔e6 58 ♘d4+ ♔e7 59 ♘b5 ♘db8 60 ♗b7 ♘c5 61 ♗d6+ 1-0

Game 42
Karpov-Polgar
Buenos Aires 2001

---

1 d4 ♘f6 2 c4 e6 3 ♘f3 b6 4 g3 ♗a6 5 ♕a4 ♗b7 6 ♗g2 c5 7 dxc5

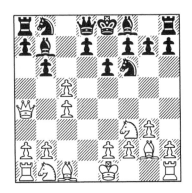

This is practically the only line played these days. After 7 0-0 cxd4 8 ♘xd4 ♕c8 9 ♘c3 ♗xg2 10 ♔xg2 ♕b7+ Black has an improved version of the hedgehog system, as with little space each exchange is normally an advantage. Nikolic-Karpov, Monte Carlo 2000 continued 11 f3 ♗e7 12 ♖d1 a6 13 ♗g5 h6 14 ♗xf6 ♗xf6 15 ♘e4 ♗e7 16 ♕b3 ♕c7 17 ♖ac1 0-0 18 f4 ♘c6 19 ♘f3 ♖fd8 20 ♕e3 ♖ac8 21 g4 d5 and Black was okay.

7...bxc5!?

More usual is 7...♗xc5, as can be seen in the two following games. After the text Black is rock solid but has few chances of an advantage.

8 0-0 ♗e7 9 ♘c3 0-0 10 ♗f4 ♕b6 11 ♖fd1 ♖d8

After 11...d6 12 ♖d2 Black has an extra option in 12...♘c6!? 13 ♗xd6 ♗xd6 14 ♖xd6 ♕xb2 15 ♖b1 ♕xc3 16 ♖xb7 ♘d4 17 ♕d1, as in Karpov-Polugaevsky, Biel 1990. Now 17...♖ad8! would have kept the balance. Notice it is important to use the appropriate rook, as 17...♖fd8 gives White the additional option of 18 ♖xa7!?, with the main point being 18...♕xc4?? 19 ♘e5! etc. What worries me most here is 12 ♕b3! ♖d8 with transposition to the main game.

12 ♕b3!

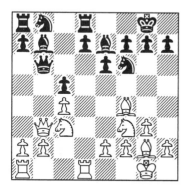

12 ♖d2 d5 13 cxd5 exd5 14 ♕c2 ♘a6 15 a3 h6 16 ♗e5 d4 17 ♘a4 ♕b5 18 b4? cxb4 19 ♘xd4 ♖xd4! and Black was winning in Olafsson-Bareev, Hastings 1990. Instead 14 ♘e5 ♘a6 15 ♖ad1 ♕e6 16 ♘c4 ♘b4 17 a3 ♗c6 18 ♕a5 d4 19 axb4 ♗xg2 20 ♔xg2 cxb4 was equal in Tukmakov-Aseev, USSR 1989, as was 14 e3 ♘a6 15 ♖ad1 h6 16 h4 ♖ac8 in Sturua-Arkhipov, Moscow 1992.

12...d6

12...♕xb3 is to premature in view of 13 axb3 d6 14 ♘b5!, forcing concessions.

13 ♖d2

White is improving his position. 13 ♕xb6 axb6 14 ♘b5 ♘e8 15 ♘g5 ♗xg2 16 ♔xg2 ♘c6 gave White nothing in Mirzoev-Dautov, Istanbul 2000, but 14 ♖d2! improves, with a chance to gradually develop an initiative.

13...♘a6

13...♕xb3 14 axb3 ♘c6 15 ♖ad1 ♘e8, as in Olafsson-Lautier, Antwerp 1998, is possibly enough for equality. But one tends to ask what the rook is really doing on d1 besides attacking the d6-pawn.

14 ♕xb6 axb6 15 ♖ad1 ♘e8 16 h4 h6 17 ♘h2 ♗xg2 18 ♔xg2 ♘ac7 19 e4 ♔f8 20 b3 ♖db8

Seems too optimistic; perhaps Black failed to appreciate the implications of his opponent's reply.

21 e5! d5 22 cxd5 exd5 23 ♘xd5 ♘xd5 24 ♖xd5 ♖xa2 25 ♖d7!

Now the white pieces are active, which cannot be said of Black's. In fact Black is in trouble.

25...♖aa8 26 ♘g4 ♖d8 27 ♘e3 ♖ac8 28 ♘f5 ♖xd7 29 ♖xd7 ♗d8 30 ♖b7 ♗c7 31 h5 ♖d8 32 ♘e3 ♖d3 33 e6 fxe6 34 ♗xc7 ♖d7 35 ♖xb6 ♖xc7 36 ♖xe6 ♖b7 37 ♖e5 ♖xb3 38 ♖xc5 ♘f6 39 g4 ♖a3 40 ♖c8+ ♔f7 41 ♘c4 ♖a7 42 f3 ♔e6 43 ♖c5 ♘d5 44 ♖c6+ ♔e7 45 ♘e5 ♘f4+ 46 ♔g3 ♖a4 47 ♖c2 ♔f6 48 ♘d7+ ♔e7 49 ♘c5 ♖d4 50 ♖a2 ♔f7 51 ♖a7+ ♔f8 52 ♘e4 ♘e6 53 ♖a6 ♔e7 54 ♔f2 ♖c4 55 ♔e3 ♖c1 56 ♖a7+ ♖c7 57 ♖a4 ♖b7 58 ♖a3 ♖c7 59 ♘g3 ♔f6 60 ♘e4+ ♔e7 61 ♘c3 ♖d7 62 f4 ♘c5 63 ♘e2 ♔f7 64 ♘d4 ♘e6 65 ♘f3 ♖b7 66 ♘e5+ ♔f6 67 ♘d3 ♔e7 68 ♔e4 ♖d7 69 ♔f5 ♖d6 70 ♖a7+ ♔f8 71 ♘e5 ♘d4+ 72 ♔e4 ♘e6 73 ♘g6+ ♔g8 74 ♔e5 ♖b6 75 ♖e7 1-0

Game 43
Borges Mateos-Spraggett
Cienfuegos 1997

1 d4 ♘f6 2 c4 e6 3 ♘f3 b6 4 g3 ♗a6 5 ♕a4 ♗b7 6 ♗g2 c5 7 dxc5 ♗xc5 8 0-0 0-0 9 ♘c3 ♗e7!

The bishop is not well placed on c5, a square that is more suited for the knight.

10 ♖d1 a6!?

This has become fashionable over the last couple of years. Black is trying to establish a hedgehog position. 10...♘a6 – the main line – is considered in the following game.

11 ♗f4 d6 12 ♖d2

With this move White is trying to put d6 under pressure but, as we shall see, Black can easily protect it. The alternative is 12 ♖ac1 ♕c7:

a) 13 ♕c2 ♖d8! (13...♘bd7 14 ♕d2 ♘e8

is a standard Hedgehog but Black wants the rook on the other side of the knight) 14 ♕d2 ♘e8 15 ♗g5 ♗xg5 16 ♕xg5 ♘d7 17 b3 ♖ac8 18 ♕e3 ♘ef6 with equality, Jakobsen-Hansen, Greve 2002.

b) 13 ♕b4 (more dangerous than 13 ♕c2) 13...♘e8 14 ♗g5 (14 ♘a4 ♘d7 15 ♕d2 ♘c5 16 ♘c3 ♘e4 17 ♘xe4 ♗xe4 was fine for Black in Hansen-Onischuk, Bundesliga 1995) 14...♘f6 15 ♗xf6 gxf6 16 ♘d5!? (forcing a draw, but it seems that White has no advantage anyway) 16...exd5 17 cxd5 ♕d8 18 ♘d4 ♔h8 19 ♘c6 ♕c7 20 ♘d4 ♕d8 21 ♘c6 ♕c7 22 ♘d4 and a draw was agreed in Ivanchuk-Lautier, Moscow 2001.

12...♕c7 13 ♖ad1 ♖d8 14 ♘g5

Others:

a) 14 ♘e1 ♗xg2 15 ♘xg2 ♘c6 16 ♗g5 ♘a5 17 ♘e3 h6 18 ♗xf6 ♗xf6 19 ♘e4 ♗e7 20 ♖c2 ♕b7 with equality in Bönsch-Stempin, Polanica Zdroj 1987.

b) 14 ♕c2 h6. Black addresses the possibility of ♘g5-e4 and ♗g5. This is not strictly necessary, but quite a common move when White has no chances of a kingside pawn storm. Grivas-Ionescu, Dubai 1986 continued 15 e4 ♘h5 16 ♗e3 ♘d7 17 b3 ♖ac8 18 a4 ♘hf6 19 ♗f4 ♘e5 20 ♘xe5 dxe5 21 ♖xd8+ ♗xd8 22 ♗e3 ♗e7 23 f3 ♘d7 and Black was okay. Normally Black should be careful when allowing White a pawn majority on the queenside, but because the pawn is on a4 there is no problem here.

c) 14 ♕b3 ♘e8 15 e4 ♘d7 16 e5 ♘xe5 17 ♘xe5 dxe5 18 ♖xd8 ♖xd8 19 ♗xe5 ♕xe5 20 ♗xb7 a5 with equality, Meister-Wegner, Germany 1987.

14...♗xg2 15 ♔xg2 ♘c6 16 ♘ge4 ♘e8!

Black should be careful and remember this lesson. White has a knight on c3 and cannot find any good use for it, so an exchange on e4 would be silly. Indeed 16...♘xe4?! 17 ♘xe4 e5 leaves the d5-square susceptible to future attention.

17 ♗g5

More sensible than 17 g4!? which, in

Zaltsman-Arnason, New York 1986, met with 17...♘a5!, a brilliant manoeuvre, albeit quite simple. There followed 18 b3 ♘b7 19 f3 ♔f8! (guarding the minor pieces and addressing the king's own security), and now White should have played 20 ♕a3 with a sensible position. Instead after 20 ♗g3?! ♕c8! Black assumed the initiative: 21 ♗f2 b5 22 cxb5 axb5 23 ♕xb5 d5 24 ♘a4 ♖a5 25 ♕b6 dxe4 26 ♖xd8 exf3+ 27 exf3 ♗xd8 28 ♖xd8 ♕xd8 29 ♕xb7 ♖d5 and Black had a clear advantage.

17...f6!

This is not really necessary. Also possible is 17...♗xg5!? 18 ♘xg5 h6 19 ♘f3 ♘a5 20 ♖d4 (20 b3? b5! is in Black's interest) 20...♖dc8 with sufficient counterplay.

18 ♗e3!

Forced. The bishop is misplaced after 18 ♗f4? ♘a5! 19 b3 f5 20 ♘g5 b5! 21 ♕a3 ♗xg5 22 ♗xg5 ♖db8, when Black has a powerful initiative.

18...♘e5 19 ♖d4 ♖dc8 20 ♘d2 f5 21 f3 ♗f6

Black is more than comfortable here.

22 ♗f2 ♘c6 23 ♖d3 ♘a5 24 e4 g6 25 ♗d4 ♗xd4 26 ♖xd4 ♘c6 27 ♖d3 ♘e5 28 ♖d4 ♘f6 29 ♕a3 ♖d8 30 exf5 gxf5 31 ♘e2 ♘c6 32 ♖h4 ♘e5 33 ♕e3 ♖e8 34 ♖h6?

What the rook is supposed to be doing up here is not clear. After 34 ♕g5+ ♕g7 35 ♕xg7+ ♔xg7 36 ♖d4 the endgame is level.

34...♕g7! 35 ♖h4 b5 36 b3 ♖ad8 37 ♘f4? ♘g6! 38 ♘xg6 hxg6 39 ♖d4

39 ♕d3 g5 40 ♖d4 d5! is also clearly better for Black because 41 cxd5? e5! is decisive.

39...e5 40 ♖d3 ♕b7?

The traditional 40th move blunder... Black can win with 40...d5! 41 cxd5 e4! 42 fxe4 fxe4 and White will suffer material losses.

41 ♔g1 ♔f7 42 ♖e1 d5 43 cxd5 ♘xd5 44 ♕c5 ♘f6 45 ♖xd8 ♖xd8 46 ♕e3 ♕d5 47 ♖e2 ♕d4 48 ♕xd4 ♖xd4 49 ♘f1 ♔e6 50 ♖c2 ♔d7 51 ♔f2 ♘d5 52 ♖d2 ♖xd2+

52...♘c3 53 ♖c2 ♖d3 54 ♘e3 ♔d6 maintains the pressure, but now we have a draw.

53 ♘xd2 ½-½

Game 44
Piket-Chuchelov
Netherlands 2000

---

1 d4 ♘f6 2 c4 e6 3 ♘f3 b6 4 g3 ♗a6 5 ♕a4 ♗b7 6 ♗g2 c5 7 dxc5 ♗xc5 8 0-0 0-0 9 ♘c3 ♗e7 10 ♖d1 ♘a6 11 ♗f4

The most normal move, but dangerous is 11 ♗e3!?, with the idea of putting the bishop on d4. This has led to problems for Black but seems to have been solved by 11...♕b8!, with the idea of overprotecting the d6-square. Georgiev-Ivanchuk, Tilburg 1993 continued 12 ♖ac1 ♘c5 13 ♕c2 ♘ce4 14 ♗f4, transposing to the main game, but 14...♕c8 15 ♘xe4 ♗xe4 16 ♕a4 ♕b7! (the obvious move) 17 ♗f1 ♖fe8 18 ♘e1 a6 was level. Here 14 ♗d4 ♗c5 looks fine for Black.

11...♕c8 12 ♖ac1 ♘c5 13 ♕c2 ♘ce4 14 ♘d4

14 ♘xe4 ♗xe4 15 ♕a4 (both 15 ♕d2 ♕b7 16 ♗d6 ♗xd6 17 ♕xd6 ♖ac8, Dautov-Smirin, Daugavpils 1989, and 15 ♕b3 ♕b7 16 ♗d6 ♗xd6 17 ♖xd6 ♖ac8, Dlugy-Adorjan, New York 1984, give Black a good game) 15...♕b7! 16 ♗d6? (this exchange favours Black; 16 ♗f1 is seen in the note above) 16...♗xd6 17 ♖xd6 ♖fc8! and Black was better in Blees-Gershon, Tel Aviv 1999. Already the threat is ...b6-b5.

In Bareev-Karpov, Tilburg 1991, 14 h3?! ♖d8 15 g4? d6! left Black in the lead as White had achieved nothing but weakening his kingside. Karpov offers 15 ♘d4 with equality.

14...♘xc3 15 ♕xc3 a6 16 ♕b3 ♗xg2 17 ♔xg2 ♕b7+ 18 ♕f3 ♖a7!

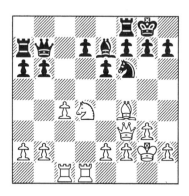

Stronger than 18...♕xf3+ 19 ♔xf3 ♖ac8 20 e4, when White has more freedom to manoeuvre thanks to his space advantage.

19 ♕xb7 ♖xb7 20 f3 ♖c8

20...♘h5!? 21 ♗e3 f5!? was an interesting alternative.

21 e4 d6

21...♘e8!? 22 h4 h5! 23 a4 ♗f6 24 ♗e3 was slightly better for White in Piket-Karpov, Monaco 1999. However, as in the main game, White failed to make anything of the modest lead, so perhaps Black should not fear it so much. Nevertheless I feel that 10...d6 is the safest option for Black.

22 ♘e2 ♘e8 23 b3 h5!? 24 h4 g6 25 ♖d2 ♖bc7 26 ♖d3 ♖c5 27 a4 ♖5c6 28 ♖cd1 ♖c5 29 ♔f1 ♗f8 30 ♘c3 ♖b8! 31 ♖1d2 ♖b7! 32 ♔e2 ♗e7 33 ♔d1 ♔f8 34 ♖c2 ♖c8 35 ♘e2 ♖bc7 36 ♖a2 ♖b7 37 ♗h6+ ♔g8 38 ♗e3 ♗f6 39 ♗f4 ♗e7 40 ♘c3 ♗f6! 41 ♘e2 ♗e7 42 ♖c2 ♖bc7 43 ♘c3 ♗f6 44 ♘b1 b5?! 45 axb5 axb5 46 ♘a3 bxc4 47 ♖xc4 ♗e7 48 ♖xc7 ♖xc7 49 ♘c4 ♖c6 50 ♔c2 f5! 51 ♖c3 fxe4 52 fxe4 ♘f6 53 ♘d2 ♖xc3+ 54 ♔xc3 ♔f7 55 ♔d3 ½-½

Summary

The 4...♗b4+ line invariably leads to a small advantage for White. 4...♗a6 is more modern and more dynamic. After moves like 5 ♕c2, 5 ♘bd2, 5 ♕b3 and 5 ♕a4 Black can easily achieve equality. The real test (if that is what you want to call it) is found in the following chapter. It is a notable feature of these lines that, after the bishop returns to b7 at a later date, it seems that White has used his extra move to his own disadvantage. The only real dangerous move considered here is 5 ♘bd2, but the idea of ...d7-d5 and ...♗b7 followed by ...a7-a5 and ...♘a6 should give Black a good game.

1 d4 ♘f6 2 c4 e6 3 ♘f3 b6 4 g3 (D) ♗a6

> 4...♗b4+ 5 ♗d2 a5 6 ♗g2 0-0 7 0-0 ♗a6 8 b3
>> 8...♗b7 – Chapter 7; 8...d5 – *Game 34*

5 ♕a4

> 5 b3 – Chapter 7
> 5 ♕c2 – *Game 35*
> 5 ♕b3 – *Game 36*
> 5 ♘bd2 (D)
>> 5...♗b4 – *Game 37*
>> 5...♗b7 6 ♗g2 c5 – *Game 38*
>> 5...c5 6 e4 – *Game 39*
>> 5...d5 6 ♗g2 ♗e7 7 0-0 0-0 – *Game 40*

5...♗b7

> 5...c6 – *Game 41*

6 ♗g2 c5 7 dxc5 ♗xc5

> 7...bxc5 – *Game 42*

8 0-0 0-0 9 ♘c3 ♗e7 10 ♖d1 (D)

> 10...a6 – *Game 43*; 10...♘a6 – *Game 44*

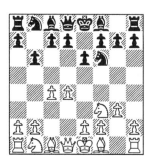

4 g3

5 ♘bd2

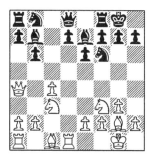

10 ♖d1

CHAPTER SEVEN

4...♟a6: Main Line with 5 b3

1 d4 ♘f6 2 c4 e6 3 ♘f3 b6 4 g3 ♗a6 5 b3

This is where the main theoretical battleground for the Queen's Indian and maybe even for 1 d4 is taking place. Black has a multitude of variations to choose from. Some of them are more experimental and lead to an unbalancing of the position, while others aim for long forced lines hoping to equalise. The balance of play currently favours Black in the sense that White apparently cannot engineer an advantage in the main lines towards the end of the chapter. But if you, like me, not only desire to play perfect chess, but also want to win some games now and again, then you might find more fun in some of the sidelines presented in this chapter, as all top players have done from time to time.

Game 45
Kasparov-Gelfand
Novgorod 1997

---

1 d4 ♘f6 2 c4 e6 3 ♘f3 b6 4 g3 ♗a6 5 b3 d5!?

This move has been played more than it deserves, or at least it has been played with an idea neither I nor practice can fully approve of. Another dubious alternative that

some might consider worth a try is 5...c5, e.g. 6 ♗g2 and now:

a) 6...d5 seems to be the only serious option. Bach-Schilow, 1997 continued 7 0-0 ♘c6 8 cxd5 exd5 9 ♗b2 ♖c8 10 ♖e1 with (probably) an edge for White in one of those 'better player wins' situations. 7...♗e7 8 cxd5 ♘xd5 9 ♗b2 0-0 10 ♘bd2 ♘d7 11 ♘c4 ♖c8 12 e4 ♘5f6 13 d5 exd5 14 exd5 was better for White in Neverov-Sazonov, Yalta 1996.

b) 6...♘c6 7 d5! exd5 8 cxd5 ♘e7?! (8...♗b4 9 ♘c3 ♗b7 10 e4 ♗a6 11 ♗f1 ♗xf1 12 ♔xf1, with some advantage to White, is a lesser evil) 9 ♘c3 g6? (9...d6 10 0-0 g6 11 ♗b2 ♗g7 merely points to the weird knight on e7) 10 ♗g5 ♗g7 11 d6 ♘c6 12 ♘d5 with a clear advantage in Popov-Zvjaginsev, St. Petersburg 1998.

c) 6...♗b7 7 d5 exd5 8 ♘h4 g6 9 ♗b2 ♗g7 10 cxd5 d6 11 0-0 b5 12 a4 b4 13 ♘d2 was better for White in Tratar-Slak, Slovenia 1994.

6 ♗g2 dxc4?!

After this move White has a large advantage. But 6...♗b4+! 7 ♗d2 ♗xd2+! is interesting (rather than 7...♗d6 8 ♘c3 ♘bd7 9 e4! c5 10 exd5 exd5 11 ♕e2+!, as in Nestorovic-Rajkovic, Belgrade 1988). Then 8 ♘bxd2 0-0 (8...c5 9 dxc5 bxc5 10 0-0 0-0 11 ♖e1 ♘c6 12 cxd5 exd5 13 ♖c1 ♕b6 14 ♕c2

♘b4 15 ♕xc5 ♘xa2 16 ♕xb6 axb6 17 ♖c6 was better for White in Nikolic-Yudasin, Tilburg 1993) 9 0-0 ♘bd7 10 ♖c1 c5 11 cxd5 (11 ♖e1 ♗b7 12 cxd5 exd5 13 ♕c2 ♖e8 14 ♕b2 ♕e7 15 e3 a5 with equality in Tischer-Eismont, Biel 1994) 11...exd5 12 ♖e1 ♖e8 13 e3 ♖c8 14 ♗h3 ♖c7 15 ♗f1 ended peacefully in Alterman-Yudasin, Haifa 1995, although I have a feeling that White might be slightly better here. Instead 8 ♕xd2 0-0 9 0-0 ♕e7 10 cxd5 exd5 11 ♘c3 ♗b7 12 ♖ac1 ♘a6 13 ♖fd1 ♖fd8 14 ♕b2 c5 15 e3 was a prototypical position in Chernin-Razuvaev, Tilburg 1994.

7 ♘e5 ♗b4+ 8 ♔f1 ♗d6

Here 8...♘bd7?? 9 ♘c6! is embarrassing. The other alternatives are:

a) 8...♘fd7 9 ♘xc4! c6 10 ♗b2 0-0 (after 10...b5 11 ♘e3! Black appears to have nothing better than 11...0-0, transposing) 11 ♘bd2 b5 12 ♘e3 ♗b7 13 ♕c2 ♕b6 14 ♘f3 ♘f6 15 ♘e5 ♗e7 16 ♘3g4?! was Karpov-Timman, Kuala Lumpur (8) 1990. Karpov himself indicates that 16 ♖c1! followed by ♗f3 and ♔g2 was better, securing an advantage.

b) 8...c6 9 bxc4! 0-0 10 ♗b2 ♗d6 11 ♘d2 ♕c7 12 ♕c2 secured White a small plus in Bykhovsky-Gofshtein, Tel Aviv 1995.

9 ♘xc4 ♘d5 10 e4 ♘e7

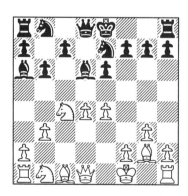

11 ♗b2

11 ♗f3?! ♘bc6 12 ♔g2 ♗xc4 13 bxc4 e5 14 d5 ♘d4 15 ♗e3 c5 is fine for Black, Jas-nikowski-Lau, Polanica Zdroj 1986, while 11 e5? ♗xe5 12 ♗xa8 ♕xd4 13 ♕xd4 ♗xd4 14 ♘c3 ♗xc3 15 ♖b1 c6 is just stupid. Black is better.

11...♘bc6 12 ♘bd2 0-0

12...e5 13 d5 ♘a5 14 ♔g1 ♘xc4 15 ♘xc4 ♗xc4 16 bxc4 0-0 17 ♗h3 f5 18 ♔g2 gave White an overwhelming advantage in Kasparov-Atlas, Catonsville (Simultaneous Display) 1996.

13 ♔g1 b5 14 ♘xd6!

An improvement at the time.

14...cxd6 15 h4 ♕b6

15...d5 is suggested as an improvement by Dokhoian, Kasparov's second, but after 16 h5! Gelfand does not like Black's position.

16 h5!?

Here White could play even better with 16 d5!, with an advantage.

16...h6?!

16...♘xd4! 17 h6 g6 18 ♘c4 ♘e2+! 19 ♕xe2 bxc4 lead to complications that are not necessarily in White's favour.

17 d5 ♘e5 18 ♘f1 b4 19 ♗d4 ♕a5

19...♗e2 20 ♗xb6 ♗xd1 21 ♖xd1 axb6 22 f4 ♘g4 23 dxe6 ♖xa2 24 ♖xd6 gives White a considerable advantage.

20 ♘e3 ♖ac8 21 ♖h4 ♖c7 22 ♕d2

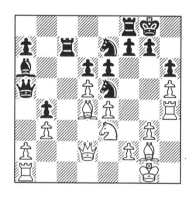

White is firmly in the driving seat.

22...♖c3?

22...♘d3.

23 ♗xc3 bxc3 24 ♕d4

Now it is over.

24...exd5 25 exd5 ♕c7 26 ♕d1 ♖c8 27 ♗e4 ♕b6 28 ♖f4 ♗b7 29 ♖c1 ♕a5 30 ♖c2 ♔h8 31 ♗g2 ♗a6 32 ♖a4 ♕b6 33 ♘c4! ♗xc4 34 bxc4 ♘f5 35 ♖xc3 ♘d4? 36 c5 ♖xc5 37 ♕xd4 1-0

Game 46
Tkachiev-Nisipeanu
Naujac-sur-Mer 2000

---

1 d4 ♘f6 2 c4 e6 3 ♘f3 b6 4 g3 ♗a6 5 b3 b5!? 6 cxb5 ♗xb5 7 ♗g2 ♗b4+

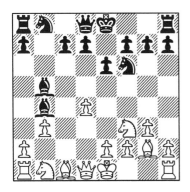

7...c5 8 0-0 ♗c6 9 ♗a3 ♘a6 10 ♘bd2 ♗e7 11 ♖c1 cxd4 12 ♗xe7 ♕xe7 13 ♘c4 0-0 14 ♕xd4 d5 15 ♘fe5 ♖fc8 16 ♘xc6 ♖xc6 17 ♘e5 ♖c7 18 ♖xc7 ♕xc7 19 ♘d3 gave White a slight advantage, due to the superiority of bishop against knight, in van der Sterren-Timman, Holland 1987.

7...d5 8 0-0 ♘bd7 9 ♗a3 ♗xa3 10 ♘xa3 ♗a6 11 ♖c1! ♕e7 12 ♘b1 ♖c8 13 ♖c2 was Wells-Dautov, Bad Wörishofen 1997, but White could have played better with 13 ♖c6! ♗b7 14 ♖c2 with an edge according to Dautov.

8 ♗d2 a5 9 0-0

Here White has a refutation according to all the books, but after 9 ♗xb4!? axb4 10 ♕d2 ♘c6! (the new move) 11 ♕g5 ♖a5 12 ♕xg7 ♔e7 13 ♕h6 ♕a8 14 ♕d2 ♘e4 15 ♕b2 d5 Black has enough compensation for the pawn and had a good game, until a draw was settled in Belakovskaia-Mastrovasilis,

Korinthos 1998.

9...0-0 10 a3 ♗e7

If Black exchanges the bishops on d2 he will experience permanent problems on the c5-square: Korchnoi's 10...♗xd2 11 ♕xd2 ♗c6 12 ♘c3 d5 13 ♘e5 ♗b7 14 ♖fc1, with a pleasant position for White, illustrates this well.

11 ♘c3 ♗c6

11...♗a6 12 ♕c2! d5 13 ♖fc1 ♘bd7 14 e4 gave White the advantage in Karpov-Christiansen, Wijk aan Zee 1993.

12 ♕c2 d5

12...♗b7!?, with the idea 13 e4 d5 14 e5 ♘e4 with counterplay has been suggested by Gershon, but I think that White has the advantage after the simple 15 ♖fc1.

13 ♘e5 ♗b7 14 ♘a4 ♘fd7 15 ♘d3

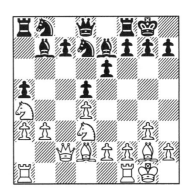

White has the advantage.

15...♗c6 16 ♘ac5 ♘xc5 17 ♘xc5 ♖a7 18 ♖fc1 ♗b5 19 e3 ♘d7?

Losing.

20 a4! ♗e2 21 ♗xa5! ♘xc5 22 dxc5 ♖xa5 23 b4 ♗f6 24 ♖a3 ♗c4 25 bxa5 ♕b8 26 ♖b1 ♕a7 27 ♗f1! ♕xc5 28 ♖ab3 1-0

Game 47
Bogdanovski-Cabrilo
Bijeljina Dvorovi 2002

---

1 d4 ♘f6 2 c4 e6 3 ♘f3 b6 4 g3 ♗a6 5 b3 ♗b4+ 6 ♗d2 ♗xd2+!?

This sideline is not as popular as one might imagine when we look at the evaluation after the opening. I think this is because the position is rather dull and Black does have a slight structural disadvantage in having a c-pawn compared to the e-pawn (both pawns are in half-open files). One difference is that f2 is a better protector for the e-pawn than b6 for the c-pawn. It is also significant that White's king can assist the e-pawn better than the Black can assist the c-pawn. These are, of course, relatively minor issues but, structurally, White does possess a slight advantage. It should not matter theoretically, but in practice such things often do.

7 ♕xd2

The only serious move. 7 ♘bxd2 ♗b7 8 ♗g2 c5 9 0-0 0-0 10 ♕c2 ♘c6 11 ♕b2 ♘xd4 12 ♘xd4 ♗xg2 13 ♔xg2 cxd4 14 ♕xd4 d5 was completely equal in Andersson-Short, Næstved 1985.

7...d5 8 cxd5

Also interesting is 8 ♗g2 and now:

a) 8...0-0 9 0-0 c5 10 ♘c3 ♘c6 11 ♖fd1 ♖c8 12 cxd5 exd5 13 dxc5 bxc5 14 ♘xd5 ♘xd5 15 ♕xd5 ♗xe2 16 ♕xd8 ♖fxd8 17 ♖xd8+ ♖xd8 18 ♖e1 ♖d1 19 ♖xd1 ♗xd1 20 ♘d2 ♘b4 21 a4?! was Gligoric-Szabo, Moscow 1956. Chekov suggests 21 a3! ♘c2 22 a4 ♘d4 23 ♗d5 ♔f8 24 f4 f6 25 ♔f2 ♔e7 26 ♔e3, with a slight advantage, as being more prudent. After 9...c6 10 ♕c2 ♘bd7 11 ♖d1 ♖c8 12 ♘e5?! (12 ♘bd2 c5 13 dxc5 is a shade better for White) 12...c5 13 ♘xd7 ♕xd7 14 cxd5 cxd4 15 ♕b2 e5 Black emerged ahead in Zhu Chen-Christiansen, Seattle 2001.

b) 8...c5 9 cxd5 exd5 10 ♕e3+ ♕e7 11 ♕xe7+ ♔xe7 12 ♘c3 ♘c6 13 dxc5 bxc5 14 ♘h4 ♘d4 15 0-0-0 ♖hd8 16 ♖he1 ♗b7 17 ♔b2 g6 18 e4, Ruzele-Balashov, Boeblingen 1998, and White looked slightly better, although it is very very slight.

8...exd5 9 ♕e3+

9 ♘c3 0-0 10 ♗g2 ♖e8 11 ♘e5! (White must be careful here: 11 0-0?! ♘e4! 12 ♘xe4

dxe4 13 ♘g5 ♘c6! 14 ♖fd1 ♘xd4 15 ♘xf7 ♘xe2+ 16 ♕xe2 ♗xe2 17 ♖xd8 ♖axd8 18 ♘xd8 ♖xd8 19 ♗xe4 c5 left White struggling for equality in Eingorn-Gelfand, Moscow 1990) 11...♗b7 12 0-0 c5 13 e3 ♕e7 14 ♕c2 ♘a6! 15 ♖ac1 ♘c7 16 ♖fe1 ♘e6 with equal play in Hansen-Epishin, Tilburg 1993. In Georgiev-Christiansen, Las Palmas 1993 Black chose the less accurate 10...♘e4?!, the game continuing 11 ♘xe4 dxe4 12 ♘g5 ♘c6 13 ♗xe4 ♘xd4 14 ♗xh7+ ♔h8 15 ♗d3 ♗xd3 16 ♕xd3 ♕xg5 17 ♕xd4 ♖ae8 18 e3 ♕b5 19 ♕c4 (Dautov's 19 0-0-0!? c5 20 ♕d5 ♕b4 21 ♔b2 looks even stronger) 19...♕xc4 20 bxc4 ♖e5!, and now Dautov gives 21 ♔e2! ♖c5 22 ♖ac1 ♖d8 23 h4 ♖d6 24 ♖hd1 ♖dc6 25 ♖d4 ♖a5 26 ♖c2, retaining a clear advantage.

9...♕e7 10 ♕xe7+ ♔xe7 11 ♘c3 ♖e8

11...♘bd7 12 ♗h3 ♖he8 13 0-0 ♔f8 14 ♖fc1 c6 was equal in Hjartarson-Agdestein, Gausdal 1987.

12 ♖c1 c6 13 ♗g2 ♘bd7 14 0-0 ♔f8 15 ♖fe1 ♗b7 16 ♗h3 ♖ad8 17 e3 h6

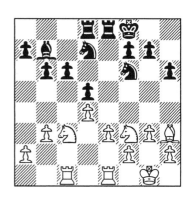

Black has an equal position. However, this endgame is far from decided and White just plays on and on, his longer arms deciding the game...

18 b4 g5 19 ♗f5 ♘e4 20 h4 gxh4 21 ♘xh4 ♘d6 22 ♗d3 ♘f6 23 a4 ♖e7 24 a5 b5 25 ♘f5 ♘xf5 26 ♗xf5 ♘e8 27 ♘e2 ♗c8 28 ♗d3 ♗d7 29 ♔g2 ♘c7 30 ♖h1 ♖e6 31 ♗f5 ♖d6 32 ♗xd7 ♖8xd7

**33 ♘f4 ♘a6 34 ♘d3 ♖e7 35 ♖h5 ♖ee6
36 ♔f3 ♔g7 37 ♔e2 ♘b8 38 ♘f4 ♖e7
39 ♖e5 ♔f8 40 ♖xe7 ♔xe7 41 ♖h1 ♘d7
42 g4 ♘f6 43 f3 ♘g8 44 ♔d3 ♖f6 45
♖h3 ♔f8 46 ♔e2 ♖d6 47 ♘h5 ♘e7 48
♘g3 ♖g6 49 ♔f2 ♖f6 50 ♖h1 ♖d6 51
♖c1 ♔g7 52 ♔e2 ♔g6 53 ♖g1 ♔g7 54
♔d3 ♔f8 55 e4 dxe4+ 56 fxe4 ♖g6 57
♘h5 ♘g8 58 ♘f4 ♖g5 59 ♘h3 ♖g6 60
♔e3 ♔e8 61 ♘f4 ♖g5 62 ♔f3 ♔e7 63
♖c1 ♔d7 64 ♘d3 f6 65 ♖h1 ♔d6 66
♘f4 ♖g7 67 ♘h5 ♖g6 68 ♘g3 ♔e6 69
♘f5 ♔d7 70 ♔f4 ♔e6 71 ♖c1 ♔d7 72
♖c5 a6 73 d5 cxd5 74 ♖xd5+ ♔c7 75
♖d6 ♔b7 76 ♖d7+ ♔b8 77 ♘d6 ♖g5 78
♖b7+ ♔a8 79 ♖f7 ♔b8 80 ♖b7+ ♔a8
81 ♖h7 ♔b8 82 ♘f5 ♖g6 83 ♘d4 ♖g5
84 ♘c6+ ♔c8 85 ♘d4 ♔b8 86 ♘e6 ♖e5
87 ♘c5 ♔c8 88 ♘xa6 ♘e7 89 ♘c5 ♔c7
90 ♖xh6 ♘c6 91 ♖h7+ ♖e7 92 ♖xe7+
♘xe7 93 a6 ♔b6 94 ♘d7+ ♔xa6 95
♘xf6 ♔b7 96 ♘d5 ♘g6+ 97 ♔f5 ♘h4+
98 ♔f6 ♔c6 99 g5 ♔d6 100 g6 ♘xg6
1-0**

In TWIC this game is quoted as ending in
a draw here. I would say that this is very
unlikely, but could have happened as a result
of time trouble. Whether the result was ½-½
or 1-0 is of no great importance except, of
course, to the players. White outplayed Black
from an equal position, which is all we need
to know.

Game 48
Petursson-Polugaevsky
Reykjavik 1987

**1 d4 ♘f6 2 c4 e6 3 ♘f3 b6 4 g3 ♗a6 5
b3 ♗b7 6 ♗g2 ♗b4+ 7 ♗d2 a5!?**

This is the choice of the ambitious player.
The typical positions in this line might be
marginally better for White, as all positions in
the QID tend to be, but results are almost
always decided by who is the better player on
the day.

8 0-0 0-0 9 ♗g5

The main line, 9 ♘c3, is considered in the
next two games.

Another option is 9 ♕c2, when Black can
equalise with 9...c5!, e.g. 10 ♖d1 cxd4 11
♘xd4 ♗xg2 12 ♔xg2 ♕c7 13 ♗g5 ♕e5 14
♗xf6 ♕xf6 15 ♘c3 ♘c6 16 ♘db5 ♖fd8 17
♖ac1 ♕e7 18 ♕e4 f5 19 ♕f3 ♗c5 20 ♘a4
♘e5 21 ♕c3 ♘g4 22 ♘xc5 ♕xc5 23 ♕d4
♘f6 with a draw in Brenninkmeijer-Hübner,
Wijk aan Zee 1992. Black should avoid 9...h6
10 a3, when 10...♗e7 11 ♘c3 d5 12 ♖fd1!
♕c8?! (12...♘a6 improves) 13 cxd5 exd5 14
♗f4 ♖d8?! (14...♘h5) 15 ♘h4! left White in
charge in Karpov-Lobron, Baden-Baden
1992, while 10...♗xd2 11 ♘bxd2 d5 12 cxd5
exd5 13 ♖ac1 ♘a6 14 e3 c5 15 ♖fd1 followed by ♘b1-c3 gives White a slight advantage according to Dautov.

9...a4! 10 bxa4

10 a3?! axb3! does not benefit White.

10...h6 11 a3 ♗a5! 12 ♗xf6 ♕xf6

Black has at least equalised.

13 e3

13 ♕d3 is probably better.

13...c5!

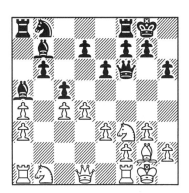

14 ♖a2

Another Polugaevsky game goes 14 ♘bd2
♗xd2 15 ♘xd2 ♗xg2 16 ♔xg2 cxd4 17 exd4
♕xd4 18 ♖b1 ♖a6 19 ♖e1 ♖c8 20 ♖e3 ♘c6
21 ♖bb3 ♘e5 22 ♖e4 ♕d6 23 ♕e2 ♕c6 24
♔g1 d6 25 ♕e3 ♕c5 26 ♖b4 ♕xe3 27 ♖xe3
and Black won the ending in Epishin-
Polugaevsky, New York 1989.

14...♖a7 15 ♘e5?!

15 dxc5 bxc5 16 ♘bd2 with approximate equality.

15...cxd4! 16 ♕xd4 d6! 17 ♘f3

17 ♘g4!? ♕xd4 18 exd4 ♗c8! 19 ♘e3 ♗d7 also gives Black something. The bishop on a5 is potentially very strong.

17...e5 18 ♕d1

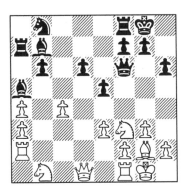

18...♘d7

Preferable is 18...♕e6! 19 ♘fd2 ♗xg2 20 ♔xg2 d5 21 ♕b3 d4! with a definite advantage for Black.

19 ♘fd2 ♗xg2 20 ♔xg2 ♕e6 21 ♖b2! ♘c5 **22 ♖b5 ♖fa8 23 ♘b3 ♘xb3 24 ♕xb3 ♖c8! 25 ♖d5?!**

25 ♖d1 ♖xc4 26 ♖xd6 ♕xd6 27 ♕xc4 ♖c7 keeps White's disadvantage to a minimum.

25...♖ac7 26 ♖fd1 ♖xc4 27 ♖xd6 ♕f5 28 ♖d8+ ♔h7 29 ♖xc8 ♖xc8 30 ♘d2 e4! 31 ♔g1?

31 ♔f1 ♖c3 32 ♕b1 ♖d3 might be terrible but it is White's only chance of survival.

31...♗xd2! 32 ♖xd2 ♖c1+ 33 ♔g2

33 ♖d1 ♕e6! picks up a rook.

33...♕f3+ 34 ♔h3 ♖g1 0-1

Game 49
Karpov-Salov
Linares 1992

---

1 d4 ♘f6 2 c4 e6 3 ♘f3 b6 4 g3 ♗a6 5 b3 ♗b7 6 ♗g2 ♗b4+ 7 ♗d2 a5 8 0-0

0-0 9 ♘c3

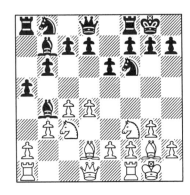

9...d5

The more flexible 9...d6 is considered in the next game. The main reason for not playing this move is an attempt to push ...d7-d5 in one go, investing the extra tempo somewhere else. After the alternative 9...♖e8 10 ♕c2 h6 11 ♖fe1 ♗xc3 12 ♗xc3 ♗e4 13 ♕b2 d5 14 ♗f1 Black has tried:

a) 14...♗xf3!? 15 exf3 ♘bd7 16 ♗d3 a4 17 ♖ad1 was Polugaevsky-Anand, Roquebrune 1992, and 17 f4! would have secured White an edge.

b) 14...♘bd7 15 ♘d2 ♕e7 16 ♖ac1 c6 17 e3 was slightly better for White in Pinter-Garcia Trobat, Spain 1993.

c) 14...c6 15 ♘d2 ♗g6 16 a3 gave White a tiny advantage in Alterman-Korchnoi, Beer-Sheva 1992.

10 ♕c2 ♘a6 11 ♖ad1! h6

11...♖c8 12 cxd5 exd5 13 ♗h3 favours White.

12 ♘e5 ♕c8 13 ♗h3!? ♕e8 14 cxd5 exd5

14...♘xd5 15 ♘xd5 ♗xd5 16 e4 ♗b7 17 ♗f4 is not to be recommended for Black.

15 ♗f4 ♖d8 16 ♕c1! ♗c8

16...♘e4 17 ♘xe4 dxe4 18 ♕c4 is only a little better for White.

17 ♗g2 ♗b7 18 a3 ♗d6 19 ♘c4!

The knight seeks fresher pastures. Black is in a bad situation.

19...♗xf4 20 ♕xf4 ♗c8 21 ♘e3 ♗e6 22

♘f5 ♗xf5 23 ♕xf5 ♕e6 24 ♕d3 ♘b8 25
b4 axb4 26 axb4 ♘c6 27 b5 ♘a5 28
♖fe1 ♖fe8 29 ♖c1 ♕d6 30 ♖c2 ♖e7 31
e3 g6 32 ♖ec1 ♔g7 33 ♘e2 ♖a8 34 ♘f4
♖a7 35 ♖a2 ♖d7 36 ♕a3! ♕xa3 37 ♖xa3
♔f8 38 ♘d3 ♔e8 39 ♘b4 h5 40 ♖ac3
♔d8 41 ♖c6! ♘e4 42 ♗h3 ♖d6 43
♖xd6+ ♘xd6 44 ♗f1! ♘e4 45 ♘xd5
♘b3 46 ♖c2 g5 47 ♗e2! ♖a1+ 48 ♔g2
♘c1 49 f3 ♘d6 50 ♗f1 g4 51 fxg4 hxg4
52 ♘f6 ♖a2 53 ♖f2! ♖xf2+ 54 ♔xf2
♘a2 55 e4 ♘c3 56 ♔e3 ♘cxb5 57 d5!
c5 58 dxc6 ♘a7 59 e5 ♘dc8 60 c7+!
♔xc7 61 ♗c4 ♘c6 62 ♘xg4 1-0

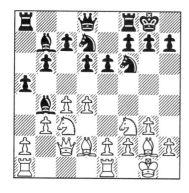

Game 50
Topalov-Adams
Fujitsu Siemens Masters Frankfurt 2000

1 d4 ♘f6 2 c4 e6 3 ♘f3 b6 4 g3 ♗a6 5
b3 ♗b7 6 ♗g2 ♗b4+ 7 ♗d2 a5 8 0-0
0-0 9 ♕c2 d6 10 ♘c3 ♘bd7 11 ♖fe1

This is the most difficult for Black to
meet. Others:

a) 11 ♖ad1 ♗xc3 12 ♗xc3 ♗e4 13 ♕c1
a4 14 ♗h3 b5 15 ♘d2 axb3 16 axb3 bxc4 17
bxc4 ♖a2 led to full equality in Morovic Fer-
nandez-Adams, Istanbul 2000. The position
is about equal, perhaps a bit better for Black.

b) 11 ♘e1 ♕c8 12 ♖c1 ♖e8 13 ♘b5
♗xg2 14 ♘xg2 ♕b8 15 a3 ♗xd2 16 ♕xd2
c6 17 ♘c3 d5 with equality in Korchnoi-
Adams, Wijk aan Zee 2000.

11...♗xc3 12 ♗xc3 ♗e4 13 ♕b2

The great expert of the QID-g3, GM
Dautov, plays the more flexible 13 ♕c1!?,
when the queen is yet to commit to a flank.
Dautov-Romanishin, Essen 2001 continued
13...h6 14 ♗h3 ♗h7 15 ♘d2 ♘e4 16 ♘xe4
♗xe4 17 f3 ♗h7 18 e4 a4 19 ♕b2 with a
pull, while 13...♕b8 14 ♗h3 c6 15 ♘h4 h6
16 f3 ♗h7 17 e4 b5 18 ♕d2 gave White
similar prospects in Dautov-Zeller, Boeblingen 1996.

13...a4

Just one of several possibilities.

a) 13...c6!? 14 ♗f1 b5 15 ♘g5 ♗g6 16
♗g2 d5 17 c5?! h6 18 ♘f3 ♘e4! led to equality in Pinter-Almasi, Budapest 1997. Avrukh
suggests 17 f3!? as an improvement. Sjöberg-
Almasi, Malmö 1994 went 15 d5?!, and now
the strongest seems to be 15...exd5! 16 cxb5
c5 17 ♗xf6 ♘xf6 18 ♘d2 ♗g6 and Black
has a pleasant grip on the centre.

b) 13...d5 14 ♗h3!? ♗f5 (14...dxc4 15
bxc4 c5 16 d5! exd5 17 cxd5 ♗xd5?! 18
♖ad1 gives White a dangerous initiative according to Chernin) 15 ♗xf5 exf5 16 ♘h4
♘e4!? 17 f3 ♘xc3 18 ♕xc3 f4 19 ♖ac1 with
a slight edge for White in Chernin-
Romanishin, Taastrup 1992.

c) 13...♕b8 14 ♗f1 (in Petursson-Lerner,
Moscow 1987 White tried 14 ♗h3 b5 15 d5
e5 16 ♘d2 ♗g6 17 cxb5 ♕xb5 18 e4 ♘c5 19
♗f1 ♕b6 and was already struggling) 14...c5
15 ♖ad1 ♖d8 16 ♗h3! a4! 17 ♘d2 axb3 18
axb3 ♗b7 19 d5 with compensation for the
pawn, should Black decide to take it, in van
Wely-Karpov, Tilburg 1996. 14...♗xf3!? 15
exf3 d5 16 ♖ac1 c6 was Hulak-Polugaevsky,
Zagreb 1987. Now 17 f4 should give White
some advantage.

14 ♗f1 c5

14...♕b8!? 15 ♘d2 b5 16 f3 ♗c6 17 b4
bxc4 18 ♘xc4 d5 19 ♘a3 ♖e8 gave Black a
good game in van der Sterren-Timman,
Gouda 1997. But we should still question
whether White could have played better.
14...♗b7 15 ♘d2 ♘e4 16 ♗g2 ♘df6 17

♘xe4 ♘xe4 18 d5 ♘xc3 19 ♕xc3 e5 20 b4 f5 offered Black sufficient counterplay in Pinter-Romanishin, Balatonbereny 1995, but it seems that White was not out to test his opponent in this game.

15 ♘d2 ♗b7 16 b4

16 ♗h3 ♕c7 17 ♖ad1 ♖a6 18 d5 e5 19 f4 ♖fa8 was the course of Kragelj-Romanishin, Pula 1994, with a good game for Black.

16...a3 17 ♕b3 cxd4 18 ♗xd4 e5 19 ♗e3 ♕c7 20 ♖ac1 ♕c6 21 f3 ♕a4 22 ♕b1

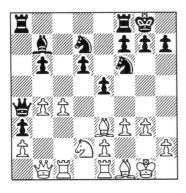

22...d5!

It is obvious that Black has outplayed his opponent in the opening and now has a better game.

23 ♗f2 e4 24 ♗d4 ♖fe8 25 cxd5 ♗xd5 26 f4 e3 27 ♘c4 ♗e4 28 ♕a1 ♕xb4 29 ♘xe3 b5 30 ♗h3 ♖ad8 31 ♖ed1 ♗a8 32 ♖b1 ♕a4 33 ♕c3 ♘f8 34 ♗e5 ♖xd1+ 35 ♖xd1 ♘d5 36 ♖xd5 ♗xd5 37 ♗xg7 ♖xe3 38 ♕xe3 ♕d1+ 39 ♔f2 ♔xg7 40 ♕e5+ f6 41 ♕e7+ ♗f7 42 ♕xa3 ♕d4+ 43 ♕e3 ♕xe3+ 44 ♔xe3 ♗xa2

As you can see it is not only club players who play on in embarrassing positions. This probably has something to do with a fighter's attitude...

45 ♔d4 ♗c4 46 e3 ♘e6+ 47 ♔c3 ♘c5 48 ♗f5 h6 49 h4 ♗e6 50 ♗c2 ♘a6 51 ♗d3 b4+ 52 ♔d4 ♘c7 53 e4 b3 54 ♔c3 ♔f8 55 ♗e2 ♔e7 56 g4 ♔d6 57 g5 hxg5 58 fxg5 fxg5 59 hxg5 ♔c5 60 ♔b2 ♔b4

61 g6 ♘b5 62 g7 ♘c3 63 ♗g4 ♘a4+ 64 ♔b1 ♗g8 65 e5 ♗h7+ 0-1

Game 51
Ehlvest-Chandler
Lucerne 1989

1 d4 ♘f6 2 c4 e6 3 ♘f3 b6 4 g3 ♗a6 5 b3 ♗b7 6 ♗g2 ♗b4+ 7 ♗d2 c5!?

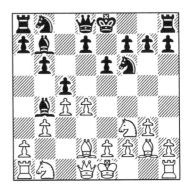

Initially this seems quite strange but, when you think about it, Black is trying to gain some control over the dark squares on the queenside, as well as opening the c-file. If you compare it with 7...a5, then 7...c5 better meets 9 ♘c3.

8 0-0

Harmless is 8 dxc5 ♗xc5 9 ♘c3 ♘e4 10 ♘xe4 ♗xe4 11 ♗c3 0-0 12 0-0 ♘c6 13 ♕d2 d5 14 cxd5 ♕xd5 with complete equality, Hjartarson-Korchnoi, Barcelona 1989.

8...0-0 9 ♗c3

9 dxc5 transposes to 8 dxc5. 9 ♘c3 cxd4 10 ♘xd4 ♗xg2 11 ♔xg2 d5 results in immediate equality, a draw being agreed in Olafsson-Petursson, Reykjavik 1989, for example.

9...d5 10 cxd5

Or 10 ♘e5 ♘c6! 11 ♘xc6 (11 ♗xb4 ♘xb4! does not trouble Black) 11...♗xc6 12 ♗xb4 (12 e3, as in Goldin-Douven, Palma de Mallorca 1989, leads to equaliity after 12...♗xc3 13 ♘xc3 ♖c8 14 dxc5 dxc4!) 12...cxb4 13 ♕d3!? dxc4 14 bxc4 ♗xg2 15

♔xg2 b5! 16 cxb5 ♕d5+ 17 f3 ♖fd8 with a complex position which should be okay for Black, Nikolic-Salov, Brussels 1988.

10 ♗xb4 cxb4 11 ♘bd2 ♘c6 12 e3 ♖c8 13 ♕b1 ♖c7 14 ♖c1 ♕e7 15 ♕b2 ♖fc8 16 ♘e5 was equal in Tukmakov-Arnason, Reykjavik 1990. I suspect that Black might have the better practical chances here.

10...exd5

Only move. 10...♘xd5 11 ♗b2 cxd4 12 ♕xd4 ♕f6 13 a3! ♕xd4 14 ♘xd4 ♗c5 15 ♘b5! ♘c6 16 b4 ♗e7 17 e4 ♘f6 18 e5 ♘d5 19 ♘1c3! was a solid plus for White in Karpov-Korchnoi, Biel 1992, and 10...♗xd5 11 a3 ♗xc3 12 ♘xc3 ♗b7 13 dxc5 bxc5 14 ♕xd8 ♖xd8 15 ♘e5 ♗xg2 16 ♔xg2 was uncomfortable for Black, if not a great deal worse, in Kishnev-Romanishin, Munich 1992.

11 ♗b2

11 dxc5 ♗xc5 12 ♗b2 ♘a6 13 ♘c3 ♘e4 14 ♖c1 ♘c7 15 ♘d4 ♖e8 favoured Black in Novikov-Hjartarson, Tilburg 1992.

11...♘e4 12 a3

Brenninkmeijer-Arnason, Groningen 1990 resulted in a level game after 12 dxc5 bxc5 13 a3 ♗a5 14 b4 ♕b6!? 15 ♘c3 ♘xc3 16 ♗xc3 cxb4 17 axb4 ♗xb4 18 ♗xb4 ♕xb4 19 ♖b1 ♕e7 20 ♘d4!? ♕d7! etc.

12...♗a5 13 ♘fd2 f5!?

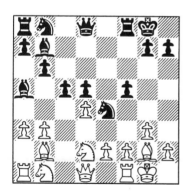

Black has had a successful opening. The situation is unclear.

14 ♘xe4 fxe4 15 ♘c3 ♘a6!

15...♘c6? 16 dxc5 ♗xc3 17 ♗xc3 bxc5 18 b4 is very good for White.

16 ♖c1 ♔h8 17 e3 ♗xc3 18 ♗xc3 ♕g5 19 ♗b2 ♖ad8 20 f4!? exf3 21 ♖xf3 ♕e7 22 ♕d2 ♖xf3 23 ♗xf3 ♖e8 24 ♖e1 ♘c7 25 ♗g2 ♘e6 26 ♖f1 ♘g5 27 ♖f5 h6 28 ♖e5 ♕f7 29 ♖xe8+ ♕xe8 30 ♕f2?

Allowing the creation of a passed pawn. Instead 30 dxc5! bxc5 31 b4 is unclear.

30...c4! 31 bxc4 dxc4 32 d5 ♗xd5 33 h4 ♘e4 34 ♕f5?

34 ♗xe4 ♗xe4 35 ♕f4 is an unattractive lesser evil.

34...c3!

Now this is possible.

35 ♕xd5

This loses on the spot. There is still some resistance left in 35 ♗a1 c2 36 ♗b2 ♘f6!? 37 ♗xd5 ♕xe3+ 38 ♔h2 c1♕ 39 ♗xc1 ♕xc1, with an extra pawn for Black.

35...♘f6! 36 ♕d4 cxb2 37 ♕xb2 ♕xe3+ 38 ♕f2 ♕xa3 39 ♕f4 ♕c5+ 40 ♔h1 b5 41 ♕d2 ♕c7 0-1

Game 52
Dokhoian-Romanishin
Yerevan 1989

---

1 d4 ♘f6 2 c4 e6 3 ♘f3 b6 4 g3 ♗a6 5 b3 ♗b7 6 ♗g2 ♗b4+ 7 ♗d2 c5 8 0-0 0-0 9 ♗xb4 cxb4

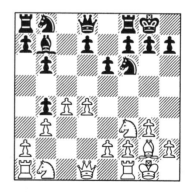

10 ♕d3!

The most serious move.

a) After 10 ♘bd2 d6 11 ♕c2 it is obvious that the queen is less well placed on c2. Shariyazdanov-Baklan, Neum 2000 continued 11...♘c6 12 e4 e5 13 d5 ♘b8 14 a3 bxa3 (14...♘a6!, a suggested of Rabinovich, seems to be more natural) 15 b4 a5 16 c5!? (this double pawn sacrifice was, of course, planned, and is rather complex) 16...♘a6 17 c6 ♘xb4 18 ♕c3 ♗a6 and Black had good counterplay in this very double edged position.

b) 10 a3 and now Black has:

b1) 10...bxa3 11 ♘xa3 a5 12 ♘e1 ♗xg2 was a short draw in Bauer-Baklan, Germany 1999. It seems that Black should be equal. There is also 12 ♘b5! to consider, fighting for e4. This seems more dangerous, although I believe Black is fine.

b2) 10...♘a6 11 e3 ♕e7 12 a4!? ♘e4 13 a5 b5! 14 ♘fd2 ♘c3! 15 ♕c2 ♗xg2 16 ♔xg2 ♘xb1 17 ♖axb1 ♖fc8 with sufficient counterplay for Black in Epishin-Petursson, Bern 1991. 11 axb4 ♘xb4 12 ♘c3 ♘e4 13 ♕c1 ♘xc3 14 ♕xc3 a5 15 ♘e5 was a draw in Yusupov-Benjamin, Saint John 1988, while 11 ♘e5 ♗xg2 12 ♔xg2 ♕b8 13 ♘d3 bxa3 14 ♖xa3 ♕b7+ 15 ♔g1 d5 16 ♘d2 ♘b8 17 e3 ♘c6 was yet another draw in Hracek-Dorfman, Hamburg 2001.

10...♗e4?

Serving only to create problems for Black. Both alternatives are superior:

a) 10...d5 and now:

a1) 11 ♘bd2 ♘bd7 12 ♖fc1 ♕e7 13 ♕e3 (13 ♘e5 ♖fc8 14 f4 ♘e8 15 e4 ♘df6 was more or less equal in Psakhis-Lutz, Baden-Baden 1992) 13...♖ac8 14 ♘e5 ♘xe5 15 dxe5 ♘d7 16 cxd5 ♗xd5 17 ♗xd5 exd5 18 ♘f3 ♖c5 19 ♕d4 ♖e8 with equality (or something very close) in Nikolic-Arnason, Moscow 1990.

a2) 11 ♘e5 ♘bd7 12 ♘xd7 ♕xd7 13 ♘d2 ♖fd8 14 ♖fd1 dxc4 15 ♘xc4 with equality in Gavrikov-Korchnoi, Swiss League 1995.

b) 10...d6 11 ♘bd2 a5 (11...♘bd7 12 a3

bxa3 13 ♖xa3 e5 14 ♘h4 ♗xg2 15 ♘xg2 d5!? 16 ♘e3 dxc4 17 ♘dxc4 gave White an advantage in Ftacnik-Romanishin, Maribor 1995) 12 ♖ad1 ♕c7 13 e4 e5 14 ♘h4 ♘c6 was equal in Gruenberg-Hjartarson, Novi Sad 1990. 13 e3!? stays flexible in the centre and seems to be stronger. After e3-e4 ...e6-e5 Black is always equal.

11 ♕e3 ♘c6 12 ♘bd2 d5 13 ♘xe4?

Later this variation was refuted with 13 cxd5! exd5 (13...♗xd5 14 ♕d3 gives White the advantage as e2-e4 is coming) 14 ♘e5 ♗xg2 15 ♘xc6 ♕d7 16 ♘e5 ♕h3 17 ♖fc1 with a clear advantage for White in Dautov-Romanishin, Kecskemet 1989.

13...♘xe4 14 ♘d2

Preferable is 14 a3 bxa3 15 ♖xa3 ♘b4 16 ♖c1 a5, with equality in Lerner-Romanishin, Nikolaev 1995.

14...♘c3

Now the threat of ...♘xd4 dictates White's moves, and Black already have an advantage.

15 ♘b1

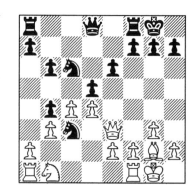

15 ♘f3 seems to be more natural.

15...♘xd4! 16 ♘xc3 ♘c2 17 ♕c1 ♘xa1 18 ♘b5 a6 19 ♘d4 ♘xb3 20 axb3 ♖c8 21 ♖d1 ♕f6 22 e4 ♖fd8 23 ♕b1 dxc4?

23...dxe4! 24 ♘c2 ♖xd1+ 25 ♕xd1 ♖d8 26 ♕e1 ♕b2! secures Black a clear advantage.

24 ♘c6 ♖xd1+ 25 ♕xd1 e5 26 ♘xb4 cxb3 27 ♘d5 ♕d6 28 ♕xb3 ♖c1+ 29 ♗f1 b5 30 ♔g2 ♕c5 31 ♗d3 ♕d6 32

♗c2 ♕c5 33 ♗d3 ♕d6 34 ♗c2 ♕c5
½-½

Game 53
Nielsen-Anand
Moscow 2001

---

1 d4 ♘f6 2 c4 e6 3 ♘f3

An important point here is that this can lead to transposition to the Catalan with 3 g3 ♗b4+ 4 ♗d2 ♗e7 5 ♗g2 d5 6 ♘f3 0-0 7 0-0 c6 8 ♕c2 b6 9 b3 ♗a6 10 ♖d1 ♘bd7, and you have the move after 10...0-0. Of course Black can also delay castling in this line but, as we shall see, this has no positive sides.

3...b6 4 g3 ♗a6 5 b3 ♗b4+ 6 ♗d2 ♗e7

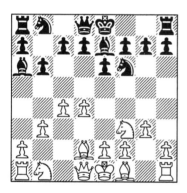

This is the main line everywhere, although, as we have seen, not Black's only reasonable line.

7 ♗g2

White also has 7 ♘c3 0-0 8 e4 as an interesting possibility, but time has shown that after 8...d5 9 cxd5 ♗xf1 10 ♔xf1 exd5 11 e5 ♘e4 12 ♔g2 ♕d7 13 ♕e2 ♘xc3 14 ♗xc3 ♘c6 15 ♖he1 ♘d8 16 ♘g1 ♘e6 17 f4 g6 18 ♘f3 ♘g7, as in Tukmakov-Vaganian, Odessa 1989, Black is fine, although, of course, there is a lot of play in the position. The main line is marked by there being very little place for individual performance or any other kind of competition between the two players, so such lines do attract a lot of players who see chess as 'going to the office'. There are many

GM between 2450 and 2550 who view chess as a random profession, playing a sort of accountant's chess. These people often play such technical lines, which are equal but not dead, and then they make their 75% score without any real risks. Here the position is just equal.

7...c6

Black has two major alternatives:

a) 7...♗b7 8 ♘c3 0-0 9 0-0 d5 (best – 9...♘a6 10 e3 d5 11 ♕e2 c5 12 ♖fd1 ♘c7 13 ♘e5 ♗d6 14 ♗e1 ♕e7 15 f4 ♖fd8 16 g4 was better for White in Van der Sterren-Sokolov, Amsterdam 1994, while 9...c5 10 d5! exd5 11 ♘e1 ♘a6 12 cxd5 d6 13 ♘d3 ♘c7 14 e4 ♘d7 15 f4 was quite pleasant for White in Timman-Franco Ocampos, Mar del Plata 1982) 10 cxd5 exd5 11 ♗c1! ♘a6 12 ♗b2 c6 13 ♘e5 ♗d6 14 ♘d3 ♖e8 15 ♖c1 ♘c7 16 ♖e1 ♘e6 17 e4 with a slight advantage for White in a typical position, Karpov-Kurajica, Tilburg 1994.

b) 7...d5 has a reputation for achieving equality, but a poor record when it comes to practical results. The position arising after 8 cxd5 ♘xd5 9 ♘c3 ♘d7 10 ♘xd5 exd5 11 0-0 0-0 12 ♖c1 ♖e8 13 ♖e1 c5 14 ♗e3 ♗b7 15 ♗h3 cxd4 16 ♗xd4 ♘f6, as in Karpov-Sokolov, Linares 1987, might be equal, but I would not like to have such a position with Black, where White has a simple blockade of the isolated pawn. All in all it might be equal from an objective point of view, but Black will find it hard in practice.

8 0-0 d5 9 ♕c2!?

This variation was previously thought to be harmless, but after 8 ♗c3 d5 9 ♘e5 had been drained of new ideas, White tried to go elsewhere to find an advantage. I do not thing that this is the way, but nor can I suggest another path. Other moves have been tried here, but none so serious that it deserves a mention in a book like this.

9...♘bd7 10 ♖d1

The most precise approach. The alternatives were:

a) 10 a4 0-0 11 a5 ♘e4 12 axb6 axb6 13 ♗f4 b5 14 ♘bd2 ♘xd2 15 ♘xd2 bxc4 16 bxc4 ♗f6 with equality Gurieli-Sokolov, Basle 2001.

b) 10 ♗f4 ♖c8 11 ♘bd2 (11 ♖d1 is, of course, still the main line) 11...c5 12 dxc5 ♘xc5 13 ♖ac1 0-0 14 ♕b2 b5 15 cxd5 ♘xd5 16 ♗e5 f6 17 ♗d4 b4 with a better position for Black in Babu-Prasad, Kuala Lumpur 1992. But White did not play the best possible lines. Meanwhile 12...♗xc5 13 ♕b2 dxc4 14 ♘xc4 ♗xc4 15 bxc4 0-0 16 ♖ad1 ♕e7 was equal in Tjiam-Van der Wiel, Holland 1993.

10...♖c8

Unless some improvement is found over the main game here, Black will have to go back to castling and slow play: 10...0-0 11 ♗f4 ♖c8 12 ♘c3 and now:

a) 12...♘h5 13 ♗c1 ♘hf6 14 e4 dxc4 15 ♘d2 b5 16 bxc4 bxc4 17 ♘a4 (17 ♕a4 ♗b5 18 ♕c2 ♕a5 19 ♘f3 h6 20 ♗d2 ♗b4 21 ♖ab1 ♗xc3 22 ♗xc3 ♗a4 23 ♕d2 ♕h5 and Black has a good position, Van Wely-Adams, Wijk aan Zee 2001) 17...c5 18 d5 exd5 19 exd5 ♘e5 20 ♗b2 ♗d6 resulted in a complex struggle in Georgiev-Mitkov, Skopje 2002, where the best player won.

b) 12...b5 13 c5 b4 14 ♘a4 ♗b5 15 ♘b2 ♘e4 16 ♘d3 ♕a5 is extremely complex, Hansen-Emms, Esbjerg 2000. Perhaps Black is equal, but it is a considerably difficult position to handle.

c) 12...dxc4!? seems to be the strongest, although both the alternatives are fine. Kramnik-Leko, Hungary 2001 continued 13 ♘d2 c5 14 dxc5 ♗xc5 15 ♘de4 ♘xe4 16 ♘xe4 cxb3 17 ♕b2 bxa2 18 ♖xa2 ♗c4 19 ♖xa7 ♗d5 20 ♘xc5 bxc5 21 e4 ♗c6 22 ♖d6 ♖a8 23 ♕a3 ♖xa7 24 ♕xa7 ♕c8 25 ♗f1 ♘f6 26 ♗a6 ♕e8 27 f3 ♗b5 28 ♕xc5 ♗xa6 with a draw. White obviously had compensation, but hardly an advantage.

Earlier White has also tried 11 a4 c5 12 ♘c3 dxc4 13 bxc4 ♗xc4 14 ♘e5 ♘xe5 15 dxe5 ♘d5 with a complex but even position

in Gelfand-Lautier, Biel 2001. White will expand with f2-f4 and e2-e4 and send his knight to d6, while Black maintains his extra pawn.

11 ♗f4! c5?!

11...0-0 still transposes to the 10th move.

12 dxc5 ♗xc5 13 ♘c3!

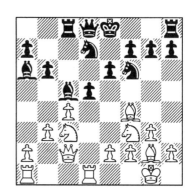

This remarkable piece of home preparation should have refuted Black's set-up and will, in the future, make Black return to 10...0-0. The latest try at the top level looked like this: 13 ♕b2 0-0 14 ♘c3 ♗b4! 15 ♘e5 b5 16 a3 ♗xc3 17 ♕xc3 bxc4 and Black had the advantage in Van Wely-Polgar, Hoogeveen 2001.

13...0-0 14 e4!

The notes that follow are based on Peter Heine Nielsen's annotations in the splendid Swedish magazine Schacknytt.

14...♘g4

14...dxc4 15 e5 ♘g4 16 ♘g5 g6 17 ♘ge4 would also give White the advantage.

15 exd5

15 ♖d2!? is a more careful alternative according to Nielsen, but after 15...e5! it seems to be just as complicated – only now I prefer Black.

15...♘xf2 16 ♖f1 e5

16...♘h3+ 17 ♔h1 ♘xf4 18 gxf4 exd5 19 ♘g5 ♘f6 20 ♘xd5 g6 21 ♖ad1 gives White a winning attack. The plan is ♕c3-h3, with numerous threats.

17 ♗c1 e4 18 ♘h4 e3!

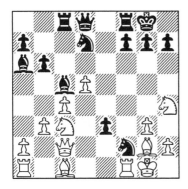

In their preparation Peter's team had focused on 18...♕f6 19 ♗b2 ♘d1+ 20 ♔h1 ♘e3 21 ♕e2 ♘xf1 22 ♖xf1 ♕d8 23 ♘xe4, and White has overwhelming compensation.

19 ♘a4 ♗d4

19...♘h3+ 20 ♗xh3 e2+ 21 ♘xc5 exf1♕+ 22 ♗xf1 ♘xc5 23 ♗b2 is not as promising as earlier exchange sacrifices but still leads to a clear advantage for White. One line is 23...b5 24 ♘f5 bxc4 25 ♗xg7, and White's attack decides.

20 ♗b2

20 ♖b1?! ♘h3+ 21 ♗xh3 e2+ 22 ♔h1 exf1♕+ 23 ♗xf1 ♗f6!, followed by ...b6-b5, gives Black reasonable chances.

20...♗xb2 21 ♕xb2?

A blunder. 21 ♘xb2! g6 is necessary according to Anand. 22 ♕c3! ♖e8 23 ♖ae1 leads to a clear advantage to White according to Curt Hansen.

21...b5 22 ♘f5 ♕g5

The move White had missed.

23 ♘d6 bxa4 24 ♘xc8 ♗xc8 25 ♕d4 ♘f6 26 ♖ae1 ♖e8 27 d6 ♘h3+ 28 ♗xh3 ♗xh3 29 ♖f4 ♕a5 30 ♖xe3 ♖xe3 31 ♕xe3 axb3 32 d7 ♗xd7 33 axb3 ♗h3 0-1

Game 54
Kamsky-Karpov
Elista 1996

---

1 d4 ♘f6 2 c4 e6 3 ♘f3 b6 4 g3 ♗a6 5
b3 ♗b4+ 6 ♗d2 ♗e7 7 ♗g2 c6 8 ♗c3 d5 9 ♘e5 ♘fd7!

9...0-0 10 ♘d2 ♘fd7 11 ♘d3 has been known to be an unnecessary extra possibility for White since Lputian-Portisch, Manila 1990. White is slightly better.

10 ♘xd7 ♘xd7 11 ♘d2 0-0 12 0-0 ♖c8

This has been the main line almost forever, but the Portisch line with 12...♘f6 13 e4 b5 has brought Black good results. Karpov-Timman, Hoogeveen 1999 continued 14 ♖e1 dxe4 15 ♕c2 ♖c8 16 ♖ad1 ♘d5 17 ♗xe4 (17 cxd5 cxd5 18 a3 ♗xa3 gives Black good compensation for the pieces, while Black also had excellent compensation after 17 ♗b2 f5 18 cxd5 cxd5 19 ♕b1 b4 20 ♘f1 ♕b6 21 f3 ♗f6 in Karpov-Polgar, Buenos Aires 2000) 17...♘xc3 18 ♕xc3 ♗f6 19 ♕c2 g6 20 ♘f3 bxc4 21 bxc4 ♕a5 22 c5 ♗b5 with a level game.

12...b5?! 13 ♖e1 bxc4 14 bxc4 ♘b6 15 c5 ♘c4 16 e4 led to a plus for White in Novikov-Hellers, Copenhagen 1991.

13 e4 c5

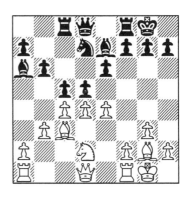

The main move. 13...b5 14 ♖e1 dxc4 15 bxc4 bxc4 16 ♕a4 ♗b5 17 ♕c2 ♖e8 18 a4 ♗a6 19 ♖ad1 ♗f8 20 ♖e3 ♕c7?! (20...c5 21 d5 exd5 22 exd5 with a slight advantage is probably better) 21 ♗f1 c5 22 d5 exd5 23 exd5 ♖xe3 24 fxe3 ♘e5 25 ♕e4 and White was well in control in Grabliauskas-Shariyazdanov, Swidnica 1997. 14...dxe4 15 ♗xe4 c5 16 cxb5 ♗xb5 17 d5 exd5 18 ♗xd5

♘b6 19 ♗g2 was also favourable for White in Shipov-Gagarin, Moscow 1994. After 19...♗f6?! 20 ♗xf6 ♕xf6 21 ♘e4 ♕g6 22 ♕d2! Black was in trouble, with ♕a5 threatened.

14 exd5 exd5 15 dxc5 dxc4 16 c6 cxb3 17 ♖e1 ♗b5?!

17...b2! was once thought to be refuted and thus replaced with the text move, but current trends go in the opposite direction. 17...b2 is considered in the next game.

18 axb3 ♗xc6 19 ♗xc6 ♖xc6 20 ♖xa7 ♗f6

20...♖xc3? 21 ♘b1! and White has a clear advantage, e.g. 21...♖c7 22 ♖xc7 ♕xc7 23 ♖xe7 ♖d8 24 ♕d5 ♕c1+ 25 ♔g2 ♖f8 26 ♖xd7 ♕xb1 27 ♖d6 and Black has a horrible ending to face which, in practice, is drawn very rarely.

21 ♘c4! ♗xc3

21...♖xc4? 22 bxc4 ♗xc3 23 ♖e3 and White wins material. The best chance lies in 21...♘c5! 22 ♕xd8 ♖xd8 23 ♗xf6 gxf6 (23...♖xf6 24 b4 ♗e6 25 ♘xb6 gave White a clear advantage in Karpov-Beliavsky, Linares 1993) 24 ♘e3!, an improvement over a previous game. Van Wely-Karpov, Cap d`Agde 1996, went 24...♘xb3 25 ♘f5 ♖c1 26 ♖xc1 ♘xc1 27 ♖b7 b5 28 ♔g2 h5 29 ♖xb5, with a promising ending for White.

22 ♖xd7 ♕f6

22...♕c8 23 ♖e3 ♗f6 24 ♕d5 b5 25 ♘a3 b4 26 ♘c4 h6 27 ♔g2 ♖c7? 28 ♘b6! and White was clearly better in Khalifman-Van der Wiel, Ter Apel 1993. Instead 27...♖c5 28 ♕b7 ♕xb7+ 29 ♖xb7 ♗c3, with an endgame with no other prospects than a fight for a draw, was the only chance.

23 ♖e4 ♕f5?

Karpov and his seconds prepared this position before the game and none of them saw the coming combination. The most amazing thing about this oversight is that a similar combination had already been played in the following game: 23...♖e6 24 ♖f4 ♕g6? (24...♕xf4 25 gxf4 ♖e1+ 26 ♕xe1 ♗xe1 27

♘xb6 is the only chance, but of course Black cannot hope for anything other than a draw) 25 ♖dxf7! ♕xf7 26 ♖xf7 ♖xf7 27 ♕d8+ ♖f8 28 ♕d5 and White won, Chernin-Veingold, Seville 1993.

24 ♖f4 ♕e6

25 ♖dxf7!

Picking up a pawn.

25...♖e8

The sacrifice could never be accepted: 25...♖xf7 26 ♕d8+ and 25...♕xf7 26 ♖xf7 ♖xf7 27 ♕d8+ ♖f8 28 ♕d5+ are both straightforward winning lines.

26 ♕f3 ♗f6 27 ♖b7 h6 28 ♔g2 ♔h8 29 h4 ♔g8 30 ♔h2 ♔h8 31 ♕h5 ♖d8 32 ♖f7 ♗d4 33 ♖f8+ ♖xf8 34 ♖xf8+ ♔h7 35 ♕f3 ♗c5 36 ♖f5 ♖c8 37 h5 ♖d8 38 ♖e5 ♕d7 39 ♕e4+ ♔h8 40 ♔g2 ♖f8 41 f4 ♖d8 42 ♕f3 ♗d4 43 ♖e2 b5 44 ♘d2 ♗b6 45 ♘e4 ♕d1?! 46 ♘f2 ♕b1 47 ♘g4 ♕f5 48 ♘e5 ♔g8? 49 ♘c6 1-0

Game 55
Gheorghiu-Cserna
Berlin 1986

---

1 d4 ♘f6 2 ♘f3 e6 3 c4 b6 4 g3 ♗a6 5 b3 ♗b4+ 6 ♗d2 ♗e7 7 ♗g2 c6 8 ♗c3 d5 9 ♘e5 ♘fd7 10 ♘xd7 ♘xd7 11 ♘d2 0-0 12 0-0 ♖c8 13 e4 c5 14 exd5 exd5 15 dxc5 dxc4 16 c6 cxb3 17 ♖e1 b2!

Once refuted, now the drawing line, killing all life in the position.

18 ♗xb2 ♘c5

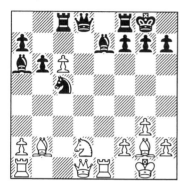

18...♘f6 19 ♘b3 ♗b4 20 ♖e3 ♕xd1+ 21 ♖xd1 ♖fd8 22 ♖d4! gives White a clear advantage due to the pawn on c6.

19 ♗a3

This was the refution of the ...b2 line, but improvements have been found. Others:

a) 19 ♘b3!? ♘d3 20 ♖e2 ♗b4! 21 ♗d4 ♗c5! was a draw in Gelfand-Anand, China 2000. The reason is 22 ♘xc5 (22 ♗c3? ♘f4! 23 ♖d2 ♘e2+ 24 ♔h1 ♕e7! 25 ♗b2 ♗xf2 is enormous for Black) 22...bxc5 23 ♗c3 ♗b5! 24 ♖e3 c4 25 ♕g4 g6 26 a4 ♗xc6 27 ♕xc4 ♗xg2 28 ♕xd3 with equality. Here 21...♘c5? 22 ♖c2! ♗d3 23 ♘xc5! ♗xc2 24 ♕g4 gave White a strong position in Dautov-Sax, Germany 1998.

b) 19 ♕g4?! ♗f6 20 ♗xf6 ♕xf6 gave White nothing but problems in Timoschenko-Bagaturov, Enakievo 1997.

c) 19 ♘c4 ♗xc4 (White is better after both 19...♘d3 20 ♖xe7! ♗xc4 21 ♖d7 ♘xb2 22 ♖xd8 ♘xd1 23 ♖dxd1!, and 19...♗f6? 20 ♕xd8 ♖fxd8 21 ♗xf6 gxf6 22 ♘e3) 20 ♕g4 ♗g5! 21 ♕xc4 ♘d3 with a further branch:

c1) 22 ♗c3 ♘xe1 23 ♖xe1 ♖e8 24 ♖xe8+ (24 ♖b1 ♖e6 25 h4 ♗f6 26 ♗b4 ♕d4 Barus-Shneider, Jakarta 1997 and Black has a clear advantage according to Khalifman) 24...♕xe8 25 ♕g4 ♗h6, planning to return the exchange, gives Black a better game

according to Khalifman.

c2) 22 ♖e2? ♘xb2 23 ♖xb2 ♗f6 wins for Black.

c3) 22 ♗e5! ♘xe1 23 ♖xe1 ♗f6! 24 ♗xf6 (Komarov gives 24 ♗h3? ♕d2 25 ♔f1 ♖ce8) 24...♕xf6 25 c7 and a draw was soon agreed in Georgiev-Komarov, Yugoslavia 1997.

19...♗d6?

19...♗b5?! 20 ♘b3 ♗f6 21 ♘xc5 bxc5 was Gheorghiu's recommendation, but after 22 ♖c1 ♕xd1 23 ♖exd1 ♗xc6 24 ♗xc5 White seems to have some chances. The a-pawn is probably falling.

19...♗f6! 20 ♖c1 ♗g5 21 ♖c2 ♗b5 22 ♘b3 ♕xd1 23 ♖xd1 ♗xc6 24 ♘xc5 ♗xg2 25 ♔xg2 ♗e7 26 ♖dc1 ♖fe8 27 ♖c3 bxc5 28 ♗xc5 ♗xc5 29 ♖xc5 ♖xc5 30 ♖xc5 g6 31 ♖c7 ♖e2 32 ♖xa7 h5 33 ♔f3 ♖c2 34 h4 ♔g7 35 ♖a6 was the course of Dautov-Alterman, Germany 1998. This endgame is a theoretical draw. Black can even lose a tempo once the a-pawn starts rolling and still make the draw. However, many players find it difficult to draw such endings in practice. One example is Georgiev, who lost it to Akopian in Las Vegas 1999. That game can be found in my book *Excelling at Chess*, page 104. Alterman also lost this endgame, but those intending to play this line should look this ending up and then they would find that there is nothing to fear. 20 ♗xc5 bxc5 21 ♖c1 ♗b5 22 ♖xc5 was agreed drawn in Shneider-Anand, Bastia 2000. Taking the difference of strength of the two players into account, one might suspect that Black was not altogether confident about his position, but I think that if Anand really wanted to win against Shneider, he would have chosen a less forcing system.

20 ♘b3 ♘d3

20...♘xb3 21 ♗xd6 ♘xa1 22 ♗xf8 and White can hope for a considerable advantage.

21 ♗xd6 ♕xd6 22 ♘c1! ♖fd8 23 ♘xd3 ♗xd3 24 ♕a4 a5 25 ♖ad1 ♕c7 26 ♗h3 b5 27 ♕h4 1-0

Summary

After 5 b3 d5 6 ♗g2, game 45 shows that 6...dxc4?! is past its sell-by date. White has found the right path to a small but very clear advantage. After 5...b5!? White will always be a little better, as his pawn structure is slightly superior. Still this line has brought many players good practical results, and is good for winning attempts, as the position easily becomes unbalanced. Also interesting is 5...♗b4!? with the idea to exchange on d2. As far as I can see this line is theoretically okay, even though the practically results indicate that it is easier to play the White side. Both 7...a5!? and 7...c5!? are probably very slightly worse for Black, but again they give positions where there remains much play, and where the better player most often succeed. The long lines with 5...♗b4+ and 6...♗e7 seems to be the main reason for Black to play 4...♗a6. There are good reasons for this: If White plays the tough lines, Black can liquidate the game to a draw, and if not, Black is probably fine all the same.

1 d4 ♘f6 2 c4 e6 3 ♘f3 b6 4 g3 ♗a6 5 b3 *(D)* **♗b4 +**

     5...d5 6 ♗g2 dxc4 – *Game 45*

     5...b5 – *Game 46*

     5...♗b7 6 ♗g2 ♗b4+ 7 ♗d2 *(D)*

          7...a5 8 0-0 0-0

               9 ♗g5 – *Game 48*

               9 ♘c3

                    9...d5 – *Game 49*; 9...d6 – *Game 50*

          7...c5 8 0-0 0-0

               9 ♗c3 – *Game 51*; 9 ♗xb4 cxb4 10 ♕d3 – *Game 52*

6 ♗d2 ♗e7

     6...♗xd2+ – *Game 47*

7 ♗g2 c6 8 ♗c3

     8 0-0 d5 9 ♕c2 – *Game 53*

8...d5 9 ♘e5 ♘fd7 10 ♘xd7 ♘xd7 11 ♘d2 0-0 12 0-0 ♖c8 13 e4 c5 14 exd5 exd5 15 dxc5 dxc4 16 c6 cxb3 17 ♖e1 *(D)*

     17...♗b5 – *Game 54*; 17...b2 – *Game 55*

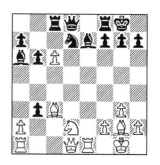

5 b3   *7 ♗d2*   *17 ♖e1*

CHAPTER EIGHT

4 g3 ♗b7

---

1 d4 ♘f6 2 c4 e6 3 ♘f3 b6 4 g3 ♗b7

4...♗b7 is the old classical move, which was much played in the days when few people believed in such modern moves as 4...♗a6. In this chapter we will consider all the classical lines as well as some of the sidelines. As you will find out, if you choose to play anything other than 5 ♗g2 ♗e7 6 ♘c3 then there is really no way to play for an advantage, or even create an interesting game. All these d5, b3 and ♖e1 lines are not dangerous for Black, once they have been looked at under the microscope.

So the real battleground is in the main lines and here it is a matter of taste. All lines should lead to an even game. But what kind of even game suits you best? Take a look and then decide.

Game 56
Karpov-Gavrikov
USSR 1988

1 ♘f3 ♘f6 2 c4 b6 3 d4 e6 4 g3 ♗b7 5 ♗g2 c5

This move is more or less refuted (this game). Other alternatives are:

a) 5...♗b4+. The difference with the Bogo-Indian is hard to find after this. After 6 ♗d2 Black has four possibilities:

a1) 6...c5 7 ♗xb4 cxb4 8 0-0 0-0 9 ♘bd2 d6 10 ♖e1 ♕c7 11 e4 e5 is very similar to Game 52, except that White has not played b2-b3. This is an advantage that secures White the better prospects in this position. 12 ♕b3 a5 13 ♕e3 ♘c6 and now, instead of 14 d5, which was seen in Gavrilov-Seferjan, Rjazan 1993, Gavrilov recommends 14 h3 ♖fe8 15 d5 ♘b8 16 ♘h4 ♗c8 17 ♔h2 ♘a6 18 f4 ♕c5 19 ♕e2 with a slight pull.

a2) 6...a5 7 0-0 0-0 8 ♗f4 ♗e7 9 ♘c3 ♘e4 10 ♕c2 ♘xc3 11 bxc3 ♖a7 12 e4 d6 13 ♖fe1 ♘d7 14 ♖ad1 ♕e8 with a modest advantage to White in Piket-Korchnoi, Nijmegen 1993, after 15 a4.

a3) 6...♗e7 7 ♘c3 0-0 (7...c6 8 e4 d5 9 cxd5 cxd5 10 e5 ♘e4 11 0-0 0-0 12 ♖e1 ♘xd2 13 ♕xd2 ♘c6 14 ♗f1 favoured White in Savchenko-Hulak, Portoroz 1996) 8 0-0 ♘a6 9 ♖c1 ♖e8 10 ♖e1 d5 11 cxd5 exd5 12 ♗f4 c5 13 ♕a4 ♘e4 14 ♖ed1 with another edge in Filippov-Kalinin, Moscow 2002.

a4) 6...♕e7 7 0-0 ♗xd2 8 ♕xd2 0-0 9 ♘c3 d5 10 ♘e5 ♘a6 11 ♖fd1, Ilincic-Damljanovic, Niksic 1997, and we have yet another of these typical positions where White is only very slightly better.

b) 5...g6?! 6 0-0 ♗g7 7 ♕c2 0-0 8 ♘c3 d6 9 e4 ♘bd7 10 b3 e5 11 ♗b2 exd4 12 ♘xd4 ♖e8 13 ♖fe1 simply led to a clear plus for

---

127

White in Milev-Simagin, Russia 1959. The weakening of the light squares on the queenside does not work well within such a King's Indian structure.

6 d5!

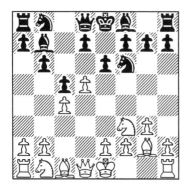

White assumes control of the centre. Either Black will have to live with an undesirable structure or fight for d5. As this game shows, White is 'fitter' for this fight.

6...exd5 7 ♘h4 b5 8 0-0!

8 cxd5 merely justifies Black's play this far.

8...bxc4 9 ♘c3 ♗e7 10 ♘f5!

10 ♗g5?! is inferior. Now White clearly has the advantage.

10...0-0 11 ♘xe7+! ♕xe7 12 ♗g5 h6

12...♘a6?! 13 ♘xd5 ♗xd5 14 ♗xd5 ♖ab8 15 ♗xc4 secures White a very clear advantage. The knight is badly placed on a6.

13 ♗xf6 ♕xf6 14 ♘xd5 ♗xd5 15 ♕xd5 ♘c6 16 ♕xc4 ♕xb2 17 e3

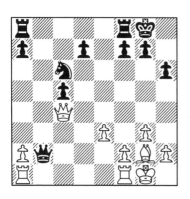

White will soon regain the pawn, after which the superiority of both his bishop and his pawn structure will guarantee an advantage.

17...♖ab8 18 ♕xc5 ♖b6?!

18...♖b5 is better. This slow play presents White with an opportunity to complete development without any concerns.

19 ♖ad1 ♘b8 20 ♗d5!

Now the game is more or less decided. The rest, as they say, is a matter of technique...

20...♕b5 21 ♕c7 ♕a6 22 ♖c1 ♕a5 23 ♖fd1 ♖b5 24 ♕d6 ♕b6 25 ♕e7 ♕g6 26 ♗e4 ♕e6 27 ♗h7+ ♔xh7 28 ♕xf8 ♕xa2 29 ♕d6 a6 30 ♕d3+ f5 31 ♖b1 ♕e6 32 ♖xb5 axb5 33 ♕xb5 ♘c6 34 ♖d5 ♔g6 35 ♕c5 ♕e4 36 ♖d6+ ♔h7 37 ♕d5 ♕b1+ 38 ♕d1 ♕e4 39 ♕d3 ♕g4 40 ♖d5 1-0

Game 57
Polugaevsky-Wojtkiewicz
Haninge 1990

---

1 d4 ♘f6 2 ♘f3 e6 3 c4 b6 4 g3 ♗b7 5 ♗g2 ♗e7 6 0-0 0-0 7 b3 d5

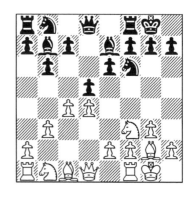

8 cxd5 exd5

Black has an easier way to equalise in 8...♘xd5! 9 ♗b2 ♘d7 (9...c5 is a good alternative: 10 ♘c3 cxd4 11 ♘xd5 ♗xd5 12 ♘xd4 ♗xg2 13 ♔xg2 ♗f6 14 e3 ♗xd4 15 ♗xd4 gave White some advantage in Aagaard-Christensen, Copenhagen 1999, but simply 14...♕d5+! would have kept the game drawish) 10 ♘bd2!? c5 11 ♖c1 ♖c8 12 ♘c4 ♘5f6 with equality in Dautov-van der Sterren, Ter Apel 1994.

9 ♗b2

9 ♘c3 ♘a6 10 ♗b2 ♕c8 11 ♖c1 ♖d8 12 a3 c5 13 dxc5 bxc5 14 b4 ♕d7 15 bxc5 ♘xc5 16 ♘e5 ♕e6 17 ♘a4 ♘fe4 18 ♘xc5 ♗xc5 19 ♕a4 ♗b6 20 ♘f3 ♖ac8 led to equality in Nikolic-Khalifman, Manila 1990.

9...♖e8 10 ♘c3 ♘a6

10...♕c8, with equality, is mentioned above.

11 ♘e5 c5 12 ♖c1 ♗f8

12...cxd4 13 ♘b5! favours White.

13 e3 ♘c7 14 ♘a4!?

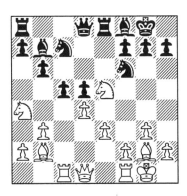

White has emerged from the opening with a small plus.

14...♘e6 15 dxc5 bxc5 16 ♘g4! ♘e4?!

16...♘xg4! 17 ♕xg4 ♕e7 18 ♖fd1 ♖ed8 was better according to Polugaevsky.

17 f3 ♘d6 18 f4! ♘e4

18...d4!? was apparently necessary.

19 ♘f2! ♘f6 20 f5 ♘g5 21 ♘xc5 ♗xc5 22 ♖xc5 ♘ge4 23 ♘xe4 ♘xe4 24 ♕d4 f6 25 ♖c2 ♕d6 26 ♖fc1 ♖e7 27 ♕a4 ♕d8 28 ♗a3 ♖f7 29 ♖d1 ♕b6 30 ♕d4 ♕a5 31 ♗b4 ♕b5 32 ♗xe4! dxe4 33 ♖c7!! ♖xc7 34 ♕d8+ ♕e8 35 ♕xc7 ♗c6 36 ♖d6 ♗b5 37 a4 ♖c8 38 ♕a5 ♗d3 39 ♕d5+ ♔h8 40 ♖d7 h6 41 g4! ♕e5 42 ♕xe5 fxe5 43 ♗d6 ♖c1+ 44 ♔g2! ♖d1

45 ♖xa7 ♗f1+ 46 ♔f2 ♖xd6 47 ♔xf1 ♖b6 48 a5 ♖xb3 49 a6 1-0

Game 58
Freitag-Oral
Graz 1998

---

1 d4 ♘f6 2 c4 e6 3 ♘f3 b6 4 g3 ♗b7 5 ♗g2 ♗e7 6 0-0 0-0 7 d5!?

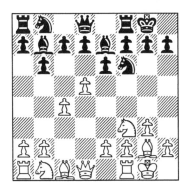

This pawn sacrifice had its heyday in the 1980's. These days it is not considered to be very dangerous but it must be remembered that it is more messy than the main lines.

7...exd5

Also possible is 7...♘a6!?, as tried in Hausrath-Tiviakov, Zwolle 2000. I suppose this was employed as a means to steer the lower rated opponent out of his 'book' ... 8 ♘c3 ♗b4 9 ♘e5 ♗xc3 10 bxc3 ♘c5 11 ♗a3 ♕e7 12 ♘d3 d6 13 ♘xc5 dxc5 14 e4 e5 15 ♖e1 ♘e8 16 ♗f1 ♘d6 and Black was doing well.

8 ♘h4!

This was Polugaevsky's discovery after the following game: 8 ♘d4?! ♗c6! 9 cxd5 ♗xd5 10 ♗xd5 ♘xd5 11 e4 ♘b4 12 ♘c3 ♗f6 13 ♘f5 ♖e8 14 f4 d6 15 ♕g4 ♘8c6 16 e5 dxe5 17 ♘e4 exf4 18 ♘h6+ ♔f8 19 ♘xf6 ♕xf6 20 ♖xf4 ♖e1+ 21 ♔g2 ♘e5 22 ♖xf6 ♘xg4 23 ♖xf7+ ♔e8 24 ♖xg7 ♘xh6 25 a3 ♖d8 26 axb4 ♖d7 27 ♖xd7 ♔xd7 and the endgame is a disaster for White, as was seen in the game Polugaevsky-Korchnoi, Buenos Aires 1980.

8...c6!

The only good move. After 8...♘e4 9 cxd5 ♗xh4 10 ♗xe4 ♗f6 11 ♕c2 White was slightly better in Gheorghiu-Unzicker, Wijk aan Zee 1981. 8...♘e8 9 ♘f5 ♘d6 10 ♘xe7+ ♕xe7 11 cxd5 c5 12 ♘c3 ♘a6 13 ♗f4 favoured White in Barlov-Ivanovic, Yugoslavia 1984.

9 cxd5 ♘xd5

Also good is 9...cxd5!? 10 ♘c3 ♘a6 11 ♘f5 ♘c7 12 ♗f4 ♖e8 13 ♗d6 ♗f8 14 ♕b3 ♗c6 15 ♗xf8 ♖xf8 16 ♖ad1 ♖e8 17 ♖fe1 ♖e5, with equality in Romanishin-Razuvaev, Jurmala 1987. In fact I think this is probably the safest line for Black. On the other hand, it does not offer much in the way of winning chances.

10 ♘f5 ♘c7

Or 10...♗f6!? 11 e4 ♘e7 12 ♘d6 ♗a6 13 ♖e1 ♗e5 14 f4 ♗xd6 15 ♕xd6 c5 16 b4 cxb4 17 ♕xb4 ♘bc6 18 ♕a4 ♕c8 with unclear play in Milos-Sunye Neto, Sao Paulo 2000. Actually I would prefer to be Black in this line, and in the game, too, but I know that a creative player will also be able to get something out of White's position.

11 ♘c3

One of the two main lines. 11 e4 d5 12 ♖e1! is Barlov's variation, which appears to lead to an unclear but equal game: 12...dxe4 13 ♘c3!? ♗c8 14 ♘xe7+ ♕xe7 15 ♗xe4 ♗e6 16 ♗f4 ♖d8 17 ♕h5 h6 18 ♖e3 was Piket-Van der Wiel, Rotterdam 1997, with

compensation for the pawn, but Black has his chances too and did okay.

White had previously played 13 ♕g4 ♗f6 14 ♘c3 ♗c8 15 ♗xe4, but after 15...♗xf5 (15...♘d5? 16 ♗h6 g6 17 ♗xf8 ♔xf8 18 ♗xd5 ♗xf5 19 ♕b4+ ♗e7 20 ♕b3 cxd5 21 ♘xd5 ♗e6 and Black resigned in Barlov-Abramovic, Yugoslavia 1994 – simply 22 ♖xe6 fxe6 23 ♕f3+ followed by ♘xe7 wins) 16 ♕xf5 g6 17 ♕f3 ♘e6 18 ♗h6 ♘d4 19 ♕g2 ♖e8 20 ♗e3 a6 21 ♘e2 ♖a7 22 ♘xd4 ♗xd4 23 ♗xd4 ♕xd4 24 ♗xc6 ♖xe1+ 25 ♖xe1 ♘xc6 26 ♕xc6 ♔g7 27 b3 there was little life left in the position in Pigusov-Tiviakov, Beijing 1997. Of course a man like Pigusov is well known for his love for exchanges. Like my first trainer, who said that the sacrifice of a pawn would only make you try to win it back, so therefore it was a waste of time...

11...d5

11...♘e8 12 ♗f4 ♘a6 13 ♕d2 d5 14 e4 ♘ac7 15 ♖ad1 ♗f6 16 exd5 ♘xd5 17 ♘xd5 cxd5 18 ♘e3 ♘c7 19 ♗xc7 ♕xc7 was already drawn in Timman-Karpov, Tilburg 1983.

12 e4 ♖e8!?

The new move. Previously known was 12...♗f6 13 ♖e1 ♗c8 14 ♕f3 ♗e6 15 g4 ♘d7 16 ♕g3 dxe4 17 ♗xe4 with compensation but no more, Romanishin-Epishin, Belgrade 1988.

13 ♗f4 ♘e6 14 ♕g4 ♘d7

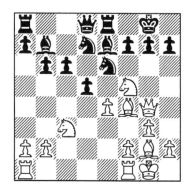

15 e5

This looks like a positional error, and now Black does not have to worry about his centre.

15...g6 16 ♘h6+ ♔g7 17 ♘f5+ ♔g8 18 ♘h6+ ♔f8 19 ♖fe1 ♗g5 20 h4 ♗xf4 21 gxf4 f5 22 exf6 ♘xf6 23 ♕f3 ♗c8 24 ♖e5 ♔g7 25 ♖ae1 ♔xh6 26 f5 gxf5 27 ♖xf5 ♔g7 28 ♖e3 a5 29 ♕g3+ ♔h8 30 ♕e5 ♘g7 0-1

Game 59
Van Wely-Korchnoi
Hoogeveen 2001

---

1 d4 ♘f6 2 c4 e6 3 ♘f3 b6 4 g3 ♗b7 5 ♗g2 ♗e7 6 0-0 0-0 7 ♖e1

This line was very popular in the mid-1990's, when Kramnik championed it. It is now known to be harmless in view of...

7...♘a6!

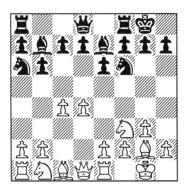

It is this move that has more or less done away with any modern interest in 7 ♖e1. Instead 7...d5 8 cxd5 exd5 9 ♘c3 might give White a little plus.

8 ♘e5

Other attempts at an advantage are:

a) 8 ♘c3 ♘e4 9 ♘xe4 (9 ♗d2 d5 10 cxd5 exd5 was equal in Barsov-Ligterink, Hoogeveen 1997) 9...♗xe4 10 ♕a4 ♕c8 11 ♘e5 ♗xg2 12 ♔xg2 c5! 13 d5?! exd5 14 cxd5 ♘b4! 15 ♖d1! d6 16 ♘f3 ♕b7!? 17 a3 b5 18 ♕b3 ♘a6 with a good game for Black, Polul-

jahov-Tiviakov, St. Petersburg 1998. White has not been able to establish the powerful centre that secures him play in Benoni structures. Necessary here was 13 ♗e3 ♕b7+!? 14 ♘f3!? cxd4 15 ♗xd4 with complete equality. 10 ♘e5 has also been played, Bator-Stefansson, Mariehamn 1997, continuing 10 ♘e5 ♗xg2 11 ♔xg2 ♕c8!? 12 e4 ♕b7 (already equal) 13 ♘xd7 ♖fd8 14 ♘e5 ♗f6 15 ♗f4 ♗xe5 16 ♗xe5 f6 17 ♗f4 e5 18 ♗d2 ♖xd4 and Black had improved his prospects. 10 d5!? is another try. Then the safe 10...exd5!? 11 cxd5 c5 12 dxc6 dxc6 13 ♘e5 ♗xg2 14 ♔xg2 ♕c8 leads to approximate equality, while the ambitious 10...♗f6 11 ♘d4 ♗xg2 12 ♔xg2 leaves Black with a modest lead in development, meaning he must act quickly in order to avoid e2-e4-e5. Delchev-Marin, Istanbul 2000 went 12...c5 13 ♘b5 exd5 14 ♕xd5 ♘b4 15 ♕d1 a6 16 ♘d6 b5 17 e4 bxc4 18 e5 ♘d3! 19 exf6 ♕xf6 20 ♗f4 g5 21 ♕g4 ♘xf4+ 22 gxf4 ♕xd6 23 ♕xg5+ ♕g6 with a draw.

b) 8 a3!? is an interesting try. White is aiming for the standard position and invests a tempo to do so. 8...d5 (8...c5 9 d5 exd5 10 ♘h4 ♘c7 11 ♘c3 d4 12 ♗xb7 ♖b8 13 ♗g2 dxc3 14 bxc3 leaves all the white pieces well placed) 9 cxd5 exd5 10 ♘c3 c5 11 ♗f4 ♘c7 12 ♖c1 ♘e6 13 ♗e5 ♘g4 was seen in Wojtkiewicz-Zagrebelny, Dhaka 1999. In many ways this fits in with White's plan to increase pressure on the d5-pawn. White was willing to surrender the bishop for the knight and now it is Black who expends energy to arrange this. 13...♕d7!? is a sensible alternative, preparing to put more weight on the d-file. After (13...♘g4) 14 dxc5 bxc5 15 h3 ♘xe5 16 ♘xe5 ♗f6?! 17 ♘g4 ♗xc3 18 bxc3! White had a slight but distinct advantage, but the improvement 16...♘c7!?, keeping the two bishops, would have given Black a fine game.

12 ♗xc7 ♕xc7 13 ♖c1 ♕d7 14 ♘e5 ♕e6 15 ♘d3 c4 16 ♘e5 ♖ab8 17 e4 dxe4 18 ♘xe4 ♗xe4 19 ♗xe4 ♘xe4 20 ♖xe4 ♕d5 21 ♕e2 f5 22 ♖e3 b5 was the course of Ibragi-

mov-Pushkov, Elista 2001, with a level game. This shows that the idea is just to get a position and then play, rather than attempt to refute Black's plans.

8...d5!

The improvement over 8...♗xg2. The difference with 7...d5 is that White's knight is not very well placed on e5 so early, so Black has no problems in equalising.

9 cxd5 exd5 10 ♘c3 c5 11 ♗f4 ♘e4 12 ♘xe4 dxe4 13 dxc5 ♘xc5 14 ♕c2 ♕c8

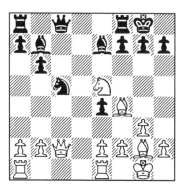

Black has equalised. The f5-square is a brilliant outpost for the queen, as is e6.

15 ♖ed1 g5 16 ♗e3 ♕e6 17 ♘c4 ♖ac8 18 b3 h6 19 ♗d4 ♗d5 20 ♗b2 ♖fd8 21 ♖ac1 b5 22 ♕c3 f6 23 ♘e3

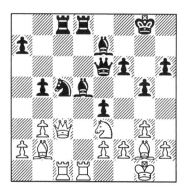

23...♘xb3 24 ♕xc8 ♖xc8 25 ♖xc8+ ♕xc8 26 ♖xd5 ♘c5 27 ♘f5 ♗f8 28 ♗h3 ♔h7 29 ♔g2 h5 30 ♘e3 ♕c6 31 ♗f5+ ♔g7 32 ♗d4 ♔f7 33 ♗xc5 ♗xc5 34

♖d7+ ♔f8 35 ♘d5 ♗b6 ½-½

1 d4 ♘f6 2 c4 e6 3 ♘f3 b6 4 g3 ♗b7 5 ♗g2 ♗e7 6 0-0 0-0 7 ♘c3 ♘a6!?

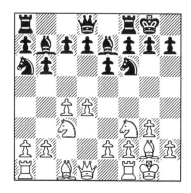

An interesting sideline. This illustrates how good this is against 7 ♖e1. When it is good here, it must be brilliant there! 7...d5 8 ♘e5 ♘a6 9 ♗f4 transposes to 8 ♗f4 in the note to White's 8th move.

8 a3

Others:

a) 8 b3 ♖e8 9 ♗b2 d5 10 ♘e5 c5 11 e3 ♕c7 12 cxd5 exd5 13 ♘b5 ♕c8 14 a3 ♘c7 led to a balanced game in Zaremba-Ibragimov, Chicago 2002.

b) 8 ♗f4 d6! (8...d5 9 ♘e5 c5 10 cxd5 exd5 11 ♖c1 ♘e4 12 ♘xe4 dxe4 13 dxc5 ♘xc5 14 ♘c4 ♘e6 15 ♗e5 f6 16 ♘d6 ♗xd6 17 ♗xd6 gave White a little something in Paunovic-Tiviakov, Cacak 1996) 9 a3 c5 10 d5 ♘c7 11 e4 a6 12 b4 exd5 13 exd5 cxb4 14 axb4 b5 with a complicated game with chances for both sides in Ribli-Markowski, Moscow 1994.

c) 8 ♕a4 ♕c8! (protecting the knight on a6 just once more) 9 ♖d1 ♘e4 10 ♘xe4 ♗xe4 11 ♗f4 d6 12 ♖ac1 ♕b7 13 ♘e1 ♗xg2 14 ♘xg2 c5 with equality in Tatai-Tiviakov, Arco 1998.

d) 8 ♗g5 c5 9 d5 exd5 10 cxd5 d6 11 ♘h4 ♕d7 12 ♕d2 b5 13 e4 b4 14 ♘d1 ♗d8, Shneider-Tiviakov, Moscow 1992, was very messy.

8...♘e4 9 ♗d2 f5 10 b4 ♗f6 11 ♖b1

11 ♖c1 c5 12 dxc5 bxc5 13 b5 ♘c7 does not look dangerous for Black.

11...♘xc3

11...c5 12 bxc5 ♘axc5! 13 dxc5 ♘xc3 14 ♗xc3 ♗xc3 15 ♕d6 ♗c6 is another route to equality.

12 ♗xc3 ♗e4 13 ♖b3

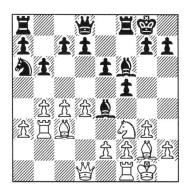

13...c6!

Part of a magnificent but not too complex plan. Black wants to establish a giant knight on d5.

14 ♗b2

14 b5?! cxb5 15 cxb5 ♘c7 favours Black.

14...♘c7 15 ♗h3

15 a4 b5 16 axb5 cxb5 17 c5 ♘d5 18 e3 a5! and Black has a positional plus.

15...b5! 16 ♘d2 bxc4 17 ♘xc4 ♗d5 18 ♕d3 ♕b8 19 ♗g2

19 f3!? ♕b5 20 ♖c1 ♖fb8 21 e4 ♗xc4 22 ♕xc4 fxe4 23 fxe4 a5! leads to equality.

19...♕b5 20 ♖c1 ♖fb8 21 f3 a5!

Black has the initiative. White was not able to counter quickly enough.

22 e4 ♗xc4 23 ♖xc4 d5! 24 exd5 exd5 25 ♖c5 ♕xd3 26 ♖xd3 axb4 27 ♖xc6 bxa3 28 ♗xa3 ♖b1+ 29 ♗c1 ♘b5

Black's pieces are literally springing to life with powerful effect.

30 f4 ♗xd4+ 31 ♔f1 ♖aa1 32 ♗xd5+ ♔f8 33 ♖d1 ♗c3 34 ♔e2 ♖xc1 35 ♖xc1 ♖xc1 36 ♔d3 ♗b2 37 ♖b6 ♖d1+ 38 ♔c4 ♘a3+ 0-1

Game 61
Andersson-Karpov
Tilburg 1983

---

1 ♘f3 ♘f6 2 c4 b6 3 g3 ♗b7 4 ♗g2 e6 5 0-0 ♗e7 6 d4 0-0 7 ♘c3 ♘e4 8 ♕c2

This line is so classical that many players still play it with some odd kind of respect for the old masters. The newer and more dangerous 8 ♗d2 is treated in the following games.

8 ♘xe4 ♗xe4 9 ♘h4 is the ultimate drawing line. After 9...♗xg2 10 ♘xg2 d5 11 ♕a4 dxc4 12 ♕xc4 c5 13 ♗e3 cxd4 14 ♗xd4 ♕c8 the position is completely equal. Apart from a blunder once deciding a game between Polugaevsky and Andersson (White), I cannot recall this line being dangerous for anything other than one's interest in chess. Yet this characteristic is precisely the reason why some people play it. By somehow reaching a technical position where they cannot create any winning chances they leave the floor free, as it were, for their opponents to create losing chances. Andersson-Karpov, Reggio Emilia 1991 continued 15 ♖fc1 ♕xc4 16 ♖xc4 ♘a6 17 ♘f4 ♖fd8 18 ♗e3 ♖d7 19 ♘d3 f6 20 ♖ac1 ♖ad8 21 ♔g2 ♔f7 with equality.

8...♘xc3 9 ♕xc3 c5

This is the most drawish line here. Equally good is 9...f5, e.g. 10 d5 ♗f6 11 ♕c2 ♘a6 12 ♖d1 ♕e7 13 ♘d4 ♘c5 14 ♗e3 ♗xd4 15 ♗xd4 d6 16 b4 ♘d7 17 a4 a5 18 bxa5 ♖xa5 with equality in Krogius-Kholmov, Kiev 1964. Meanwhile Andersson-Akesson, Skelleftea 1999 went 10 b3 ♗f6 11 ♗b2 d6 12 ♖ad1 a5 13 ♘e1 ♗xg2 14 ♘xg2 ♘c6 15 ♕d2 ♕d7 16 d5 ♘d8 17 ♗xf6 ♖xf6 18 dxe6 ♘xe6 19 ♘f4 ♘xf4 20 ♕xf4 ♖e8, again with complete equality. It should be said such positions can be seen a million or so times in GM games, and some players, like Andersson, continue to play them because they know them so well.

10 ≝d1

Black also has nothing to fear after the line 10 b3 ≗f6 11 ≗b2 cxd4 12 ②xd4 ≗xg2 13 ≗xg2 ②c6 14 ≝e3 ≝c8 15 ≝fd1 ≝d8, as in the encounter Beliavsky-Adams, Belgrade 1995.

10...d6 11 b3 ≗f6 12 ≗b2 ②d7

This is the most flexible choice, but another route to equality is well known, namely 12...≝c7 13 ≝d2 ≝d8 14 dxc5 dxc5 15 ≝f4 ②a6 16 ≝xc7 ②xc7 17 ②e5 (17 ≗xf6 gxf6 18 ②e1 ≗xg2 19 ≗xg2 ≗f8 20 ≝d3 ≝xd3 21 ②xd3 ≗e7 22 ≝d1 ②e8 23 g4 was equal in Hort-Karpov, Buenos Aires 1980) 17...≗xg2 18 ≗xg2 ≗xe5 19 ≗xe5 ②e8 20 f4 f6 21 ≗c3 ≗f7 22 g4 ≝xd1 23 ≝xd1 ≗e7 24 ≗f3 ≝d8 with a draw to follow in Timman-Karpov, Amsterdam 1980.

13 ≝d2 ≝e7 14 dxc5 ≗xb2 15 ≝xb2 dxc5 16 ≝d3 ≝ad8 17 ≝ad1

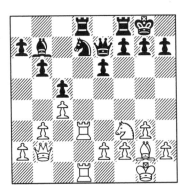

17...②b8 18 h4 ≝xd3 19 ≝xd3 ≝d8 20 ≝d2 ≝xd3 21 ≝xd3 ½-½

Game 62
Pinter-Tompa
Hungary 1993

---

1 d4 ②f6 2 c4 e6 3 ②f3 b6 4 g3 ≗b7 5 ≗g2 ≗e7 6 ②c3 ②e4 7 ≗d2

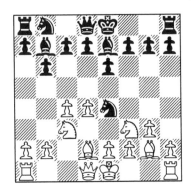

7...≗f6!

I believe this is the best way to deal with these lines. 7...0-0 8 d5!? is considered in the next game. Note that if 7...0-0 8 0-0 then it is interesting to play 8...d5!?, for if you want to play such positions this is certainly the right place to push to d5. Actually these lines are considered to give White a slight plus in ECO, but I guess that is primarily because there was originally a guy who tried a line and secured a modest advantage and then he has been quoted for it ever since. Perhaps White is a little better, but then he always is in these situations. Korchnoi-Polugaevsky, Moscow 1972 continued 9 cxd5 exd5 10 ≝c1 ②d7 11 ≗f4 c5 12 ②xe4 dxe4 13 ②d2 f5 14 ②b3 ≗d5 15 dxc5 with a draw.

8...d6 9 d5! ②xd2 10 ②xd2 e5 11 f4! exf4 12 gxf4 ②d7 13 ②f3 ≗f6 14 ②d4 ≝e8 15 e4 gave White a substantial advantage in Vaganian-Furman, USSR 1971.

8...f5 is considered in the last game.

8 0-0

8 ≝c2 ②xd2 9 ≝xd2 looks like a loss of time, and I suspect that that is what it is. After 9...0-0 10 0-0 d6 11 e4 (11 d5 ≗xc3 12 ≝xc3 exd5 13 ②h4 d4! 14 ≝xd4 ≗xg2 is equal, as pointed out by Makarichev) 11...②d7 12 ≝ad1 g6 13 h4 ≗g7 14 h5 ≝e7 15 ≝fe1 ≝fd8 16 hxg6 hxg6 17 ≗h3 c5 18 d5 ②e5 19 ②xe5 ≗xe5 Black had no problems whatsoever in Tukmakov-Nielsen, Copenhagen 1996.

8 &c1 has not been tested since Black came up with 8...&xd4! 9 ♘xd4 ♘xc3 10 &xb7 ♘xd1 11 &xd1 c6! 12 &f4 0-0 13 &d6 &e8 14 &xa8 ♕c8 15 b4 ♘a6 16 b5 ♕xa8 17 bxa6 c5 18 ♘f3 ♕e4 with sufficient counterplay in Karpov-Salov, Rotterdam 1989, a game Black went on to win after a fierce struggle.

8...0-0 9 &c1 c5

9...d5 is a tempo too late. After 10 cxd5 exd5 11 &f4 ♘a6 12 &e5 &e8 13 &xf6 ♕xf6 14 e3 c5 15 ♘e5 ♕e7 16 &e1 ♘c7 White should not play 17 ♘d3?! (Korchnoi-Salov, Belgrade 1987) but 17 ♕a4!? ♘xc3 18 &xc3, with the idea of 18...c4 19 &xc4 b5 20 &xc7 bxa4 21 &xe7 &xe7 22 &c1 with a small advantage to White according to Korchnoi.

10 d5 exd5 11 cxd5 ♘xd2

Also possible is 11...♘xc3!? 12 &xc3 d6 13 ♘d2 &e8 14 ♘e4 &e7!? 15 g4 b5 with a messy game in Rogers-Speelman, Oropesa del Mar 1996.

12 ♘xd2

12 ♕xd2 &e8 13 h4 d6 14 ♘g5 &a6 15 ♘ge4 &e5 16 &fe1 g6 17 a4 ♕e7 18 b3 ♘d7 resulted in stone-cold equality in Epishin-Oms Pallise, Sevilla 2000.

12...d6 13 ♘de4!

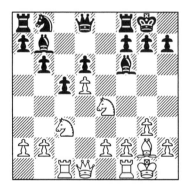

This is the only dangerous move. White should remember how strong the bishop is on f6. After 13 ♘c4 &a6 14 ♕b3 &xc4 15 ♕xc4 ♘d7 16 e3 a6 17 a4 ♕e7 18 ♕e2 &fb8

19 &a1 &e8 only Black had realistic prospects of pushing for a win in Vyzmanavin-Khalifman, USSR 1990.

13...&e5!

13...&e7?! had been played quite often before 13...&e5 took over. Actually, I wonder why? The bishop does not look better than the knight once it gets to e7. (I would suspect that even 13...♘a6 is better than this). White earned himself a clear advantage in Karpov-Salov, Linares 1993: 14 f4 ♘d7 15 g4! a6 16 a4 &e8 17 g5 &f8 18 ♔h1! etc. Shneider-Beliavsky, USSR 1990, went 16 g5 b5 17 ♘g3 &e8 18 h4 &f8 19 h5 with the better game for White. Let us compare the bishop with the knight now – why run away from the exchange like that?

14 ♕d2

14 f4 &d4+ 15 ♔h1 &a6 16 &f3 &e8 (16...♕e7 is even better according to Almasi) 17 g4 ♕e7 18 g5 ♘d7 19 e3 &xc3 20 ♘xc3 b5 21 &g3! f5! and Black was slightly better in the game Yusupov-Almasi, Germany 1994. It should be noted that the line itself does not give Black the advantage – White should be able to improve on this, but the positive trend seems to be with Black, nonetheless.

14...&a6 15 ♔h1

15 &fe1 g6 16 f4 &d4+ 17 e3 &g7 18 a3!? ♕e7 19 b4 ♘d7 20 g4! h6 21 g5!? was unclear in Brenninkmeijer-van der Weil, Holland 1991.

15...♕e7 16 f4 &d4 17 &fe1

The most natural. After 17 &f3 ♘d7 18 e3 &xc3 19 ♘xc3 b5 20 &f1 &ab8 Black had good counterplay in Horvath-Zagrebelny, Budapest 1993, while 17 b4 g6 18 b5 &c8 19 e3 introduced an early draw in Yermolinsky-De Firmian, Seattle 2000.

17...g6 18 e3 &g7 19 g4

19 a3 ♘d7 20 b4 cxb4 21 axb4 &c4 22 ♘e2 &fc8 23 ♘g5 &xe2 24 &xe2 a5 gave Black a better game in Van der Sterren-Yemelin, Hamburg 1997.

19...h6 20 g5 hxg5 21 ♘xg5

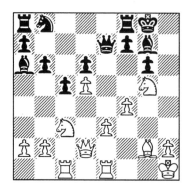

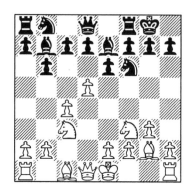

The game is rather unclear.

21...♘d7 22 ♕f2 ♗h6!

22...♘f6 23 ♕h4 followed by e3-e4-e5 would be very dangerous for Black.

23 h4 ♗xg5 24 hxg5 f6! 25 gxf6 ♕h7+ 26 ♔g1 ♘xf6 27 ♕g3 ♖ae8 28 ♗h3 ♔g7 29 ♖cd1 ♖h8 30 ♗g2 ♕h4 31 ♕xh4 ♖xh4 32 a4?! g5! 33 fxg5 ♘d7 34 ♖a1 ♗d3 35 ♘b5 ♖g4 36 ♘xd6 ♖f8 37 e4 ♖xg5 38 ♘f5+ ♔f6 39 ♖e3 ♘e5 40 ♖g3! ♖fg8 41 ♖xg5? ♖xg5 42 ♘e3 ♗xe4 43 ♖f1+ ♔e7 44 ♖f4 ♗xg2 45 ♘xg2 ♘d3 46 ♖e4+ ♔d6 47 ♔f1 ♘xb2 48 a5 ♖f5+ 49 ♔g1 ♖xd5 50 a6 ♖d1+ 51 ♔f2 ♖a1 52 ♘f4 ♖a4 53 ♖e6+ ♔d7 0-1

Game 63
Romanishin-Korchnoi
Lvov 2000

---

1 d4 ♘f6 2 ♘f3 e6 3 g3 b6 4 ♗g2 ♗b7 5 c4 ♗e7 6 ♘c3 0-0

This move makes a lot of sense. Black wants to see if White's move order holds any real threats to his wellbeing.

7 d5!

7 ♕c2 is, as always, answered with 7...c5! and Black equalises with 8 d5 exd5 9 ♘g5 ♘a6 10 cxd5 ♘b4 11 ♕d2 ♘fxd5 12 ♘xd5 ♗xg5 13 ♕xg5 ♕xg5 14 ♗xg5 ♗xd5 15 ♗xd5 ♘xd5 16 0-0-0 ♘b4 17 a3 ♘c6 18 ♖xd7 ♖fe8 19 ♔d1 f6 20 ♗d2 ♖ad8, as in Bogdanovski-Marin, Yerevan 1996.

7...♗b4

7...♘a6 8 0-0 ♘c5 9 ♘e5 a5 10 ♗e3 exd5 11 cxd5 ♗a6 12 ♕c2 ♗d6 13 f4 gave White the advantage in Atalik-Stoica, Herculane 1996.

8 0-0!?

This line allows the exchange on c3, after which Black is okay. The critical lines arise after 8 ♗d2! and now:

a) 8...♗xc3 9 ♗xc3 exd5 10 ♘h4 ♘e4 (10...c6 11 ♘f5 dxc4 12 ♕d6 ♔h8 13 ♘xg7 ♔xg7 14 ♕f4 h6 15 g4 gave White a promising attack in Halasz-Lendwai, Miskolc 1990) 11 cxd5 ♘xc3 12 bxc3 d6 13 0-0 ♘d7 14 e4 ♘c5 15 ♕d4 ♗a6 16 ♖fd1 ♕d7 17 f4 with a slight advantage to White in Karpov-Ivanchuk, Linares 1993.

b) 8...c6 9 0-0 ♗xc3 10 ♗xc3 (10 dxc6!? dxc6 11 ♗xc3 ♘bd7 12 ♕c2 also looks better for White and the two bishops) 10...cxd5 11 ♘h4 ♘e4 12 cxd5 ♘xc3 13 bxc3 ♕c7 14 c4 ♘a6 15 ♖c1 with an advantage according to Ribli.

c) 8...♘a6!? 9 0-0 ♘c5 and now 10 ♘e1 ♖e8 11 ♘c2 ♗xc3 12 ♗xc3 exd5 13 cxd5 ♘ce4 14 ♘e3 ♘xc3 15 bxc3 ♖xe3! 16 fxe3 d6 17 ♕d4 ♘d7 18 ♖f4 ♕e7 19 ♖af1 ♘e5 gave Black brilliant play for the exchange in Razuvaev-Tiviakov, Rostov 1993. It is hard to find any use for the rooks as all the files are closed or semi-closed. An improvement for White is 10 ♘h4!, e.g. 10...♖e8 11 ♖c1 a5 12 a3! (12 ♖e1?! d6! was good for Black in

Van Wely-Tiviakov, Gausdal 1992)
12...&xc3 13 &xc3 exd5 14 cxd5 &a6! 15
&e1 with a modest plus for White thanks to
the strong and uncontested dark-squared
bishop. 14...&ce4 has been analysed by Barlov. After 15 &f5 &xc3 16 &xc3 &a6 17 d6!
White has the initiative. Note 17...&xe2 18
dxc7! &c8 19 &d6, and White wins in a million ways. White is on top after 15...&xd5?
16 &xg7 &g5 17 g4 etc.

8...&xc3

There are alternatives, but this is the
move.

9 bxc3 &a6 10 &h4 &b8!

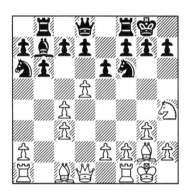

Time has shown this to be the strongest
option. 10...e5 11 e4 d6 12 f4 exf4 13 &f5
&c8 14 &xg7?! &xg7 15 &d4 &g8 16 gxf4
&c5 17 e5 &g4 was good for Black in Filip-
pov-Tiviakov, Elista 1995, but simply 14
&xf4 would have kept White slightly better.

10...&c5 11 &a3 &b8 12 &xc5 bxc5 13
&b1 exd5 14 cxd5 &a6 15 &e1 d6 16 &xb8
&xb8 17 &d2 &e8 18 e4 gave White some
pressure in Shneider-Brynell, Aars 1995.

11 e4 d6 12 &e3

12 f4 &d7 13 &f3 e5 14 fxe5 (14 &e3
&ac5 15 &d2 &a6 is equal) 14...&xe5 15
&xe5 dxe5 16 &a3 &c5 17 &xc5 bxc5 18
&a4 &d6! with a good game for Black in
Filippov-Savon, St. Petersburg 1996.

12...&e8 13 &e1 &d7 14 f4

After 14 &f3 &ac5 15 &c2 &f6 16 &d4
&h6 17 h3 &a6 18 &f1 exd5 19 exd5 &g6

Black had nothing to fear in Romanishin-
Markovsky, Biel 1995.

14...&ac5 15 &f2 &a6 16 &f3

White decides to forget about the c4-pawn
and generate his own chances on the kingside.

16...e5!

16...&xc4 17 &d4 &d3 18 &f1 &xf2 19
&xf2 &xf1 20 &c6 gives White something
to bite on. Now the d4-squares is protected.

17 f5!?

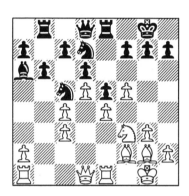

White refuses to compromise.

**17...&xc4 18 &e3! b5 19 g4 f6 20 h4
&c8 21 &e1 c6 22 dxc6 &xc6 23 &c2
&c7 24 &g3 &b6 25 g5 fxg5?**

I qualify this move as a suicide attempt!
Actually, Black built up his position in order
to be able to push ...d6-d5, and he had to do
it now! Then White would be at a crossroads:
25...d5 26 &xc5! &xc5 27 &h5 &h8 28 &e3
&e7 29 &d1 d4 30 cxd4 exd4 31 &xd4 &d7
with equality is a suggested improvement
from Korchnoi.

**26 hxg5 d5 27 &xc5! &xc5 28 &h5 &d7
29 f6?**

29 &e3!.

**29...d4 30 fxg7 &f7 31 &h3 &xc3 32
&xc3 dxc3 33 &xc3 &xg5 34 &e3 &f6
35 &f1 &xe4 36 &a3 &g3 37 &f2 &xg7
38 &xa7 &f8 39 &b6 &g5 40 &a7 &e6
41 &d5! &xf2 42 &xf2 &h5 43 &b8+
&g7 44 &xb5 &f6 45 &b7+ &h6 46
&xf6? &xf6+ 47 &f3 &xf3+ 48 &xf3**

♗d5+ 49 ♔g3 ♗xa2 50 ♗e4 ♗f7 51 ♔g4 ♗g6 52 ♗b7 ♔g7 53 ♔g5 h6+ 54 ♔g4 ♔f6 55 ♗c8 ♗f5+ 0-1

Game 64
Yermolinsky-Gulko
Seattle 2000

---

1 d4 ♘f6 2 c4 e6 3 ♘f3 b6 4 g3 ♗b7 5 ♗g2 ♗e7 6 ♘c3 ♘e4 7 ♗d2 0-0 8 d5!? f5 9 ♕c2

9 0-0 transposes to the main lines.

9...♘d6

It is also possible for Black to play for equality with 9...exd5 10 ♘xd5 ♘c6 11 0-0 a5 12 ♖ad1 ♗f6 13 ♗e3 ♔h8 14 ♘xf6 ♖xf6 15 ♘g5 ♘b4 16 ♕b1 ♕e8 17 a3 ♘a6, as in Horvath-Atalik, 1991, which ended in a draw after 26 moves.

10 ♗f4

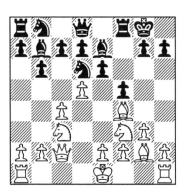

A possibly better shot for an opening advantage is 10 b3 ♗f6 11 ♖d1 ♕e7 12 0-0 ♘a6 13 ♘e1 c6 14 dxc6 dxc6 15 e4 ♘b4 16 ♕b1 c5 17 ♗f4 ♘f7 18 ♘b5 e5 19 ♗c1 ♖ad8 with a complex struggle in Van der Sterren-Salov, Wijk aan Zee 1998, where White might get to occupy d5 at the right moment if he plays his cards right.

10...♘a6

10...♘xc4 11 ♘b5 ♗b4+ 12 ♔f1 ♗xd5 13 ♘xc7 ♘c6 14 ♘xd5 exd5 15 ♘g5 gives White some initiative, while 10...♗f6 11 0-0 ♕e7 12 ♗xd6 cxd6 13 ♖ac1 (13 ♖fd1 g6 14

♘d4 e5 15 ♘db5 ♖c8 16 e4 was a little better for White in Ivanchuk-Salov, Linares 1993, although Black can improve) 13...♘a6 14 dxe6 dxe6 15 ♖fd1 ♖ac8 16 ♕a4 ♖fd8 was completely equal in Epishin-Korobov, Ohrid 2001.

11 0-0 ♘xc4 12 dxe6 ♘b4

12...dxe6 13 ♕b3 ♗d5 14 ♘xd5 exd5 15 ♘d4 ♕d7 16 ♕b5 ♕xb5 17 ♘xb5 ♖ad8 18 b3 gives White a small plus.

13 ♕c1

13 ♕b3? ♘a5! 14 ♕a4 dxe6 is better for Black.

13...d5

Black cannot enter 13...dxe6 14 ♖d1! ♘d5 15 ♘d4 ♕c8 16 ♘xe6 ♘xf4 17 ♕xf4 as he clearly has severe problems.

14 b3 ♘a5

14...♘d6 15 a3 ♘a6 16 ♘e5 looks good for White.

15 ♘e5 ♖f6?!

15...c5!? 16 ♖d1 ♗f6 and Black should be able to keep the balance. Now he has to play some precise moves in order to equalise.

16 ♕b1!

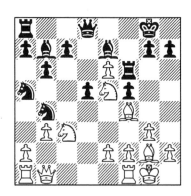

16...d4

16...c5 17 a3 ♘a6 18 ♖d1 and d5 is weak.

17 ♗xb7 ♘xb7 18 ♖d1 c5?!

18...♖xe6 19 ♕xf5 ♖f6 20 ♕g4 ♗d6! 21 ♘e4 ♗xe5 22 ♗xe5 ♖g6 23 ♕f3 ♘c6 gives Black an acceptable position, although it is still White who is dictating events.

19 e3 ♖xe6 20 ♕xf5 ♖f6 21 ♕g4 ♘d6?

This is just bad. Necessary was 21...♗d6!
22 exd4 cxd4 23 ♘b5 when White's prospects are slightly preferable.

22 exd4 cxd4 23 ♖xd4 ♘c2 24 ♘c6

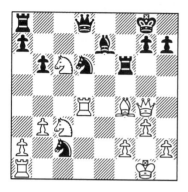

**24...♕f8 25 ♘xe7+ ♕xe7 26 ♘d5 ♕f7
27 ♘xf6+ ♕xf6 28 ♖xd6 ♕xa1+ 29 ♖d1
♕f6 30 ♕d7 ♖f8 31 ♕d3 ♖c8?! 32
♕d5+ ♔h8 33 ♗e5 ♕g6 34 ♕d8+ ♕e8
35 ♕d7 1-0**

Game 65
Khalifman-Korchnoi
St Petersburg 1997

**1 d4 ♘f6 2 c4 e6 3 ♘f3 b6 4 g3 ♗b7 5
♗g2 ♗e7 6 ♘c3 ♘e4 7 ♗d2 f5 8 d5 ♗f6**

I am not too fond of this line. 8...0-0
transposes to Game 64.

9 ♕c2 ♕e7

9...♘d6 gave White a better game after 10
♗f4 ♕e7 11 ♗xd6 cxd6 12 0-0 0-0 13 ♖fd1
g6 14 ♘d4 e5 15 ♘db5 ♖c8 16 e4 in Ivanchuk-Salov, Linares 1993.

10 ♖d1

White is concentrating his play on the d5-
pawn. Both alternatives are worse. 10 0-0
♗xc3 11 ♗xc3 exd5 12 cxd5 ♗xd5 looks
acceptable for Black, Hulak-Naumkin, Palma
1989, while Tyomkin gives 10 ♘xe4? fxe4 11
♕xe4 exd5 12 ♕f4 ♘a6! 13 ♘d4 0-0 14 ♘f5
♕c5 as being better for Black. Clever guy.

10...exd5

Khalifman writes in his notes: '...the text

move was played before and brought Black
good practical results. I think it's strategically
dubious...'

The alternative is 10...♘a6 11 0-0 ♘d6
(11...♘ac5 12 ♘b5 0-0 13 ♘xc7 ♖ac8 14
♘b5 exd5 15 cxd5 ♗xd5 16 ♕b1 gave
White a plus in Naumkin-Marinelli, Formia
1995) 12 ♘b5 (12 dxe6!? dxe6 13 ♕a4+ ♔f7
14 ♗e3 favoured White in Petursson-
Rozentalis, Malmö 1993) 12...♘xb5 13 cxb5
♘c5 14 dxe6 dxe6 15 ♗b4 ♗e4 16 ♕c1 and
White was slightly better, Olafsson-
Rozentalis, Lyon 1994. Rozentalis generally
plays a lot of these typical QID positions
without too much hesitation, as he knows
them very well.

11 cxd5

11 ♘xd5?! ♗xd5 12 cxd5 ♕c5! 13 ♕xc5
bxc5 14 ♗c1 ♘a6 and Black is better
(Olafsson-Arnason, Kopavogur 1994).

11...c5?!

This move finds a refutation in this game.
Better is 11...0-0 12 0-0 ♘a6 (probably the
best – White has only a slight advantage now)
13 ♗f4 ♘xc3 14 bxc3 ♖ae8 15 ♘d4 ♕c5 16
♕b3 ♔h8 17 ♗e3 with an for White according to Khalifman.

12 dxc6! dxc6

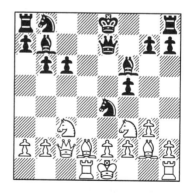

13 ♘xe4!

This was a new move. The e-pawn is now
terribly weak.

**13...fxe4 14 ♘h4! ♗xh4 15 gxh4 0-0!
16 ♕c4+ ♕f7 17 ♕xf7+ ♖xf7 18 ♗xe4**

White is close to winning the ending.
**18...c5!? 19 ♗xb7 ♖xb7 20 ♗c3 ♘c6 21
♖g1 ♖e8 22 ♖g5 ♖e4 23 h5 ♖be7 24 e3
♘d4 25 ♔f1 h6 26 ♖d5 ♘b5 27 ♗e1
♖f7?! 28 ♖d8+ ♔h7 29 ♖1d7! ♖f5 30
♖d5 ♖f6 31 ♖b8! ♖d6 32 ♖f5 ♖f6 33
♖xf6 gxf6 34 ♖d8 c4? 35 a4 c3 36 axb5
cxb2 37 ♖d1 ♖c4 38 ♗d2! ♖c5 39 ♖b1
♖xb5 40 ♗c3 ♖c5 41 ♗xb2 ♖b5 42 ♔e2
a5 43 ♔d3 a4 44 ♔c2 ♖c5+ 45 ♗c3 b5
46 ♔d3 ♖xh5 47 ♗xf6 1-0**

Game 66
Ivanchuk-Timman
Wijk aan Zee 2001

**1 ♘f3 ♘f6 2 c4 b6 3 g3 ♗b7 4 d4 e6 5
♗g2 ♗e7 6 ♘c3 0-0 7 0-0 ♘e4 8 ♗d2
f5**

Because of the trouble I feel Black faces in
this line I highly recommend 8...♗f6.

9 ♕c2!

This quieter variation is an attempt to increase the tension. After 9 d5 ♗f6 10 ♖c1
♘a6 Black normally equalises completely.
The theory goes as follows: 11 a3 c6! 12 dxe6
dxe6 13 ♕c2 c5 14 ♖fd1 ♕e7 15 ♘e1 (15
♘xe4 ♗xe4 16 ♕a4 ♘b8 17 b4 ♘c6 18 b5
♘d8 19 ♗c3 ♗xc3 20 ♖xc3 ♘f7 was equal
in Beliavsky-Brodsky, Koszalin 1998)
15...♘xd2 16 ♗xb7 ♕xb7 17 ♕xd2 ♖ad8 18
♕e3 ♕e7 with equality in Hansen-Korchnoi,
Malmö 1996. Or 11 ♗e1 c5! (the new way to
play) 12 dxc6 dxc6 13 ♕b3 ♘ac5 14 ♕c2
♕e7 15 b4 ♘xc3 16 ♗xc3 ♗xc3 17 ♕xc3
♘e4 18 ♕b2 c5 with complete equality, Be-
liavsky-Stefansson, Istanbul 2000.

9...♗f6

9...♘xc3 10 ♗xc3 ♗e4 11 ♕a4 d6 12
♖ac1 ♕d7 13 ♕d1! c5 14 ♕d2 ♘c6 15 ♖fd1
and White had a little something in Skem-
bris-Huzman, Beersheba 1993.

9...♘xd2 10 ♕xd2 ♗b4 11 ♖ac1 ♗e4 12
a3 ♗xc3 13 ♖xc3 ♕f6 14 ♘e1 ♗xg2 15
♘xg2 ♘c6 was very slightly better for White
in Stahlberg-Castaldi, Hamburg 1955.

10 ♖ad1

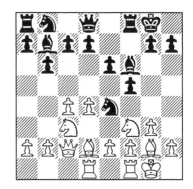

10...♘a6

This is certainly not the main move, and in
this game Black is nowhere near equality.
The alternatives are:

a) 10...♘xc3 is the critical line given in
Chess Informant, and also the most natural.
But I think Black needs to come up with a
new concept somewhere to play like this. 11
♗xc3 ♗e4 (11...♕e7 allows 12 d5! ♗xc3 13
♕xc3 ♘a6 14 ♘d4 ♘c5 15 b4 ♘e4 16
♗xe4 fxe4 17 dxe6 dxe6 18 b5, when White
is just a whole lot better, Ovsejevitsch-Rehm,
Berlin 1997) 12 ♕c1!, Azmaiparashvili-
Gulko, Elenite 1995. The queen is much
better placed here than on d2 because it
leaves the way clear for the traditional plan
with ♗h3 followed by ♘d2, driving the
bishop away from e4 and seizing control of
the centre. Now 12...♕e8, to prevent ♗h3, is
answered with 13 ♖fe1 with the idea of ♗f1.
However, it could be argued that the inclusion of these points benefits Black as well as
White. Instead the game continued (12 ♕c1!)
12...d6 13 ♗h3! ♕e8 (Gulko does not like
this move and improves it with 13...♘d7!? 14
♘d2 ♗b7 15 e4 c5! with counterplay – he is
probably correct, although it is far from clear
that Black has a potentially equal position,
and 16 d5 seems good for White to me) 14
♘g5 ♕h5 15 ♘xe6! and now White found
the strong combinatorial continuation
15...♕xh3 16 f3 ♗b7 17 ♘xc7 and Black

was in trouble, although he went on to win.

Earlier 12 ♕d2 leads to a more or less equal position after 12...d6 13 ♘e1 ♗xg2 14 ♘xg2 ♕e7!, when the idea behind developing the queen first is seen after 15 ♕c2, when Black has the deep reply 15...♕f7! intending 16 e4 fxe4 17 ♕xa4 d5! followed by 18...♘c6 and Black has good and natural counterplay. Karpov -Polugaevsky, Amsterdam 1981 went 15 ♘f4 ♘d7 16 d5 ♗g5 17 dxe6 ♗xf4 18 ♕xf4 ♕xe6 19 ♖fe1 ♘c5 and Black fine.

b) 10...♕c8 11 d5! ♘d6 12 b3 ♘a6 13 ♗f4 favoured White in Lundin-Skold, Sweden 1967.

c) 10...d6 11 d5 ♗xc3 12 ♗xc3 ♘xc3 13 ♕xc3 e5 14 b4 saw White assume an advantage on the queenside in Larsen-Levitt, London 1990.

d) 10...c5 11 d5 ♗xc3 12 ♗xc3 exd5 13 cxd5 d6 14 ♘h4 ♘xc3 15 bxc3 ♕f6 16 f4 ♘a6 17 ♗h3 g6 18 e4 was also better for White in Navrotescu-Marin, Bucharest 2001.

11 ♘e5!

11 a3 c5 12 d5 ♗xc3 13 ♗xc3 exd5 14 cxd5 d6 15 ♘h4 ♘xc3 16 bxc3 achieved nothing in Gritsak-Brodsky, Ordzhonikidze 2000.

11...♘xc3 12 ♗xc3 ♗xg2 13 ♔xg2 ♕c8 14 ♖fe1 ♕b7+ 15 ♔g1 ♗xe5

This is a tough decision, after which the pressure down the d-file and the potentially very strong bishop gives White an advantage.

Interesting was 15...c5!? 16 dxc5 ♘xc5 17 b4 d6, which Fritz came up with, although it looks like White is better after 18 ♖xd6 (18 bxc5 dxe5! gives Black a good game) 18...♕e4 19 ♕d2 ♗xe5 20 ♗xe5 ♕xe5 21 f4! (21 bxc5 ♕xc5 and Black is fine) 21...♕e4 22 bxc5 bxc5 23 ♕d3! etc.

16 dxe5 ♖f7

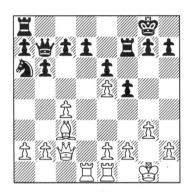

17 b4 c6 18 ♖d6 b5 19 ♖ed1 bxc4 20 a3 ♖c8 21 ♗e1 ♘b8 22 a4 c5 23 b5 ♕e4 24 ♕xe4 fxe4 25 ♗c3 ♔f8 26 ♔g2 ♖c7 27 ♗d2 ♖c8 28 g4 c3 29 ♗e3 a6 30 ♖c1 axb5 31 axb5 ♔e8 32 ♖xc3 c4 33 h3 ♖f8 34 ♗a7 ♔e7 35 ♖d4 e3 36 fxe3 ♖c7 37 ♗b6 ♖b7 38 ♗c5+ ♔e8 39 b6 ♖g8 40 ♖a3 d5 41 exd6 e5 42 ♖a7 1-0

A tough struggle, where the knight never got into the game.

Summary

4...♗b7 still seems to be playable according to theory. The older attempts to get an advantage with 7 d5 and 7 b3 do not trouble Black and neither does 7 ♖e1 ♘a6!. The most dangerous tries are the logical developing moves with 6 ♘c3 and 7 ♗d2 in reply to 6...♘e4. Black should have a good grasp of the theory to play these lines, but if he does, then he can also count on equality. My investigations have clearly indicated that ...♗f6 is a better defence than ...f5, but who knows what time will show.

1 d4 ♘f6 2 c4 e6 3 ♘f3 b6 4 g3 ♗b7 5 ♗g2 *(D)* **♗e7**

     5...c5 – *Game 56*

6 ♘c3

     6 0-0 0-0 *(D)*

          7 b3 – *Game 57*

          7 d5 exd5 8 ♘h4 – *Game 58*

          7 ♖e1 – *Game 59*

          7 ♘c3

               7...♘a6 – *Game 60*

               7...♘e4

                    8 ♗d2 – 6 ♘c3

                    8 ♕c2 – *Game 61*

6...♘e4

     6...0-0 7 d5 ♗b4 – *Game 63*

7 ♗d2 *(D)* **0-0**

     7...♗f6 – *Game 62*; 7...f5 8 d5 ♗f6 – *Game 65*

8 0-0

     8 d5 f5 9 ♕c2 – *Game 64*

8...f5

     8...♗f6 – 7...♗f6

9 ♕c2 – *Game 66*

5 ♗g2

6...0-0

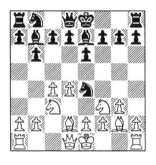

7 ♗d2

INDEX OF COMPLETE GAMES